ANALYTICAL

PHILOSOPHY OF

ACTION

Action seems like a leak from another realm or world into this world – an intervention such as God would bring about were he able to bring about changes in the world without transgressing the laws of nature...We stand within and without Nature!

Brian O'Shaughnessy, 'Observation and the Will'

Domine, quinque talenta tradisti mihi: ecce alia quinque superlucratus sum.

Matthew 25:20–1

ANALYTICAL PHILOSOPHY OF ACTION

BY

ARTHUR C. DANTO

Professor of Philosophy, Columbia University

CAMBRIDGE

AT THE UNIVERSITY PRESS

1973

Published by the Syndics of the Cambridge University Press
Bentley House, 200 Euston Road, London NW1 2DB
American Branch: 32 East 57th Street, New York, N.Y.10022

Library of Congress Catalogue Card Number: 72–91364

ISBN: 0 521 20120 9

Printed in Great Britain
by Alden & Mowbray Ltd
at the Alden Press, Oxford

TO
SIDNEY MORGENBESSER

CONTENTS

PREFACE

In the middle band of six tableaux, on the north wall of the Arena Chapel in Padua, Giotto has narrated in six episodes the missionary period in the life of Christ. In each panel, the dominating Christ-figure is shown with a raised arm. This invariant disposition of his arm notwithstanding, a different kind of action is performed by means of it from scene to scene, and we must read the identity of the action from the context of its execution.[1] Disputing with the elders, the raised arm is admonitory, not to say dogmatic; at the wedding feast of Cana, it is the raised arm of the prestidigitator who has caused water to become wine; at the baptism it is raised in a sign of acceptance; it *commands* Lazarus; it *blesses* the people at the Jerusalem gate; it *expels* the lenders at the temple. Since the raised arm is invariantly present, these performative differences must be explained through variations in context, and while it may be true that context alone will not constitute the differences and that we must invoke the Christ's intentions and purposes, still, we cannot overestimate the extent to which context penetrates purpose. *Expulsion* at Cana would be as incoherent with Christ's mission as blessing the money-lenders would be; acceptance at the graveside of Lazarus would not be Christ's way, and admonition at the gate of Jerusalem would be only puzzling. The identity of the actions is such that were we to imagine, through some artistic catastrophe, that the marvelous pictorial context were washed away in each instance leaving only the Christ-figure with a raised arm, the latter would be neutralized and reduced to an anatomical posture, a mere flexed and angled limb. It will perhaps make the motive of the present study clear if I say that it is just my aim to wash away the contextual factors which convert movements into gestures and vest the disposition of limbs with high spiritual significance. I want to isolate those bare, neutral actions before they are colored by the sorts of meanings they are shown to have on the Arena walls and in common life. The 'before' is of course logical, as my enterprise is analytical. One reason for this preoccupation with *basic* actions, as I shall term them, is to be able to appreciate the points in the logical architecture of action at which those factors enter, through

ix

which the actions are converted into something more human and more social, and taken up into the fabric of communication, and deposited as part of human history.

A parallel preoccupation in the theory of knowledge would demand a similar erasure of the apparatus of interpretation which penetrates and renders significant the objects of perception: say, for convenient if complicated instance, the Arena frescoes at Padua. Imagine not knowing the identity of the characters depicted there, so that the filter and focus provided by the grasped allusions Giotto counted on to achieve his striking artistic economies were obliterated in a kind of cultural aphasia. So that one would see whatever one in fact sees when one knows the stories and iconography, but in a deep sense one would not know what was happening. One's perception might be stained, if we take aphasia in its pathological sense, with the nagging thought that there was some purposefulness with no discernible purpose, as the aphasiac might know that what was before him had a meaning he no longer could eke out. But *my* interest is only in noting the possibility of a perception invariant to and independent of interpretations, of what Wittgenstein termed 'seeing as'. Then this sort of perception would be ours if we had no degree of acculturation or if there were no culture, as bare arm movements would be done with no ulterior gestural signification under the same admittedly unrealistic assumptions. Then, as with actions, one might locate where in the logical architecture of perception these differentiating features enter, through which things are seen *as* what it requires a special education to understand. It is fair, I believe, to say that most of the classical problems of perception arise this side of that point at which perception takes on this crucial coloring and specialization, and a model of my preoccupations with action may be found in the sort of treatment of perception one meets in Locke or Hume.

As the same (sort of) arm-rise might be an admonition or a blessing, an affirmation or a rejection, it is obvious that the description of it as an arm-rise underdetermines the description of it *as* this gesture or that: a description may be given of it which is neutral to its description as a *significant* bit of behavior. So the predicates which apply to it in this neutral sense are logically independent of and scarcely then definable in terms of the predicates through which it is described in human or cultural terms. Whether in the sphere of perception or of action, philosophers may seek for descriptions of what is perceived or what is done in terms which presuppose no special cultural information, and which may then be counted as universal, being invariant to every possible coloration history or culture may add. It would in a deep sense exclude what we regard as characteristically human to seek to eliminate or reduce these variational descriptions, and it would be futile to pretend that we could possibly explain the most characteristically human gestures or the contents of our experience in terms so austere and universal. But as we may be interested in man, both as perceiver and performer, invariantly as to his cultural and historical location, it is in just such terms that we must conceive him.

This is not, I might add, the only or the most important parallel to be drawn between action and cognition, and one strain which runs throughout my book is that these two typical ways of relating to the world – acting upon and coming to know it – have frequently parallel structures – that what I here term the 'logical architecture' of knowledge and of action are of a piece, or nearly of a piece. A preface is a place only to announce, not to analyze or speculate upon the philosophical import of such a claim. Whatever its explanation, I have sought to use the two concepts of action and of knowledge as guides to each other's structure, and so the book is as much a treatise of aspects of knowledge as it is of aspects of action. I might add, indeed, that this has in some way limited the topics of which I treat, for I have had very little concern with those features of the concept of action which are parochial in the sense that they have no correspondence in the theory of knowledge.

These parallels, as well as the central concept of this book, that of the *basic action*, I first developed in a paper which the exigencies of publication split in two: 'Basic Actions', *American Philosophical Quarterly*, II (1963) and 'What We Can Do', *Journal of Philosophy*, LX (1963). At least the idea of basic actions aroused a certain interest, and through a series of invitations to present my views, the idea has undergone, under the fire of criticisms, considerable modification. Some of these appeared in further papers and other contexts, but the present book, for worse or better, supersedes whatever I have written on this subject. I think very few words from any of these have entered the present book unaltered. I presume permission to use those few.

This book, meanwhile, presented the sort of problem painters know, who must transform a scribbled inspiration from a scrap of paper into something formal and on a large scale. Something is always lost, some freshness and speed, but the systematic enlargements and what they reveal are plainly worth the sacrifice. Many of the ideas I thought (and others hoped) would follow naturally from the concept of basic actions did not follow at all, and often only their contraries were even compatible with it. And other ideas I had hoped I might remain neutral towards, in fact demanded a stand, since certain problems could not have been otherwise solved. Thus I became, in the course of writing, a Materialist and a Determinist of sorts.

There have been far too many helpful critics for me to acknowledge all the illuminations I owe them. I am, however, in the special debt of Professor Robert Audi, who read the entire manuscript through and peppered it with questions. Fragments of certain versions were beneficially perused by George Sher, Eric Steinberg, and Toni Vogel Carrie. The American Council of Learned Societies and the John Simon Guggenheim Foundation provided support and encouragement, and liberated enough time for a full if penultimate draft to be completed.

Paris and New York   A.C.D.
1972

KNOWLEDGE AND ACTION

In the ringing, invidious disjunction between those who have only tried to understand the world and those who seek to change it, Marx apostrophized an ancient juxtaposition. We may see it, for example, in the main counterposed funerary figures of the Medici Chapel in Florence: Giuliano, muscular as a horse, called from thought to action, sits poised for movement, while facing but not seeing him, Lorenzo – *Il Pensieroso* – is lost through thought to action, and sits curled beneath a sheltering helmet, immune to outward stimulation. Lorenzo is outside, as it were, a world Giuliano has just entered, and broods upon the meaning of that which Giuliano is content to live. Respectively external and internal to the world, they emblemize the lives of contemplation and of action to which men have in all ages felt themselves alternatively summoned. Inevitably, so universal a polarity must be reflected in philosophy in terms of alternative anthropologies: theories of what man *essentially* is, whether a cognitive or a practical being. Western philosophy, in a powerful tradition from Plato to Descartes, endorsed the former view. Exemplarily, we are knowers of a fixed reality, our essence fulfilled through the acquisition of ideas whose clarity is their guarantee of truth. This theory of man generates accordingly a theory of reality and of our relation to it. Marx, in opposition, perceives us as agents, included in rather than set against a reality he believed plastic enough to be altered: reality is something we help shape, it has an essentially historical dimension, it is not something fixed and given, of which we might as knowers hope to achieve a final representation in thought. So his injunction to change the world is underwritten by an implicit metaphysics of world and men, if men are to be effective as agents.

The human epic, from the Cartesian viewpoint, is liberation from doubt through understanding crowned with knowledge, and any limitation upon our powers of either comprehension or cognition qualifies the outcome of the epic. From the Marxist viewpoint, the human epic is liberation from the forces of history by becoming their master and replacing fatality with freedom,[1] with similar restraints where there are limits. Neither epic is realizable if the applicable limits are absolute, if we are constrained in the one case by an ignorance which is indefeasible and in the other by an insurmountable impotency. The philosophical translations of these threats lie in a certain sort of Skepticism, which entails a logical incapacity ever to know; and a certain sort of Determinism, which correspondingly entails a logical incapacity ever to change the world. Cartesians see us as external to a world we seek to know, and Skepticism then insists that the gap between the world and us is cognitively insuperable. Marxists see us as one with the world, so the problem of Skepticism cannot then arise. But the paralyzing form of Determinism holds that we are so internal to the world that any change to be brought about through our agency is logically foreclosed, the Marxist dream of freedom swamped by an inevitability we cannot modulate. So our counterposed philosophies yield ironically inverse hopes if their epics are to come true: that we may after all come sufficiently into the world to achieve cognitive success, and stand sufficiently outside it that we may attain mastery over it. Skepticism is overcome by closing a gap between the world and us, and Determinism by opening up another. We are successful as knowers only if we are within and without the world at once, and similarly if we are agents. Speaking broadly and rhetorically, each of the opposing philosophies of man requires a dimension of the other, for their subject – which is us – is a complex entity, simultaneously Giuliano and Lorenzo, complexly related to a correspondingly complex world.

It is in part to map these complexities, to get a better philosophical picture of man as related to the world through knowledge and action, that I shall employ the concepts of knowledge and action as mirror-images of one another, having parallel but inverse structures.

II

A case of central concern to theorists of knowledge is that in which a man *m* knows something *s through* some other thing that he knows. He may, thus, know that *s* through *e*, where *e* is evidence for *s*. It does not follow that *s* could not be known true without there being anything through which it is known, though *m* perhaps can come to know that *s* only through something else that he knows. Nor does it follow that

2

there are specific things through which whatever else we may come to know are known, though it may be true of *m* himself that there are specific things through which he knows whatever else is known by him to be true.

Of correspondingly centrality in the theory of action are cases in which a man *m* does something *through* some other thing that he does. He moves a stone, say, by pushing against it, and the stone is thus moved by him through the application of mechanical force. It does not follow that what he does in this way could not have been done without there being something through which it is done, though it may be true that *m* can have moved the stone in no way other than through something else done by him. Nor does it follow that there is some specific sort of action through which whatever further things we do must be done, though *m* himself may be constrained by his limited endowment of powers to achieve his further ends through a restricted range of actions.

I shall begin my inquiry by considering that class of actions of which moving a stone by pushing against it is an unspectacular exemplar. And since this class of actions appears to share a degree of structure with a prominent class of cases in epistemology, I shall consider the two together, using what we have at hand in the theory of knowledge to guide us through our exploration in the theory of action. For since philosophers have been more sedulous of certitude than of effectiveness and – obsessively intellectualistic! – because they have feared ignorance more than impotency, they have bent their labours more to the clarification of knowing than of changing the world. So we have in their collective deliberations a sort of chart to the topography of the concept of action, providing the parities hold.

In the theory of knowledge, now, there is an analysis to be found which, variations in detail notwithstanding, is sufficiently widely accepted that we may refer to it as the Standard Analysis of Knowledge.[2] It consists typically of three sorts of entries, with individual differences between epistemologists showing up more in their mode of construing these entries than in any serious departure from the schedule of entries as such. In general, a man *m* is said to *know that s* (which I abbreviate, where convenient, to *m*K*s*)[3] when each of a psychological (or I shall prefer to say, a *representational*), a *semantic*, and an *explanatory* condition is satisfied. Thus, to cite one widely canvassed analysis, *m*K*s* only if

K-1   *m* believes that *s*.
K-2   *s* is true.
K-3'   *m* has adequate evidence for *s*.

Item K-3' quite clearly collapses two pieces of information together, namely that there is something which both is known by *m* and which is adequate evidence for *s*. Call this *e*. Then K-3' should be replaced with its constituents:

K-3   *m* knows that *e*.
K-4   *e* is adequate evidence for *s*.

The appearance of the word 'knows' in K-3 warns us that we cannot generalize upon this version of the Standard Analysis without circularity or infinite regression. But as our concern for the present is just with those cases in which we know something (*s*) through something else that we know (*e*), generalization is less important than congruity with the case at hand. Let us therefore bracket K-3, so to speak, and exclude it from consideration until the matter of generalization becomes pressing. This leaves us, then, with a model of knowledge which consists of three distinct types of component and three distinct relations. The components are these: the person *m*, the sentence *s*, and what I shall call the *object* of *s*. The relations hold between *m* and *s*; between *s* and its object; and between *e* and *s*. These relations are respectively psychological, semantical, and explanatory. A few words must be said on each.

(A) The sentence *s* is one of a class of philosophically crucial entities which I designate *semantical vehicles*.[4] The criterion of the semantical vehicle is having a representational property or being a representation.[5] Amongst representational entities in this sense are, in addition to sentences: pictures, charts, stories, theories, names, concepts, and (as this term was used in the seventeenth century) *ideas* (*idées*, *Vorstellungen*). I am less concerned with a complete list than with having these examples appear on any complete list. One of the things shared as a property by these (and any) semantical vehicles is their capacity to bear semantical values, of which the conspicuous examples are Truth and Falsity. The representational property (or descriptive meaning) of a vehicle is presumed invariant to the semantical value it in fact bears. Thus what a picture represents (what it is a picture *of*, what it is *about*) may be determined without knowing whether there exists in the world what-

4

ever it is which would give a *positive* semantical value to it if (a) it were
denoted by the picture and (b) it *matched*, within suitable limits of
verisimilitude, the picture in question.⁶ And the meaning of the picture
does not entail the existence of a matching denotatum: a picture of
Mary Magdalene is, by common iconographic convention, a picture of
a woman with long hair and a vial. Any student of art history may learn
to identify and 'read' the pictures as of Mary Magdalene. But whether
there was indeed such a woman, and, if so, whether she matches the
pictures of Mary Magdalene, demands more than iconographic exper-
tise. It requires that we turn from pictures to the world, and carry out
some operations of matching. And, with appropriate variations for
other members of the class, this is so with the other semantical vehicles.
To know what a sentence *means* demands only the powers the mastery
of language engages, but to know which of the sentences we understand
are *true* (or bear the positive semantical value for sentences) demands a
turn from language to the world, and calls upon other powers. The
Problem of the External World was, at its inception in the writings of
Descartes, simply this: that though he had access to his ideas, and understood them well enough, neither of these was adequate to ensure that
any of them were correspondent with anything external to themselves.
So he might have perfect understanding of his ideas but no knowledge
whatever, unless he could enter the space *between* his ideas and that
external reality and check for correspondences. And this, as he set
matters up, was not open to Descartes.

Descartes' insulating space, I have elsewhere argued,⁷ is but a travesty
of the space between language, or between semantical vehicles generally, and the world, where the world is what determines which
semantical value these vehicles bear. I shall speak of the *object* of a
semantical vehicle as that in the world which confers a value upon that
vehicle depending upon whether the appropriate semantical relations
are satisfied. Thus Mary Magdalene herself is the object of a Mary-
Magdalene-picture, which is then 'true' or 'false' depending upon
match of picture with saint. If a Mary-Magdalene-picture lacks an
object, it either is degenerately false through failure of denotation, or
(if you prefer) the question of truth or falsity does not arise. And so,
with appropriate modifications, with Mary-Magdalene-stories, -de-
scriptions, -theories, and the like (with *no* modification if sentences are
pictures, as Wittgenstein once believed,⁸ in which case a Mary-Mag-
dalene-sentence is a picture, if true, of a *fact* with Mary Magdalene

herself as a component). We may say that Mary Magdalene her very self is what these pictures, stories, and descriptions *represent*, providing we appreciate that they remain Mary-Magdalene-representations as a class whether, in *this* sense, they represent Mary Magdalene or not. There are, thus, two distinct notions of representation, confusion of which has perhaps darkened more philosophical waters than any nearest competitors. One is a *relational* sense, from which it follows that, if *v* represents *x*, *x* must exist: in this sense the Magdalene herself would be represented by the class of her pictures, descriptions, and the like, and we may then speak of her as the *object* of these vehicles. The other is non-relational, or at least does not have an *object* as the relatum. In this non-relational sense, Mary-Magdalene-representations would be just the representations they are, independently of whether they represent in the relational sense. If, of course, they do represent in that sense, we may speak of them as 'true' or 'false' depending upon satisfaction of other conditions, e.g. degree of fit between the saint and pictures of her. The two senses of representation correspond rather closely to Frege's distinction between reference and sense. To be sure, Frege thought both of these relational, Venus being the reference of 'the Evening Star' and a thought its sense. For the moment it little matters how we make this distinction so long as it is honored, and so long as vehicles' senses are distinguished from their references. Neither does it matter that there should be other sorts of meaning than *representational* meaning. The latter alone is relevant to the present analysis.[9]

Returning to the Standard Analysis, then, *s* is a semantical vehicle, which means that it has a certain representational property. Moreover, it clearly succeeds in representing the world in the relational sense of 'representation': it has an object, which makes it true. Without such successes there is no knowledge.[10]

(B) There is a further ambiguity in the concept of representation, which is this. So far I have restricted representation to semantical vehicles which, since they have representational properties, may succeed in bearing one or another semantical value. But we often speak of *ourselves* as representing something, viz. through our descriptions, or stories, or pictures, or theories. So when Caracci paints the Magdalene, Caracci represents. I shall say that a *belief* is a way in which we represent the world: to believe the Magdalene died in Spain is to represent the world in a certain way. When a man believes that *s*, *s* is *his vehicle* of representation, and his belief is true when the appropriate semantical

6

relation is satisfied between vehicle and object, viz. the object makes the vehicle *true*.

It seems only plausible that knowledge is at least in part a matter of interpreting or representing the world the way the world really is, so that there is no knowledge if there is no representation. So I shall suppose the Standard Analysis to require a relation between a person *m* and a semantical vehicle. Whether this relation is in fact *belief* may be moot, but few, I think, would deny that he who knows something must *somehow* represent the world, whether his doing so is to be termed a belief or not. It will be convenient to suppose it *is* a belief. A true belief puts us in relation to the world through a semantical vehicle the world makes true. But this is by common philosophical consent not enough for knowledge, which is why a third relation between ourselves and the object is required. In the Standard Analysis, this is mediated through a piece of evidence to which we are related in a way our bracketing of K-3 enables us to overlook for the moment. To the third relation I shall turn in a moment, but only after laying out an analysis of the concept of action which has enough parity of structure with the Standard Analysis of Knowledge to justify our further elucidation of the latter.

I shall employ the expression '*mDa*' as convenient shorthand for '*m* makes happen the event *a* by *doing a*'. The term 'D' makes graphic the assertion that *a* was done, and hence is an event properly redescribable as an action. It is a generalized action-marker, standing for whatever *verb* of action we might employ in common discourse. Suppose *a* is an event which consists in a stone traversing an interval of space and time at an angle oblique to the surface of the earth. Then D may take *lifting* as an instance, if *m* makes *a* happen by lifting. Or if *a* is an event consisting in *m*'s eye closing, D may take *winking* as an instance. In each of these cases, of course, it is plain that *a* could happen though '*mDa*' were false.

The locution '*mDa*' covers over the stiltedness of the expression '...makes...happen by...-ing' and permits us to treat actions in a generalized manner by treating 'does' for the moment as an auxiliary of action verbs, much as 'knows' may be an auxiliary of cognitive verbs. In so doing, I follow the illustrious precedent of Anselm of Canterbury who in discussing the Latin verb *facere* treats it in similar auxiliary fashion:

This verb *facere* is commonly put for every verb, of whatever signification soever,

7

completed or uncompleted, even for *non facere*. Thus, when it is asked concerning someone *quid facit*? 'What is he doing?': closely considered, 'do' is here put for every verb than can be given in answer, and whatever verb is so given, is put for 'do' ... So when the answer is, He is reading, or writing, this is as much as to say: he is doing this, to wit, reading or writing.[11]

A singularly felicitous though unwitting gloss on this notion is provided by J. L. Austin:

The beginning of sense, not to say wisdom, is to realize that 'doing an action', as used in philosophy, is a highly abstract expression – it is a stand-in used in the place of any (or almost any?) verb with a personal subject, in the sort of way that 'thing' is a stand-in for any (or, when we remember, almost any) noun substantive, and 'quality' a stand-in for the adjective.[12]

Austin adds a caution against abuse of the word:

We treat the expression, 'doing an action', no longer as a stand-in for a verb with a personal subject, as which it no doubt has some uses, and might have more if the range of verbs were not left unspecified, but as a self-explanatory, ground level description.[13]

What I wish to achieve, by sweeping whatever is actional in any verb with a personal subject into the auxiliary 'D', is to make it plain that it does *not* stand on its own and requires a 'ground-level' verb, and to put it in a position where whatever it contributes conceptually may be logically isolated. After all, so much is already presupposed in regarding action as an analyzable, i.e. non-primitive, concept.

Now at this level, the following has a certain naturalness in its initial favor as a candidate analysis of actions as a class:

A-1   *m* intends that *a* happen.
A-2   *a* happens.
A-3   *m* does *b*.
A-4   *b* is adequate for *a*.

As with the counterpart analysis of knowledge, this one has a hostage against generalization in A-3, but since our interest lies in those actions we do *through* other things that we do, it is the adequacy to these cases that must serve as our criterion. I accordingly will put A-3 in just those temporary brackets which confine K-3.

III

Since Plato, it has been philosophically ceded that knowledge cannot be identified with true belief, since what I believe may be true by accident, as it were, and I am right only in the way a blind man is who wanders onto the right path by hazard. For almost parallel reasons, action must be something in excess of having what we intend to happen *in fact* happen, for its so happening may have nothing to do with us nor be due to any of our doing, but only to a fortuitous coincidence between what happens and what we would have wished to have happen. For this reason, a great deal of stress in either analysis falls upon the *fourth* condition, and it is the office of the term *adequacy* to fill the space between true belief and knowledge in the one case, and between a satisfied intention and an action in the other. That 'is adequate for' happens to relate *sentences* in the analysis of knowledge and *events* in the analysis of action suggests that either it is radically ambiguous or that our analyses are insufficiently refined. Since, however, this is the third relation it remains to us to elucidate, we might consider the two analyses together, and see if we cannot bring them into closer line.

In epistemology, these questions have been elegantly pondered in recent times in consequence of a sequence of counter-examples introduced (or re-introduced) into the literature by Edmund Gettier against the theory that knowledge is a matter of *justified* true belief.[14] Preservation of the Standard Analysis against such counter-exemplification has developed into a minor philosophical industry.[15] The gist of the counter-examples is this. A man knows something which justifies him in believing *s* to be true, and *s* is indeed true. But its being true has nothing to do with what justifies him in believing it to be true, and hence our intuitions balk at crediting him with *knowledge* that *s*. Thus I see *n* wearing a new suit, which justifies me, suppose, in believing that *n* has bought a new suit. And he has bought a new suit! Only it is not the one he is wearing, which has been bought by his twin brother who loaned it to *n* while his own is being altered, *n* having to turn up suitably garbed to his new, respectable job. What I believe is this: $(\exists x) (x$ is a new suit and *n* bought *x*.) This is not entailed by what I know, namely that *n* is wearing a new suit, but it is entailed by what I seem justified in believing on the basis of what I know, namely that he bought the suit he is wearing, which in the event is false.[16] All the counter-examples are of this sort. And it is not difficult in a general way to work out counter-examples parallel to these for the theory of action. Thus *n* flicks the switch and the light goes on, as it usually does, and it seems plausible to say that *n* made it happen that the light go on by flicking the switch. In this case, however, the circuit between this switch and the light has been lost by an inept electrician who has wired it to a switch in the next house, happily but coincidentally flicked by *n*'s neighbor simultaneously. So *all n* did was flick the switch, though we would ordinarily say that he turned the light on, believing, as we do, that flicking the switch is adequate for this. It is so only if an intermediate event happens, namely something in the circuit which causes the light to go on. This indeed happened, but in total independence of *n*'s action. So the causal gap between what he did and what happened parallels the logical gap between what he knows and what is true in the case of knowledge. And each analysis in consequence needs repair – unless, of course, one adopts the heroic strategy of denying that if these counter-exemplifications hold, what I know (or what *n* does) is in fact 'adequate'. And in the case of *knowledge* this would mean that in the case described I was *not* justified in believing that *s*. But this might merely have the consequence of intolerably narrowing the domain of justified beliefs to the boundaries of the domain of knowledge itself, and I then am justified in believing only what I know. One way to achieve this would be to require of *e* that it entail *s*,[17] but this is an extreme demand and might exclude many cases we would intuitively want to class as knowledge. A weaker relation between *e* and *s*, as well as a looser criterion of justified belief, ought to be consistent with the analysis of knowledge, and the proposal I am about to make appears to me the natural coagulant for the haemorrhage the Gettier examples have induced in the Standard Analysis. I do not suppose that what follows is the final word, but only that it provides the framework within that word must at last be given. It will be enough if it enables us to generate our structures.

I propose that *e* is adequate evidence for *s* only if the truth of *e* is explained – I shall subsequently say *non-fortuitously* explained – through the truth of *s*: that *e* is true because *s* is true. I am not saying that *e* might not have been true had *s* been false, but only that it in fact is true just because *s* is true.[18] Introduction of an explanatory nexus between *s* and *e* fits, I believe, scientific as well as common practice, where theories are supposed to imply their evidence, and explain the phenomena which are thereby constituted evidence, so that nothing would be evidence which was not in principle explainable with reference to that for which it is taken as evidence. It fits, as well, that pattern of scientific inference identified by Peirce[19] and developed by N. R. Hanson in which an hypothesis is *abducted* from a phenomenon, viz. when, were it true, the phenomenon would be understood as a matter of course. This, to be sure, marks out only a condition for evidential *adequacy*, and though I put no restrictions here upon what specific criteria a sentence *e* must satisfy in order that it might serve as evidence, one may think for a moment of philosophical programs which do insist that there is a severely restricted set of things through which I know whatever else I know, say certain inner states of myself. Then *e* is drawn from a set of sentences satisfied exclusively by such inner states, whatever these may be. If anything is to be known *through* these, it must be because it will explain the occurrence and character of the inner state taken in evidence. Thus the Cartesian program in epistemology would be fulfilled if the occurrence and character of my ideas could be explained with reference to external things, themselves 'objects' of the ideas which then are evidence for those objects. What especially impressed Descartes was my incapacity to deduce the explanation of my ideas from the ideas themselves, or even deduce the fact that they *have* an explanation, and though I have a natural impulse, he claimed, to believe that my ideas are caused by their objects, they may have wholly different or no causes, and my impulse is not to be trusted. This, which is the Problem of the External World, arises here chiefly because of the unnatural restrictions Descartes fatefully placed upon what can be counted as evidence; but my interest in the case is exhausted through exhibiting it as a dramatization of the need which the concept of explanation serves to satisfy in our analysis. What *e* is evidence for is *always* 'external' to *e* – nothing is presumably explained through *itself* – and of course there are always the problems to be faced of alternative explanations, overdetermination, and the like. But these we need not confront at this point.

One intuitive feature, however, is worth stressing: we may defeat a claim that *s* explains *e* by demonstrating that *e* would have been true whether *s* had been true or not, and hence that the truth of *e* is wholly independent in the present case of the truth of *s*. If I see a round spot on the billiard table, and infer that there is a white ball on the table, I may be right that there is such a ball, though in fact it is hidden behind a cushion and the white spot happens to be a freak illumination which would have been there whether or not the white ball was there: the presence of the white ball explains nothing so far as concerns that spot. This seems always to be the mark of the Gettier cases: the explanatory hypothesis, a justified one surely, that *n* had bought a new suit, was victim to the fact that the suit he bought is not the suit he wears, and the one has nothing to do with the other. So I shall gloss 'adequate' in K-4 as: 'is (non-fortuitously) explained by'.

We cannot extend this immediately to the case of action, if only because it seems to invert the natural order of things to explain the happening of *b* through the happening of *a* when the fact is that *m* made *a* happen (in part) through doing *b*, so that, if anything, it is with reference to *b* that we would most naturally explain *a*, viz. discounting final causes. But nothing prevents us from inverting A-4 to accommodate our intuition, and say that *b* is adequate for *a* if *b* explains *a*, that is, that *a* happened here because *b* happened. Certainly, the same defeating condition applies here as in the case of cognition, namely reference to *b* is defeated as explanatory of *a* if it can be demonstrated that in the present instance, *a* would have occurred anyway, whether or not *b* had occurred, so that its occurrence is independent of *b*'s and their co-occurrence mere coincidence. Since *a* and *b* are supposed to be *events*, it seems natural to appreciate 'explains' in A-4 as '*causally* explains'. And the two models could be brought into further congruity by specializing explanation in the case of cognition in a similar way. This would not be a causal theory of knowledge so much as a causal theory of *evidence*, an analysis of knowledge which has a causal component, just as the analysis of action is less a causal theory of action than a model for a class of actions which would have a causal component. The concept of explanation perhaps is richer than the concept of causation – it must be if we explain *laws* with reference to higher order laws – but it is not clear that we shall have need of any save the concept of causal explanation. So I shall have causation primarily in mind as I continue to construe these cases of action and cognition in which explanation figures as it is being made to do here.

The concept of non-fortuitous explanation, meanwhile, requires some comment, although it is easier to furnish examples of what one wishes to have ruled out by it than it is to make the principle of exclusion formal and explicit. Let me give examples for each of the two domains. (A) *m* flips a switch, intending that the lights go on, and they do. The switch is dead, but the click reminds the custodian in the next room that it is time to turn the lights on, which he does, illuminating the room as *m* intended. The flipping of the switch by *m* then enters into the explanation of the lights going on, setting up a causal chain, but it is just *m*'s good luck that what he intended should happen in fact happens. (B) *m* believes that *n* has acquired a new suit on the basis of observing him to be wearing one: and *n* indeed has acquired a new suit, though not the one he is wearing. Yet had he not acquired a new suit, he would not be wearing this one. For *his* suit was splashed by a passing oil-truck, and his compassionate identical twin loaned him his virtually identical suit so that he may show up for his interview in suitable habit. So he would not be wearing this new suit, in the light of the circumstances, had he not acquired a new suit first: what *m* truly believes enters into the explanation of his evidence, but there is no knowledge here. Now in both (A) and (B) the successes are lucky in a way which is inconsistent with the concepts of action and cognition in a sense which it is the explicit function of the concept of non-fortuity to exclude. A *deus ex machina* is no less one for having been prayed for. Now it will not do to say that an explanation of *j* by *i* is fortuitous if there is something *l* such that *i* explains *l* and *l* explains *j* and *i* cannot explain *j* alone: for this, though it fits the case at hand, equally fits any case in which there is an explanatory chain, e.g. where by flicking the switch, hence closing a circuit, *m* lights the bulb. What we need rather is some criterion for distinguishing fortuitous from non-fortuitous explanatory chains, all the more difficult to find, I believe, since each supports a true counterfactual. What *appears* to distinguish them is that fortuitous explanations have a *chance* factor at some point, e.g. the passing truck in (B) and the custodian within earshot in (A). It is *not* a matter of chance that in the normal case (though this may be circular) flipping a switch closes a circuit. But I propose no analysis of chance occurrences here.

We must note that the various entries in the two analyses are not altogether independent. In some respect, K-1 and A-1 appear independent of K-2 and A-2 respectively. A man's beliefs and his intentions are independent of the *truth* of what is believed and the *fulfilment* of what is intended, and of course the converse is true as well: a sentence may be true and an event take place independently of whether we believe the one or intend the other. But K-2 and K-4 do not seem independent in this way, since the truth of *s* is an explanatory condition of the truth of *e*, and A-2 and A-4 are similarly dependent since *b* is an explanatory condition for the occurrence of *a*. So A-4 would be false if A-2 were false, and K-4 would be false if K-2 were false.

IV

A question arises whether we should wish to add to the analysis and

K-5   *m* believes that K-4

A-5   *m* believes that A-4.

The reason for such a wish, in the case of action at least, is a desire to distinguish between *a* being an action of *m* or being only the *consequence* of an action. If *a* happens because *b* happens, then we should be obliged to say that if this makes *a* an action, it makes whatever else happens because *b* happens an action as well. And *m* does whatever may be a consequence of whatever he does. A similar consideration in the theory of knowledge directs us to distinguish between a man knowing something because something else he knows is a consequence of it; and his knowing whatever it is of which what he knows is a consequence. The former is a kind of omnipotency and the latter is a kind of omniscience.[20]

It seems plain enough that we have some control over this if we pay attention to the representational element in either analysis, namely what *m* intends to be the case and what he believes to be the case. So we might say that *a* is an action of *m*'s and not a mere consequence of an action only if he intended that *a* happen; and that *s* is a piece of knowledge and not the mere consequence of a piece of knowledge only if *m* in fact *believes* that *s*. If we are to employ these representational elements as determining the boundaries of what *m* does which is a consequence of his actions, and of what he knows which his knowledge is a consequence of, then I think we must invoke A-1 in explanation of A-3. That is to say, *m* does *b* because he intended that *a* should happen. And this, I think, entails or at least strongly implies A-5. For it is not plausible to suppose a man did something, intending that something else should happen, unless he believed that his doing the former would make the latter happen, would, in historical retrospect, enter in as an explanation of the latter. So A-1 explains A-3, and these together imply A-5.

But something very close to this is needed in the analysis of knowledge as well. Philosophers have been somewhat obsessed with adventitious truth, as we might call it, as a disqualification of knowledge – truth which is conferred upon *s* in such a way as to have nothing to do with the basis upon which *m* believes that *s* – but adventitious belief is perhaps at least as disqualifying a lapse.[21] For if he believes what is true though for reasons having nothing to do with what makes it true, then even though he is in possession of adequate evidence, we would hardly credit him with knowledge. Suppose a man believes a certain alleged sixteenth-century painting to be fake, which it is. And he has plenty of evidence for his belief: the pigment dissolves instantly under acetone; the costumes are vaguely Empire; the panel is plywood stamped 'Made in Hoboken'; the dealer is a notorious swindler. He knows all this, but it fails to make an impression: *he* believes the painting a fake because the figures remind him of Rouault's (in fact they are not in the least like Rouault's). So it is not enough to hold a true belief and to have adequate evidence: one has to hold the belief because of the adequate evidence if there is to be knowledge: the right sort of evidence has to enter in the right sort of way into the explanation of the fact that the man believes as he does. So I think that when the conditions K-1 through K-4 hold, we would want to add that K-1 is true because K-3 is true, and this implies that K-5 is true as well. If m believes that s because he knows that e, it is reasonable to suppose he believes that e is adequate evidence for s. So K-1 and K-3 imply K-5, and m, in such a case, may appeal to K-4 in justification of K-1. It is with reference to K-4 that m believes that s on the basis of what he knows, namely e. And, returning to action, it is with reference to A-4 that m would justify his doing b: he does it because he believes it to be adequate for a, which he intends should happen.

It will be noted that whereas it is K-1 we speak of as being justified in the case of knowledge, it is A-3 that we speak of as being justified in the case of action. This can hardly be an accident, since beliefs and actions are the natural candidates for justification, rational belief and rational actions being the two chief (and perhaps only) actualizations of rationality in men. But what is striking in these two patterns of justification is that they are the inverse of each other. In knowledge we justify a man's belief on the basis of what he knows together with his explanatory hypotheses; in the case of action we explain what he does in terms of his intentions and his explanatory hypotheses. This is the second inversion between the two analyses. The first comes in the explanatory hypotheses themselves. In the one case we explain what is known in K-3 with reference to what it is that is said to be known *through* this. In the other case, we explain, with reference to what is done in A-3, that which we do *through* doing it, and the line of explanations runs outwards from what we do, rather than inwards, as in the case of knowledge.[22]

But these inversions are quite what we must expect if we think for a moment about how we intuitively regard action and knowledge respectively. It is the aim of knowledge to interpret the world in the sense of fitting our representations to the way it is. It is the aim of action to *change* the world in such a way that it is fitted to our representations of it. We may adapt a delightful example from Miss Anscombe's *Intention* to bring the differences out sharply. A man is given a shopping list, with 'potatoes' as one of the itemized purchases he is to make. He brings tomatoes home, however, and, accused of having failed in his mission, he decides to set things right by crossing out 'potatoes' and writing 'tomatoes' in instead. A case of comparable but precisely inverse dottiness would be found were a man asked to *list* what has just been brought into the kitchen, writing down 'potatoes' when in fact there are none of these, but in fact only tomatoes. Accused of failure, he decided to set things right by throwing the tomatoes out and replacing them with potatoes. His is the madness of the poor portraitist who lops an inch off the Duchess's nose to make his portrait of her come out right.

Let us make these inversions explicit and round off our analyses by adding

K-6   K-1 because K-3

and

A-6   A-3 because A-1.

In the light of these, it is instructive to contemplate cases in which all the elements of the analysis are true except K-4 and A-4. These are the cases where beliefs and intentions are true by accident, and so are illusions of cognitive and practical success respectively. But now if we suppose K-2 and A-2 false in addition, we get the more common failures which are the tragic counterparts to those cognitive and practical victories which the Standard Analyses of Knowledge and Action define: of believing that *s* on the basis of knowing that *e*, believing that *e* is adequate evidence for *s*; and of doing *b* because one believes that this is adequate for *a*, which one intends shall happen. These are cases of misinterpretation and misperformance respectively, the case of those who fail to interpret the world right, or who fail to change it as they should wish. Heeding the Eleventh Thesis on Feuerbach is no talisman against failure, and those who fail to interpret the world right are doomed to fail in changing it as they should wish, or else having it change adventitiously, and through no directed effort of their own.

The 'because' in K-6 and especially in A-6, meanwhile, has been of some concern to philosophers. Have we here but a straightforward case of causation, in which m's intention *causes* his action? And in which his knowing something *causes* him to believe something? Or in invoking a man's intention in explanation of his action, are we bringing in a pattern of explanation of a different logical sort from that by means of which we explain a happening, say, through its causes? In one respect it is premature to attempt an answer to these questions, first because (!) we have said nothing about the causal relation as such, and secondly because the 'cause' in K-6 – itself a piece of knowledge on m's part – and the 'effect' in A-6 – a piece of action on m's part – have been bracketed thus far in our analysis. Suppose, however, that we considered 'observation' as an instance of the kind of knowledge bracketed here: then m's observing that which makes e true might cause him to believe that s in a sense of 'cause' no different from that in which, say, a ball causes a window to break. And even if believing were a state of m and causality a relationship between *events*, still, being *put* into a state is an event, though the state itself may endure indefinitely, like the state of being broken in the window's case. With intentions, themselves regarded as states, the matter is more, or seemingly more complex, since the *termination* of an intention, though an event, does not need to cause an action: for a man might simply stop intending one thing and come to intend another. Well, so might a man begin to believe something without being caused to believe it through having come to know something, without this defeating the claim that there are cases where knowing that e may cause a man to believe that s. And so, supposing preservation of structure, with intentions. Thus one may, with a measure of ingenuity, maintain that only straightforward causation is involved here, even if one's intention may constitute one's *reason* for acting, in the one case, and one's knowledge, in the other case, may constitute one's reason for believing. Perhaps not every reference to reason is also a reference to a cause, but in at least these models, there is no obvious discouragement to the thesis that m's reasons *are* causes. There may, to be sure, be cases in which men act for causes which are not reasons, and similarly believe for causes which are not reasons, but these would neither of them be rational or reasoned actions and beliefs. But all of these are intricacies we might better shelve for the present, until we remove the brackets from our analyses, and get some better control over the concept of causation.

V

By the *object* of an action or a cognition, as these are structured by the analyses we have just drawn, I shall mean so much of the world (or of history) as confers truth upon that which the agent or the knower respectively intends or believes to be true, and exclusive of the fact that he knows or does them. Thus the spatial translation of a stone makes true what *m* intends, when *m* intends that the stone in question move. But of course it does not alone make true the sentence '*mDa*' – where *a* = the spatial translation of the relevant stone – for *a* satisfies but one of the conditions laid down by the analysis of action, and the satisfaction of this condition does not entail the satisfaction of all the others. So it is quite possible that *a* should have occurred and *mDa* be false, in much (or exactly) the same way in which *o* – the object of a cognition – should have existed though *mKs* were false, and *o* is what makes *s* true. So we may consider these objects apart and independent from the actional and cognitive contexts in which they in fact are embedded.

This may seem linguistically parochial to the metaphysical realist, as it makes what is or happens in the world relative to sentences made true by whatever is or happens in the world: and the world's contents and events, it may be charged, have boundaries and individualities independent of our descriptions and representations. Be this as it may, it is at least plain that *we* cannot speak of the boundaries and individuations of actions or cognitions save with reference to the representations of the person to whom action or knowledge is ascribed. This is secured by the first entry in either analysis, but it contributes to the logical complexities of sentences which ascribe knowledge or action to *m*, since these refer at once to an object *and* a representation. And because such sentences as *mDa* and *mKs* are at once about the world and about someone's representation of the world, they are semantical mongrels, sharing certain logical features with sentences straightforwardly about the world, and others with sentences straightforwardly about representations. If we think of *mKs* and *mDa* as logical compounds of sentences 1–6 in either analysis, then one of the components of each analysis – A-1 and K-1 – is quite clearly about a representation, and another – A-2 or K-2 – is *almost* as clearly about the world. Let us note certain differences.

One difference, clearly, between '*m* knows that *s*' and '*m* believes that *s*' is that the latter does not and the former does entail that *s* is true. And one difference between '*m* intends that *a* happen' and '*m* does *a*' is that the latter entails as the former does not that *a* happens. So '*m* knows that *s*' and '*m* does *a*' are false if *s* is false or *a* does not occur, and both the ascription of action and of cognition, in contrast with the ascription of belief or intention, are semi-truth-functional. Again, it is notorious that it does *not* follow from '*m* believes that *i* is F' that ($\exists x$) (*m* believes that *x* is F) – for the latter would be false if there is no such individual; and were the entailment licit, men could not be said to have beliefs about non-existent things, and worse, we could deduce the existence of anything anyone believed to exist: every believer would constitute adequate evidence for the existence of that in which he believed. So quantification into *s* in such contexts as '*m* believes that *s*' is ruled out. Such contexts are what Quine speaks of as *opaque* to quantification.[23] The reason for this is plain. Ascription of belief is really about a man's representation, not about what would make the representation a *true* one. And reference to a representation is not reference to what the representation refers to if, indeed, it succeeds in referring. But with knowledge, matters are less well defined. For it does seem as though, from '*m* knows that *i* is F' we can infer (Ex) (*m* knows that *x* is F). It seems that way because the former entails the truth of '*i* is F' and the latter entails the existence of *i* and hence the truth of ($\exists x$) F*x*. And so knowledge-ascriptions appear, again in Quine's phrase, *transparent* to quantification. But this is because knowledge-ascriptions are at once about representations *and* objects, about the world *and* about a man's representation. If we think only about that part of the analysis of knowledge which is about the world, quantification, with its existential implications, seems unexceptionable. And so, with suitable alterations, with ascriptions of action in contrast with ascriptions of intention.

Nevertheless, it would be a mistake to suppose, on the basis of this, that knowledge- and action-ascriptions are *simply* transparent. For if we turn to another form of operation upon terms in referential position, we find a considerable ambiguity. It is a well-known feature of belief-sentences that, if *m* believes that *i* is F, and if the term '*i*' is co-referential with the term '*j*', it is by no means logically assured that *m* believes that *j* is F. But in the ordinary transparent context, interchange of co-referential expressions is guaranteed to preserve truth-value, and indeed this defines a transparent context. Again, the reason why this will not do in belief sentences is plain. They are about representations, and *not* about what would make these representations true. That m represents i as F is a true description of *his* representation. And if it is true, then it in fact is *false* that he represents j as F. He may *in addition* represent j as F, but this would be another representation. So the only way in which we can effect interchanges in belief-sentences will be through interchanging terms referring to the same element of a representation, rather than through interchanging terms which refer to whatever the element itself might refer to. For with belief-sentences we are talking about representations as such, rather than about whatever it is that the representations might refer us to. Exactly the same opacities extend to the case of knowledge. It does not follow (to use an example of Kneale's[24]) from the fact that the Pope knows that twelve is the number of Apostles, that the Pope knows that the sum of the fourth and fifth prime numbers is the number of Apostles – even though twelve is the sum of the fourth and fifth primes. The typical Pope can be assumed cognitively competent regarding the New Testament (indeed infallible), but not necessarily even cognitively aware of identities in number theory. In ascriptions of knowledge, the mode of representation is crucial: the Pope knows the truth only relative to his representation of it. And so, I am afraid, with us all. Now it is absurd to suppose that knowledge-ascriptions are transparent with respect to quantification and opaque with regard to substitution. And so some uniform policy of logical operation must be agreed upon.

This matter becomes crucial when we turn to the concept of action. Suppose mDa and suppose that what m intends to be true is s, and that a makes s true. Let t be a term in referring position in s and let t' be co-referential with t, and let s' finally be the result of substituting t' for t. Then a makes true s' since it makes true s. But do we wish to say that a 'under the description s'' is what m did? That s' describes his action? It describes a truly. But it does *not* describe his *action* if s is what m intended and reference to his representation is a truth-condition for the ascription of action. The issue of strict, in contrast with limited liability is essentially a matter of whether we insist upon making literal and explicit reference to the *content* of a man's intention, or if we insist instead upon the event we explain as having occurred through his having done it, without literal reference to *his* representation. The great Greek legends of Atrius and Oedipus show that the gods punished by a criterion of strict liability. Atrius intended to eat what was served him but not to eat his children, though in eating what was served him he ate his children. Oedipus intended to make love to the queenly lady, though not to make love to his mother, but in making love to the queenly lady he made love to his mother. A like strictness in the domain of cognition would require that Oedipus and Atrius *know* they were respectively loving a mother and eating a child, which would mean that each *knowingly* committed a foul act. But of course the tragedies evolve in part because the crucial description is allegedly hidden from the perpetrator. Strict liability in action and limited liability in cognition is the formula for tragedy (or comedy), but it is hardly a formula for logicians concerned with patterns of unexceptionable inference, and a consistent policy must be invariant to the two domains. Either we do everything which can be truly said of *what* we do, and know everything about what can be truly said of *what* we know, or reference to our representations defines the limits of practical and cognitive responsibility. I opt for the latter.

Reference to representations considerably complicates the semantics of knowledge- and action-ascriptions, largely because we require a very much more exacting mode for individuating representations than we need in connection with their objects. This requirement falls as much upon anyone who takes liabilities strictly and knowledge- and action-sentences as transparent, as it does upon me. For what he insists upon is that it is the *same* thing under *different* descriptions, and hence reference to the *same* thing cannot account for the differences in the descriptions. If *s* and *s'* are equally made true by the object *o*, it does not follow that *s* and *s'* are the same description. 'Masaccio paints the Brancacci Frescos' is made true by what makes true 'Maso di Ser Giovanni di Chastello Sangiovanni paints the Brancacci frescos' – if Masaccio indeed is Maso di Ser Giovanni di Chastello Sangiovanni. But the *sentences* are conspicuously different if only as designs. We may get some sense of the difference if we think of the perhaps overdeterminate paradigm of direct quotation, where the words within quotes must be the same words as those spoken by him we quote. Obviously, we make certain allowances here: we may quote a man in print though he spoke, and we may quote a man in English who speaks only French. But we are not at license to interchange co-referential or even synonymous expressions, for then we misquote him. So quotations rigorously circumscribe the sentences a man utters, and may be regarded, in effect, as *pictures* of the words they reproduce. In something like this, in ascribing a belief that *s* to a man *m*, or an intention that *s* to a man *n*, we are virtually *depicting* their alleged representation of the world. If believing or intending are instances of thinking,[25] and thinking were inner speech as it is made out to be in the *Theaetetus*, then the conventions of belief- or intention-ascription would collapse virtually into those of quotation, and the sentence '*m* believes that *s*' would furnish in the sentential shape *s* what is tantamount to a picture of *m*'s soul.[26] And in virtue of the representational components in knowledge- and action-ascriptions, much the same sort of picture of what the subject in question represents, or *how* he represents the world is given. But in addition to this, of course, knowledge- and action-ascriptions bridge the space between representations and objects. For it is through succeeding in action and cognition that we bring our representations, however specific, into alignment with the world. And conversely, it is because action- and knowledge-ascriptions are really rather elaborate conjunctions of sentences, as the fact that the analysis of each has involved so far the isolation of six distinct entries should prove; and it is because these entries are of different semantical sorts, that the logical behavior of these ascriptions may appear anomalous. Ascription of knowledge that *s*, for example, contains at least one opaque entry and at least one transparent one, e.g. '*m* believes that *s*' and '*s*' respectively. With *s* standing alone, all the operations admissible for free-standing sentences apply: substitution of co-referential and of synonymous expressions *salva veritate*, quantification, and the like. But none of this works with '*m* believes that *s*'. The explanation is that here *s* is mentioned rather than used, but since both use and mention are collapsed in '*m* knows that *s*', the latter appears to be opaque and transparent at once! Exactly such considerations apply with action ascriptions as well. What is crucial to *our* purposes, however, is that we individuate actions and cognitions alike in part by individuating the representations of the subject, and then through this those bits of history and reality which are respectively done and known by him.

VI

The first entry in each of our analyses is one in which *m* stands in a certain relation to a representation, for to believe that *s*, or to intend *a*, is to be in a certain representing way: to be, I should want to say, in a *representational state* which (in the case of belief) *s* pictures if '*m* believes that *s*' is true. Now to represent is to hold what I will term a *truth-*

attitude toward a representation, which will vary according to the mode of representation, e.g. whether one hopes, or believes, or intends that *r*, where *r* is the representation in question. A truth-attitude is a belief regarding the semantical value of the representation, the belief that *s* is *true*, for example, when one believes that *s*.

In belief, a man refers his representations to the world. If he believes, for example, that as an astrological species Capricorns are industrious, he spontaneously supposes this a feature of the world, and this spontaneous supposition is one mark of belief as a mode of representation. It remains a fact that *m* believes what he does regarding Capricorns even though the Zodiac is false and the divisions it imposes are utterly permeable, for the falsity of *r* leaves unaffected the truth of '*m* believes that *r*'. So it is quite consistent to say, out of one's superior knowledge, that *m* believes what is false. But *m* cannot say this of himself. He cannot, because to believe that *r* is to believe that *r* is true, and to believe that *r* is false is exactly not to believe that *r*.[27]

We are thus in no position to refer our beliefs to ourselves as mere ornaments of the soul, things we happen merely to have. So long as they are beliefs we must refer them to the world, and hence they cannot survive a change in truth-attitude: no longer to believe that *r* is true is no longer to believe that *r*. And, in part because other modes of representation are typically held against a certain background of belief, they too have corresponding truth-attitudes. Thus, if I hope my friend has survived the crash, I must at least believe it is not false that he has survived the crash, and the hope dies with the knowledge that it *is* false that he has survived. I cannot wish that *r* were true if I know that *r* is true: I only can be *glad* that it is the case. Nor can I *fancy* that *r* if I believe that *r* is true. Nor can I regret that something has happened which I believe has not in fact happened. And so forth. It is an interesting question whether there are semantically neutral modes of representation. Descartes, for whom the vehicles of representation were *idées*, evidently believed it possible though difficult to restrain his 'vagabond mind' from holding truth-attitudes towards these: to represent himself as in his dressing-gown in a heated room, for example, without believing either that he was or was not in a dressing-gown in a heated room. He proposed to *believe* nothing (no *idée*) which was not first clear and distinct, and by this criterion, should there be obscure or indistinct *idées* only, he must curb himself from holding with regard to any of them a definite truth-attitude. For then, though he will have foregone ever being right, he will at least have avoided ever being *wrong*. And Descartes' successors, the Phenomenologists, in speaking of the *bracketing* of experience, must similarly suppose it possible to represent in a semantically neutral way, for what after all are we bracketing *except* truth-attitudes? Perhaps a man can inventory the representational contents of his mind without paying attention to the mode of representation in any case, nor accordingly to the truth-attitudes he holds towards these representations. But except for these philosophical suspensions, truth-attitudes are co-present in most modes of representation, and I would like now to pay special attention to the attitudes which go with *intention*.

I believe it analytical to the concept of intention that, if *m* intends that *r*, *m* intends to make happen that which will make *r* true. There are just the same absurdities in saying that one intends that *r* but that one will not do what is required in order that *r* be true, as there are in saying one believes what one believes not to be true. Intention then *commits* one to act, and it is for this reason that it is counted a particular sort of failure when what a man intends to be true, say *r*, is made true through no action of his, or, what comes almost to the same thing, is made true by something he does only unintentionally, as when, intending to kill my enemy, I run him over on my way to do him in. As matters worked out, I would not have killed him had I not intended to, but I did not kill him intentionally, and the *latter* requires accordingly something in excess of a given event having an intention as its cause, even though the event makes true what a man intended *be* true and in fact he made it be true himself. The latter case is like doing what you promised without keeping your promise, as one does by being where one had promised one would be, only by accident, so to speak, having forgotten one had promised to be there. It is built into the notion of keeping a promise that *r*, that he who makes *r* true does so *because he made the promise*.[28] But then, as in intention, something more is required than that his having made the promise in some way caused him to do what he had promised to do. This is why intentions and promises cannot simply be regarded as causes if we are to speak of actions as intentional, or as discharging a promise. And it is why, I think, those who might wish to insist that reasons and causes are distinct could justify their view, not because reasons are *not* causes, but that we seem to demand something more of a reason than that a man's having it should cause him to do a certain thing which then causes that to happen which answers to his reason.

My reason for shooting at *m* may be that I wish him dead – he has seduced my aunt, say – but something strikes my arm as I by squeezing the trigger, sever the chandelier above his head which kills him when it falls. But this does not so much show that reasons are not causes, as that it should not be an *accident* that events causally traced to a man's reason should make the latter come out true. And we find more or less the same vexations here as we did in our previous analyses, where it had to be non-fortuitous that something explained something else. It is perhaps because implicit rejection of a mediating accident is involved here, that philosophers insisting upon a distinction between reasons and causes have supposed that reasons are *essentially* or *necessarily* connected with what they are reasons for. In any case, we can modify our claim this way: if *m* intends *r*, he intends that *r* should be made true by him because he intends that *r*, and that this not be accidental. So if *r* is made true through some other route, his intention will not have been fulfilled. It will be once more like being right for the wrong reasons. And we shall later note that not only must one believe what one believes to be true, but true for the reasons one has for believing it.

Intention commits us, however portentous this may sound, to changing the world as belief commits us to the view that the world is as we represent it. This suggests, then, a sort of complementarity between belief and intention which perhaps explains the complementarity between knowledge and action which Marx refers to in the Eleventh Thesis on Feuerbach. If one knows that *s*, *s* is true and what makes it true is then a *fait accompli*. So *s* cannot be regarded by him who knows that *s* as something he can intend. One cannot intend to make true what one believes already is true, and to believe that *s* already is true is to consider action with regard to *s* as logically foreclosed. So it is as though, with obvious qualifications, one cannot simultaneously believe that *s* and intend that *s*, since the truth-attitudes appropriate to belief and to intention here conflict. I cannot intend to live forever if I believe I am immortal: for then there is nothing for me to do which could make an effective difference. The truth of *s* leaves no logical space in which steps can be taken to make *s* true: and if whatever is to be true already is so, nothing can be done of the sort we have been analyzing in this chapter. For all actions are foredoomed to failure or superfluousness. The only option given us is to know the truth, but not to make it.

So intentions imply a view of history not only in which not everything which will be true is already true, but in which one is able to be effective in shaping events to fit one's representations. One must believe that history is not in effect over before it has happened, that it is open and in some deep respect up to us. It is in this sense that intentions imply the falsity of Fatalism, which holds the shape of history to be foregone and *accompli*, that whatever will be true has been forever true.[29] And it is in this sense that actions, if they occur, refute Fatalism. For actions imply intentions, and intentions imply through their truth-attitudes that Fatalism is false. If we make *r* true by acting, *r* cannot have been true before we made it true. This does not mean that actions do occur. It is only that if they occur, all their presuppositions must be satisfied, and whatever conflicts with these must be false.

But it follows that if *m*D*a*, then, since this entails that *m* made happen that (*a*) which confers truth upon his erstwhile representation *r*, no one, until the action was completed, could have known that *r*. No one can have known, because knowledge that *r* entails that *r* is true, and if *r* were true before *m* made happen what made *r* true, then it is false that that is what *m* did. So knowledge and action, with regard to the same representation, are logically inimical: where there is room for action, there is none for knowledge; and where there is room for knowledge there is none for action. It is in this respect that the man of action and the man of thought are logical antagonists. If the world is a *fait accompli*, our sole option is to interpret it correctly, to find out what is the case.[30] If we can change the world, however, it is not a *fait accompli*, and to attempt merely to interpret it is foredoomed to failure. We can only know the truth when it has been made. Knowledge presupposes closure at just those points at which action presupposes openness. And as we are constrained to suppose ourselves impotent regarding the past – we cannot do what has already happened – so are we constrained to suppose ourselves ignorant with regard to the future – we cannot know what has not happened. To believe that there are actions is to believe that what we at last can know will have come about in part because of what we have done: that the shape of the past is contingent upon the shapes we project onto the future.[31]

The Future is what we cannot know and the Past is what we cannot alter. So we are at once constrained to a Skepticism regarding the future and a Fatalism regarding the past. The former is entailed by that conceptual feature of knowledge which entails that if a man knows that *s*, then *s* must be true and its object accordingly exist. So if we knew the future, the future would exist and its alteration would be as impossible as by common consent the alteration of the Past is allowed to be. By contrast, if we *could* alter the past, then it could not be knowable nor fixed, but would be characterized by just that plasticity which by common consent defines the Future. There are philosophies of knowledge which treat the future in terms appropriate to the past and philosophies of action which treat the past in terms appropriate to the future. The former, of course, must suppose action impossible or redefine it as a form of knowledge, and the latter must regard knowledge as impossible or regard it a form of action. If action and knowledge are at once distinct and parallel, as we have argued in this chapter that they are, then, if we are to be regarded agents and knowers at once, the world itself must be at once sufficiently fixed for knowledge and sufficiently plastic for action. This is entailed, and in some measure defined, by the simultaneous applicability of the two models we have developed here.

If the models are simultaneously applicable, of course, we face a question. In order that *m* do *a*, he must do *b*, and in order that he know that *s*, he must know that *e*. These moments of action and cognition, which are *parts* of the models of action and cognition we have elaborated, have so far been bracketed. Now we must face what we have held to one side. For let the world be as fixed and as plastic as may be required, there is neither knowledge nor action unless we can do that *through* which we do such things as the model characterizes, and know things *through* which we have such knowledge as fits the Standard Analysis. To these matters we now must turn.

BASIC ACTIONS AND BASIC COGNITIONS

The class of actions and cognitions logically surveyed in Chapter 1 were those in which a man does or knows something *through* some other thing that he does or knows, and hence actions and cognitions which *contain*, as it were, other actions and cognitions as components. Actions and cognitions thus characterized I shall designate as *mediated*. It is the mark of a mediated action mDa that there be an event b, distinct from a; that b itself be done by m; that a happen because b happens; and that that doing of b by m be a component of mDa. Correspondingly, it is the mark of a mediated cognition mKs that there be some sentence e distinct from s; that e itself be known by m; that e be true because s is true; and that knowing that e on the part of m be a component in mKs. It is clear that neither all actions nor all cognitions can be mediated ones.

If, in each case in which I do something, I must do something else *through* which the first thing is done, then nothing could be done at all. And so again with knowing. For in either analysis, an infinite regression is generated – and a vicious one, for the difficulty is not that it is impossible that an infinitude of distinct things should be known or done. It may be possible, or at least not interestingly impossible, that an infinitude of things should be done even in a finite interval,[1] or that an infinitude of distinct things known even by a finite mind. It is rather that one could not enter the chain of actions or cognitions if, always as a condition for doing so, one must know or do something first: for *that* condition then has a condition that one do or know something *else* first, and this runs viciously to infinity. So if there are mediated actions and cognitions, there must be actions and cognitions which contain no further actions and cognitions as components. These are actions we do but not *through* any distinct thing which we also do, and cognitions had but not through something which we also know. Such actions and cognitions as these I shall call *basic*, and mediated ones are accordingly non-basic.

Mediated actions are not the only sorts of non-basic actions, and it will be useful to sketch two other sorts of non-basic action.

(1) A composite action might consist only of basic actions performed in sequence or together, as in a dance. Thus suppose one moves a right leg back from an initial position and a left arm forward. Then one moves these to the initial position, and does the same things with the left leg and the right arm. And this completes the dance. Amongst the events which compose the dance, there is no *causal* connection. The aggregate of basic actions is integrated into the composite action by virtue of the rules of the dance. And one performs the composite actions by performing the basic actions in the appropriate order.[2]

There is an analogous sort of composite cognition. Suppose '*x* is an apple' may be analyzed into a set of predicates on *x*, each of which may be observed to hold of *x* through a basic cognition. Then, if one knows basically each of the appropriate sentences, there is nothing further one must know in order to know that *x* is an apple, except the rules of meaning by which '*x* is an apple' is analyzed into the set of predicates on *x*.[3]

There are theories of knowledge according to which whatever we can know must be so analyzable, if the knowledge in question is not basic, so that all cognitions either are composite or basic. And so are there theories of action according to which all actions are basic or composite, that is 'analyzable without remainder' into sequences and sets of basic actions.[4]

(2) A man blesses someone by raising his arm. The blessing is something he does *through* raising his arm, and so seems non-basic, but clearly there is no event distinct from the raising of the arm in which the blessing consists, e.g. the blessing is not *caused* by the rising of the arm. What we have is a basic action performed in *conformity with a rule* which licenses a redescription of it as a blessing, providing the agent is in a position to play the role of blesser. Let us call such actions *gestures*.

There are non-basic cognitions which correspond to gestures. Suppose I *perceive* a man blessing someone. Then it may be said that what I really see is that he raises his arm. I do not in addition see something separately describable as a *blessing* which he does. What I do, in effect, is to bring what I perceive under a rule of interpretation, according to which it is a blessing. That it is a blessing is not something I know *through* knowing the man to have raised his arm. Rather, I know it is a blessing through knowing what rule applies. It is like knowing that the shape A is the first capital letter of the alphabet, viz. that it is the letter 'A'. The *letter* 'A' is the *shape* A *covered by a rule*.

Now clearly, there are neither composite actions nor cognitions on the one hand, nor gestures and their cognitional counterparts on the other, unless there are basic actions. For these have basic actions and cognitions as components. So, that there are non-basic actions and cognitions other than mediated ones does not change the analysis. But the concept of mediation yields the regressive argument to basic actions, and only mediated actions and cognitions comprise a non-conventional, that is, a causal or a logical liaison between what is known (or done) and that through which it is known (or done).

II

If *m*K*e* is a basic cognition, then *m* knows directly that *e*, in the respect that there is nothing *f* through knowing which, *m* knows that *e*: he *simply* knows that *e*, again in the respect that there is no further cognition which is a component in his so knowing. So, if he *believes* that *e* is true, there is at least nothing to which he could appeal to justify his so believing except the fact that he knows that *e* is true, which would be a curious justification if, as in the model for the Standard Analysis of Knowledge, belief that *e* would be a component in knowledge that *e*. Such justification would have an air of circularity which we can only dispel by turning, for a moment, away from language towards the world. Once more let us regard the *object* of a cognition as that which confers truth upon whatever is believed by him to whom cognition is ascribed, so that *o* is the object of *s* if *s* is made true by *o* and believed by *m*. In *mediated* cognition, we may say that *m* is then cognitively related to the object of *s* through the object of *e*, where *e* expresses his evidence for *s*. Let the object of *e* be *x*. In direct or basic cognition, then, *m* is cognitively related to *x* in a direct way, that is to say, not through being related cognitively to any other object. The reason he is cognitively related to *o* when he is cognitively related to *e* will in general be because *o* and *e* themselves are related, e.g. because, perhaps, *o* *explains* *x*. Or because *o* has caused *x*. But whatever the case, *m*'s cognitive relation to *x* is *immediate* and direct when there is no mediating object. Since this is a cognitive relationship, let us say that *m* *cognizes x*. And now the air of circularity disappears. For *m* believes that *e* because he cognizes *x*, where *x* is what makes *e* true. And he knows directly that *e* because he cognizes directly what makes his belief that *e* a true one.

Though *cognize* is a term of art, it has some natural exemplifications in *perception, intuition, experience,* and the like, and if we think, for example, just of the first member in this little list, we get a very natural reading for '*m* knows directly that *e*'. It is that *m* believes that *e* because he perceives that which makes *e* true. Thus I know that there is a piece of paper before me if I perceive a piece of paper. Other conditions no doubt are required, but whatever these may be, it is the direct cognitive relation which interests me, and which I shall concentrate upon here. Obviously, a man *may* cognize something without believing that to be true which is made true by what he cognizes; and he may believe something true without cognizing what makes it true. But we shall speak of direct knowledge, and hence basic cognition, only when a man believes something *because* he cognizes whatever makes his belief a true one.

Parallel considerations apply to action. Here that which corresponds to the *object* in knowledge is an *event*, e.g. *a*, if *m*D*a* is true. And in the realistic vein just adopted for discussing cognition, we may similarly speak of *m* as mediately related to an event, or directly related to one. In a mediated action, thus, he is related to the event *a* through being directly related to the event *b*, where *b*, we suppose, causes *a*: and hence he is mediately related to *a*. But in the basic action, there is no event to which he is directly related save that event he is said to have done. He does *b* directly only in the sense that, in contrast with mediated action, there is nothing which is itself an action of his and a component in the doing by him of *b*. It is wholly consistent with this characterization of a basic action that *m* may (directly) do *b* because he intended to, even if we think of his so intending as actually the cause of his basic action. For the basic action then is an effect, and the intention, since a cause, is not a component of the effect, nor hence a component in the basic action itself. So we may consider basic actions apart from intentions, much as we may consider basic cognitions apart from such beliefs as they may cause. Thus I might directly cognize something which makes the sentence *e* true, and yet I do not, for whatever reason, believe that *e*. However otherwise complicated direct cognition and direct performance may be, they are in the one specified sense simple.

It follows from our regressive argument that not all actions can be mediated actions; that if mediated actions occur, so must basic actions; and that each mediated action has at least one basic action as a component. Exactly parallel consequences for the concept of mediated cognitions may be drawn, and we may accordingly insist that it will be through basic actions, on the one hand, and basic cognitions on the other, that we do and know whatever further things we do and know. But it does not follow, in the case of cognitions, that there is some special and restricted class of things which we both know directly to be the case, and on the basis of which we know whatever else we know. A similar disclaimer must be made in the theory of action, but the issues are perhaps clearer in the theory of knowledge, and I shall consider its application here first.

It has sometimes been maintained by epistemologists that there are *basic sentences* or *propositions*. These appear to play a role in the structure of empirical knowledge comparable to that played by *axioms* in deductive structures. Thus, it was thought that it is through knowing the axioms to be true that we know to be true the theorems they entail, though the axioms themselves cannot be known through one another – since they are independent – nor through the sentences of the system they generate. So, in a way, with basic sentences. If j is a basic sentence, then there is no sentence or set of sentences, distinct from j, through which j may be known. Hence, if m knows that j, this must be a basic cognition, and unless one knows j basically to be true, one cannot know it to be true at all (and often cannot even be said to understand it). Thus basic sentences require basic cognition, but my concept of basic cognitions does not entail the existence of basic sentences.

There may, to be sure, be basic sentences. 'I am in pain' may be an example, not in the sense that a man cannot be in pain without knowing that he is, but rather that if he knows that he is in pain, he must know this directly and not through anything else. It may be incoherent with the concept of pain that one should come to know through the mediation of evidence that one is in pain. But such examples would be mere connoisseur specimens for the epistemologist unless basic sentences also played that role which immediately licenses the analogy with axioms, namely that they should be vehicles for formulating the evidence upon which the entire edifice of knowledge rests. Then not only will there be nothing through which they are known, but whatever else is known must be known through them. It follows, of course, that all basic sentences are mutually independent. If one adds that basic sentences must be immune to error as was often held, then, for those philosophers (and they were legion) who accepted them, the foundations of knowledge would be secure. The incorrigibility of the basic sentence would correspond to the 'self-evidence' attributed in an earlier era to the axioms of a system, whose inherent certitude was then transmitted along the rigorous logical channels, the *proofs* in a system, to the system's farthest theoremic reaches.

With such structures and conceits we need concern ourselves here not at all. Perhaps J. L. Austin is wholly correct in his polemical claim that it is not the office of any special class of sentences to formulate evidence.[5] The fact that *e* formulates my evidence for *s* does not rule it out that, under different circumstances, I might have come by my knowledge that *e* indirectly, and through the mediation of evidence. That we must always start somewhere does not entail that there is some particular place from which we must always start. Basic cognitions thus no more commit us to basic sentences than the claim that everyone has some parent commits us to the claim that someone is the parent of everyone.

So it is with actions. If *m* does *x*, a mediated action, there must be some event *y*, distinct from *x*, which *m directly* does. But it does not follow at all that under different circumstances, he could not have done *y* indirectly instead. Or better: it does not follow that another event of the same type as *y* could not be done by *m* as a mediated rather than as a basic action. Though I raise my arm, for example, and do so as a basic action, I could raise my arm as a mediated action by doing something which then causes it to rise. So if *y* is an event which *m* makes happen directly, it does not follow that *y* belongs to a type of event, all instances of which are such that if they are done, they must be done directly. So from the fact that certain things must be done directly if anything is done by mediation, it does not follow, and indeed it may be false, that there are certain things which, unless done directly, could not as a type be done at all. There may, of course, be such a type, much as there may be basic sentences. But it would be only a curious fact that such a type were to be found. A theory of action which paralleled the familiar theories of knowledge which have an essential place for basic sentences would be one in which not only are there such things, but that whatever further we do must be done through these. And nothing in the concept of basic actions commits us to so narrow a basis for actions.

Suppose, then, curiosities of the sort just alluded to apart, whatever we do as a basic action is something which might also be done as a mediated action, through the mediation thus of some other event. It is an interesting question whether the converse of this is also true: that whatever we in fact do as a mediated action we might also do as a basic one. A corresponding question may be asked in the theory of knowledge. Could we know directly, and through a basic cognition, anything we in fact or under different circumstances know only through the mediation of evidence? I shall make no effort to answer either question until I have introduced the concepts of gifts and powers, which I do in Chapter 5, but we can at least contemplate for a moment an exhaustive array of possibilities, of which there are just four.

Let us speak of event-types and their exemplifications: arm-moving is an event-type exemplified by actual moving arms; stone-moving is an event-type exemplified by actual moving stones, etc. Any two arm-moves, thus, exemplify the same event-type. Without pausing to do more than appeal to obvious intuition, we may distinguish four sorts of event-types. (1) m may make happen events exemplifying the first type either through basic or mediated actions; (2) exemplifying the second type only through basic and never through mediated actions; (3) exemplifying the third type never through basic but only through mediated actions; and (4) exemplifying the fourth type through *neither* basic *nor* mediated action. A comparable array may be constructed for the theory of knowledge, which it would be pedantic to execute. Regarding (4), m is absolutely impotent for events of this type, as he would be absolutely ignorant for the corresponding type in the case of cognition. We know from our argument that not all events can be of type (3), for then there would only be mediated actions, which is impossible. The interesting question, however, is whether the differences pertain to the types themselves, or whether they pertain instead to us. A fair perspective on this question may be derived from considering the somewhat irregular case of God.

Discounting sophistries, of course, case (4) would be empty for God, supposing him omnipotent and omniscient. Able to know and do whatever can be known or done, there remains an interesting difference between God and ourselves in the *manner* of cognition or action. It has been argued,[6] for example, that we may know mediately and through inference whatever God knows, so that (4) in at least the case of knowledge is empty for us as well: we can know whatever God knows. But whereas we may know mediately, God can, and indeed must know everything directly: in God's case all cognition is basic, and hence case (3) for cognition is logically empty in the divine circumstance. But so is case (3) in the theory of action. 'How can you suppose', Philonous asks in the second dialogue[7] between him and Hylas, 'that an all-perfect Spirit, on whose will all things have an absolute and immediate dependence, should need an instrument in his operations, or, not needing it, make use of it?' Case (3) cannot be empty for us, unless (4) is non-empty, which goes against the happy principle that we can do whatever God does and *as a basic action*: which would make us indiscernible from God. We are, to complete this conceit, in the image of God so far as we have some basic actions and basic cognitions available to us. So are we in his image in the respect that the limits of what we can know and do are one with his limits. The difference must be made up by mediated actions and cognitions, from which it follows that case (3) cannot be empty for us. Indeed, we may imagine an indefinite extension of our mediated powers of action and cognition alike, though, as we shall see in the appropriate place, an extension of our *basic* powers is a matter of an altogether different order. Our basic powers are, as it were, given us, it being up to us to extend through the mediation of means and instruments, and of evidence in the case of knowledge, the larger boundaries of our performative and cognitive reach.

Such reflections, though I regard them as sound, are more entertaining than compelling at this point, and I have indulged them solely for the purpose of bringing in the structures they reveal. And one part of the structure, I believe, is this: events which exemplify the same event-type may be either basic or mediated actions, in case they are made to happen through doing; and one cannot accordingly determine from the event itself which of these is so. In other words, whether an event, supposing it to have been done, is done as a basic or a mediated action must be decided by something external to the event itself. Thus the event *a*, in the model of Chapter 1, is a mediated action through the fact that it is embedded in a context which the conditions A-1 through A-6 define. The problem before me now is to determine what embedding context is required for *b* if it is to be a basic action. I pursue that now, quitting until later pursuit of our analogy with cognition. Meanwhile, since *b* is one or the other sort of action depending upon the context it is embedded in, one cannot tell from the event that it *is* embedded, nor hence that it is an action.

III

In the philosophy of Bishop Berkeley, a striking distinction is drawn between spirits and ideas. Spirits are active, ideas are inert. Spirits have ideas, ideas are had by spirits.[8] The *esse* of ideas, Berkeley famously argued, is *percipi*. The *esse* of spirits is then *percipere*. It follows that spirits cannot be perceived, and hence, each of *us* being a spirit, we can have of ourselves no idea. Ideas are opaque, spirits are perfectly diaphanous. Nothing in *what* I perceive tells me that I am perceiving it: the fact that I perceive *x* is never a differentiating feature of *x*. Spirits (us) then are logically external to the ideas we have, and a complete description of the set of all ideas (the world) would not reveal that there were spirits. In brief, a spirit cannot think himself into the world if the world is the set of all his ideas. My perceiving a world is never part of the world I perceive. Of my perceiving the world – and hence of myself – I only have what Berkeley somewhat unhelpfully called a 'notion'.

Philosophers since Hume have been restless with Berkeley's distinction, perhaps rightly so. But the structure these distinctions imply is almost unavoidable in the concepts which involve human beings, no less so in the concept of action than in that of perception. Thus it is, as we may see in our canvass of positions, that it is an external rather than an internal fact of an event that it should be *done*. If such an event as an arm going up is neutral, for example, as to whether or not it was raised, as perhaps it must be if 'It rose because he raised it' is genuinely explanatory,[9] then the fact that it was raised is not revealed in the event itself. And what then is true for this event is true for all. So we would stand, as agents, external to a world which has in part the shape it has because we have performed actions. As agents, indeed, we would stand to the world in something like the relationship in which God might: logically external to what depends upon us for its existence, but which shows no internal differentiating trace of our existence. The world would have to be evidentially neutral as to whether or not God exists, so it is easy to deny and impossible to prove from any feature of the world that there is a God. At best it would be derivable only from the *fact that* the world exists, not from any feature of the *way* it existed. We are, then, related to events explained with reference to our having done them, like so many Berkeleyan spirits, like so many *dieux cachés*.

With these heady notions in mind, let us then begin to examine the sort of structures we are dealing with, and in order to preserve analytical credentials such reflections are apt to put in jeopardy, let us ponder a set of cases much in the center of recent philosophical interest, namely speech acts. With these, perhaps, the distinction between basic and mediated actions is not immediately applicable (though the distinction between basic actions and gestures *is*). But for the moment, since our interests are structural, they will contribute to perspicuity, and enable us to return to our questions with an enhanced sense of logical architecture.

Consider, to begin with, assertions. Though we sometimes refer to sentences as assertions, in fact it is better to say that the sentence is what is asserted, to be distinguished from the asserting of it, the latter being, so to speak, an action we perform *with* a sentence. Hence the sentence itself is only redescribed as an assertion when it is asserted, but its being asserted is not something one can tell from anything intrinsic to the sentence itself. The sentence, taken as such, with its syntactical and other properties, is neutral with regard to whether or not it is asserted, in the sense that nothing *internal* to the sentence is modified through the fact that it is asserted: assertion does not *penetrate* what is asserted. This was recognized by Frege, since whom we have a special sign – the *Urteils-streich* – which Frege introduced specifically to emphasize that there are no sentences from whose inner content it follows that they are asserted: nothing about s as such entails $\vdash s$.[10] So s is neutral in that it does not determine its assertoric context, and the *Urteilsstreich* does not in this respect penetrate what it operates on by transforming it into an assertion.

Now asserting is an action, with sentences. And we might easily consider the appearance of s – whether on paper or in the air – as a sentential event which radically underdetermines its status as an assertion. It is in this respect that no evidence from s gives us a basis for supposing it was an assertion, and there are a number of other such cases. According to Ramsey, for example, the fragment 'It is true that...' serves to emphasize, without contributing to the meaning of the sentences it is attached to.[11] According to Austin, 'I know that...' serves to give the speaker's word regarding the sentence it is attached to, without in any way penetrating the latter's content.[12] And as much might be said regarding some of our more conspicuously punctuational apparatus such as the exclamation point or the mark of interrogation. These expressions and symbols do not stand on their own, nor refer on their own behalf: 'The assertion sign', wrote Frege, 'cannot be used to construct a functional expression; for it does not serve in conjunction with other signs to designate an object. "⊢2 + 2 = 4" does not designate anything; it asserts something.'[13] So the mere fact that the *Urteilsstreich* appears on the page does not mean that it belongs, so to speak, in the same plane of discourse as the expressions it fronts: it transforms into actions typographical events which we otherwise merely understand. Austin wanted very much to stress that 'I know that' is *not* descriptive but performative, so that the entire descriptive content of 'I know that *s*' is borne by *s* alone. It is in just this sense that we may distinguish *m*'s doing of *b* from the event *b*, which is an action through being an event which is done, but is such that from it alone it cannot be determined that somebody did it. If the world of things and events is, as Berkeley said it to be, Divine Visible Language, nothing *in* the world would enable us to know *that* it was said or meant.

But surely, it will be argued, even granting that the symbols of asserting, giving one's word, and the like are not in their own right descriptive, and so do not in their own right belong to that which is asserted or avowed, even so, when an assertion occurs, *more* occurs than simply the sentential event. And surely we can describe this further thing? For consider these descriptions: 'The sentence *s* is asserted'; 'The speaker gives his word that *s*'; 'The sentence *s* is emphasized.' These do not respectively assert, avow, or emphasize the sentences referred to. They do not even in the second instance, in case the speaker referred to in the sentence is the speaker of the description in question, for the matter of self-reference here only complicates without altering the essential analysis. Since all of these are descriptions of actions which occur, each may be regarded as a case of *mDa* for some man *m* and some (sentential) event *a*. And now the question is, under what conditions will these descriptions be true? No doubt they will be false if the requisite sentential event fails to occur. But since the sentential event underdetermines its redescription as a (speech-)act, what further than the sentential event must happen for it to be an action?

There is a strong temptation to say: *nothing* in addition happens: all that happens is the sentential event. For it is not as though there were two events when a sentence is emphasized, viz. the sentence and the emphasis. Nor again can there be two events, one the sentence and the other the assertion of it. For then the second event might easily occur on its own. But there can be no act of Pure Assertion or of Pure Emphasis. We assert (emphasize, avow, etc.) *something*. Like verbs of action generally, these verbs are ineluctably transitive. This, I think, gives us our problem. On the one hand, what makes a sentential event an assertion is not some distinct event, related to it in a certain way, and certainly not a distinct event which is *itself* an action. For then all the same questions arise again, with that event. On the other hand, since it seems plain that the sentential event can occur without being an action, something in excess of the event itself is required in order to fill the space between being an event and being an action. Something must be left over when we subtract, as it were, the event which is done from the doing of the event. But then this remnant, whose logical representation may indeed be an operator of some sort, apparently cannot consist of a distinct event, so that an assertion (for example) would be the coupling of two events. For, of course, this throws us back onto the other horn, since it does not appear plausible to suppose that the natural candidates for such events can occur on their own: there is no *pure* doing, no doing which is not the doing of *something*.

One heavily favored resolution of this problem has been this. An event is an action only 'under a certain description'.[14] This is a striking suggestion, as it has the air of transforming a metaphysical fury into a benign linguistic distinction. So let us examine the deflection of a question which appears to concern two sorts of events into a question which rather concerns two sorts of descriptions. Does it mean that the event itself is neutral as between descriptions? Then what *licenses* the difference in them? To this question I now turn.

IV

Let us suppose that there is a class of basic descriptions of an event *e*, where a description is basic providing only that its truth does not entail the occurrence of any event other than *e*. We may equally well speak of basic descriptions of objects as those which, when true of an object *o*, do not entail the existence of an object other than *o* itself. Thus 'is a father' is not a basic description of *o*, since it is true of *o* only in case there is an object, distinct from *o*, which is *o*'s child. Nor is 'the killing of Bayard' a basic description of an event consisting of driving a knife through Bayard's throat, for the description entails the occurrence of an event distinct from this one, namely the *death* of Bayard, and while it is clear that an event consisting in driving a knife through Bayard's throat might occur without Bayard's death, a *killing* of Bayard could not take place without Bayard dying. And in particular, no description of *e* which is an implicit explanation of the occurrence of *e* may be counted a basic description of *e*, inasmuch as events are explained with reference to the occurrence of events other than themselves. Hence no description which has a causal implication, whether *e* is taken as cause or as effect, may be assumed a basic description of *e*. Nor, for the matter, of *o*. Part of why 'is a father' is not a basic description lies in the fact that it implies a certain causal history, participation in which is a necessary condition for fatherhood to descend upon *o*. Hence 'is a cause' or 'is an effect' are plainly not basic descriptions of any event whatever, nor are any descriptions where rules of meaning entail these.

A description of an event or an object which is not a basic description will simply be called a non-basic one. Plainly, some non-basic descriptions of *e* imply an explanatory account of *e* – or an explanatory account in which *o* figures – but I do not suppose that all non-basic descriptions are in this respect explanatory. Locative descriptions like 'northernmost suburb of New York', or identificatory descriptions like 'A's oldest daughter' need not be explanatory, but for the moment the marshalling of kinds of non-basic descriptions is of smaller importance than is the logical fact that all such descriptions are implicitly polyadic, with implicit references made to objects or events distinct from the one to which they are applied, and such that the descriptions fails if the requisite references fail. 'My eldest daughter' is a description of Elizabeth which applies to her only on condition that there is at least one other person, herself my daughter, and younger than Elizabeth. So though the description is *of* Elizabeth, implicit reference is made to me and to another daughter of mine. It was the teaching of those who held a theory of Internal Relations that there are no basic descriptions, unless of the universe as a whole, and this consisting of the set of all non-basic descriptions of its parts. And *each* such description would have a polyadicity specified by the number of parts there are, implicit reference being made to each of these whenever an explicit description is given of any one. In what follows, I shall simply suppose this doctrine false, and assume that there are basic descriptions of objects more circumscribed than the universe as a whole.

The logical relations between the set of non-basic and the set of basic descriptions is subtle, but I shall suppose more or less this. Whatever non-basic description is true of *o* entails that some basic description must be true of *o* as well. Thus nothing can be an eldest daughter which is not female, and 'is female' is a basic description of Elizabeth. To be sure, it may be argued that it *does* make implicit reference to distinct biological characteristics, but these are characteristics of Elizabeth; they are *parts* of *her*; and there is no implication carried by the concept of the basic description that the individual so described is to be partless. This does not mean that basic descriptions cannot be given of parts, but only that a description of Elizabeth (or of whom- or of whatever) is no less basic for the fact that she has parts themselves basically and non-basically describable, and that *some* non-basic descriptions of these may make implicit reference to Elizabeth. 'A family' is a basic description of a group, though plainly a family has parts which are its members. 'Leading family' is not a basic description of that same family, since implicit reference is made to families lower down in the order of prestige. But 'leading family' entails the basic description 'family', however variant and flexible the criteria of familyhood may be.

There is, I believe, no entailment from basic to non-basic descriptions. Though a non-basic description D may entail a basic description D' of *o*, the *truth* of D' is always consistent with the falsity of D or, more guardedly but perhaps more profoundly, the existence of *o* is logically compatible with the non-existence of any individual distinct from *o*, just as – and we shall hear more of this shortly – the occurrence of *e* is logically consistent with the non-occurrence of any event other than *e*. It is a brute fact of logic that no sentence of the form Rxy is equivalent to a conjunction of sentences Fx and Gy, and hence that it is consistent with Fx and Gy that Rxy should be false. But even if this were by some logical miracle to be faulted, Fx and Gy are logically independent if x and y are distinct, and any supposed counter-example to this would find an implicit reference to y in Fx, or an implicit reference to x in Gy, and hence it will have been false that these were respectively *basic* descriptions of x and y. So I shall take it for granted that the truth of any description basic of *o* is logically consistent with the falsity of any non-basic description of *o*. And that this is perfectly general.

Inasmuch as basic descriptions imply no explanation of that to which they apply, it immediately follows that one could not deduce what causes, if any, or what effects, if any, an object or an event has, so far as the latter is specified under basic descriptions alone. It is no less important for being trivial that Hume proposed a general incapacity to deduce what must be the effects of a thing from what we may take Hume to have regarded as a basic description of that thing.[15] For any description of it which makes reference to its causes (or effects) is a non-basic description. And no set of basic descriptions, however extended, entails one of these.

Now it is often difficult to determine whether a description is basic or non-basic without knowing to what it is applied. For often, we redescribe an object or an event in terms of relations it in fact has with other objects or events. Thus *m*D*a* may be a basic description of an event of the sort specified by the Standard Analysis of Action, or a non-basic description of one of the event-components of that mediated action. We may say, for example, that *a itself* is an action, even that it is a mediated action, and in so describing *it* we are making implicit reference to at least one other event, distinct from *a* and in consequence of which *a* happens. From the basic description *m*D*a* it of course follows that *a* occurred if the description is true; and it is quite out of the question that *m*D*a* shall have occurred and *a* not. For *a* is a part or component of the larger, let us call it *molecular* event of which *m*D*a* is a basic description. Of course *m*D*a* may equally be a non-basic description of *b*, if *b* is the event because of which *a* happens, and as such it is a non-basic description of it in that if it is true of *b* – or even of the doing of *b* by *m* – it entails if true that another event, distinct from *b*, shall occur, namely *a*. Now from the *basic* description of *a*, of course, it does not follow that *m*D*a*, which is in a sense the explanation of why, from the mere information that *a* occurs, we cannot tell whether it was (redescribable as) an action or not. And similarly with *b* under *its* basic description.

But the question now before us is whether, in describing *b* as a *basic action*, we are giving a basic description of *b*, or whether, as in the case of a mediated action, describing *b* as a basic action is a *non-basic* description of it, and so makes implicit reference to some event other than *b*, through being related to which *b* is a basic action. If the latter should be the case, then reference to something being an action 'under a description' does not resolve the problem of the last section, for its *being* an action depends upon its being a part or component of some larger structure, the other elements of which then remain to be identified. And in that case, though an event of the same type as *b* might occur though *not* as a basic action (though from the basic description of *b* it could not be determined whether it were a basic action or not), the difference between such an event which is and such an event which is not a basic action cannot be resolved with reference to descriptions alone. For one description of *b* may make implicit reference to other things and other events necessary for *b* properly to be redescribed as a basic action, and another description of *b* may make no such reference. Only if a description of *b* is a basic description of it is no ulterior reference made: but in that case, of course, no event of the same sort as *b* can occur which is *not* a basic action. And this is unplausible if we reflect back, for a moment, upon sentential events of a sort which appear to underdetermine their status whether as an assertion or as a bare utterance. And, moreover, it destroys as an *explanatory* pattern a claim that *m*'s arm rose *because* he raised it.

Non-basic descriptions are often covert metonymies: a whole is meant though only one of its conspicuous parts or attributes is mentioned; and when this rhetorical condensation is forgotten, a singular confusion is generated. Thus, though two descriptions, one basic and the other non-basic, are given of the same event, if the non-basic description is a metonymy, it is perilous indeed to suppose the two descriptions joinable by the identity operator commonly licit between two descriptions of ostensibly the same thing. Suppose *b* is an event and '*m* raises his arm' and '*m*'s arm rises' are two descriptions of *b*, and that the former is non-basic. Then, because they appear each to refer to *b*, they appear joinable by ' = ' – and this then encourages certain philosophical theses regarding identity, e.g. that a basic action just *is* a bodily movement: 'just as Venus is one planet equally and appropriately described as the morning star and the evening star'.[16] In the chapter which follows, we shall pay a close attention to the concept of identity. But here I am concerned only to point out the dangers of treating the identity operation as straightforward when at least one of the expressions is a metonymy. For if *b* is referred to by two descriptions between which the identity operator is legitimately inserted, nothing can be true of *b* 'under the one description' which is not true of it under the other. If *b* is identical with *x*, whatever is true of *b* is true of *x*, and conversely. But in that case, as has been pointed out by Davidson,[17] certain philosophers who insist upon the identification of (basic) actions with bodily movements are inconsistent in claiming that bodily movements are caused but that actions are *not* caused. Either the identification must be surrendered, and all the philosophical advantages this appears to bring, or else some curious logical properties are to be associated with identity in this special case, so that though a given event *c* causes *b*, it does *not* cause *x*, though *b* and *x* are identical! And this leaves us unclear as to what might be meant by identifying actions and bodily movements in the first place. As a matter of incidental interest, it is just those philosophers who insist that when *b* is an action, there is no event, distinct from *b*, in which the doing of *b* consists, who are also concerned to distinguish actions from bodily (or *mere* bodily) movements in this inconsistent manner.[18] They cannot have it both ways, but in fact the anomaly disappears when it is recognized that one of the descriptions is a metonymy, between which and another, let us suppose *basic* description, no ligature of identity is legitimate, though the two descriptions appear to refer to the same event. Let me now explain why.

Let '*m* raises his arm' describe the event which '*m*'s arm rises' also describes, but the former describes it as a basic action and the latter, suppose, as a bodily movement. But if a basic action should prove to be a whole in which this event is only a part, then the non-basic description of just the event itself as the basic action is really a metonymy, the proper reference of which is this whole. Now description of the whole as the basic action it is will be a basic description, but description of a *part* which implicitly refers to the whole will be a non-basic description of the part. Note, now, that if *b* is the event in question, and *b* is part of a whole consisting of a basic action, then it could be true that *b* is caused *without* being true that the *basic action* itself is caused! If, metonymically, we refer to *b* itself as a basic action, we then would find ourselves inconsistently saying that *b* is caused and uncaused. But the inconsistency dissolves when the metonymy is recognized; and when it is recognized, we directly appreciate that the description of *b* as a basic action and the description of it as a bodily movement cannot be connected through identity. Once we break the identification, then all sorts of positions are possible, e.g. that the basic action, in which *b* is a component, should have a wholly different set of causes, if it is caused, than *b* itself should have, since they are distinct events, albeit related as whole to part.

Deflecting the problem onto the plane of descriptions, then, leaves us just where we were when we undertook it so hopefully a few pages back. The question before us remains still that of what, in addition to *b*, we are referring to when we (now metonymically) describe *b* as a basic action. We may be as reluctant as we were before to suppose that we are referring to a separate event, a pure doing, for example, which could occur on its own, licensing a redescription of *b* as a basic action when suitably related to *b*. On the other hand, perhaps the reluctance should weaken.

44

V

The view that there are events neutral to the difference between whether or not they are *actions*, looks fascinatingly analogous to the more widely appreciated view in epistemological theory that there are perceptual objects neutral to the difference between their being veridical or illusory. And indeed, the philosophical recipes for arriving at these neutral objects are strikingly similar. Subtract from the fact that you perceive a deer the fact that the deer exists, suggests Lewis, then the remnant is what you actually perceive,[19] and (we may add) this remnant then is neutral with regard to the existence or non-existence of a *deer*. Subtract from the fact that you raise your arm the fact that your arm goes up, suggests Wittgenstein.[20] Then (we may add) your arm going up is neutral to the difference of whether or not it is *done*. In the theory of perception, neutralization of the data, call them 'percepts', gives rise immediately to the question of the External World, namely whether, from one's percepts alone, one can determine whether there is a world external to them to which they 'correspond'. And thus stated, the problem is of course insoluble. Analogously, the neutralization of events immediately gives rise to what we might call, in the light of one of the solutions it is natural to consider, the problem of the Internal Agent, namely whether one can tell, from the fact that an event occurs, that someone made it happen by doing. So stated, the problem is insoluble. For all our neutral percepts tell us, there is no world outside, and for all we can tell from neutral events, there are no agents and hence no actions.

The two structures might be brought into greater parity by considering the analogue to the Representationalist theory of perception in the topic of action. Representationalism is the view that a *percept* is veridical only when it is caused by its correspondent object. Hence *veridical perception* involves a relation between m, a percept, and an object, and the percept is veridical when the object *causes m* to have a percept which *corresponds* to the object. But the percept itself is neutral as to the latter: 'veridical percept' is a non-basic description of a percept. The analogous theory in the topic of action is as follows. A successful action involves a relation between m, a volition, and an event, the latter being an action when it is caused by and corresponds to the volition. But the event in question is itself neutral as to whether these relations hold, and 'is an action' is a non-basic description of the event which is, of course, underdetermined by its basic descriptions. That the two theories are inverts of each other – causality running inward from objects to percepts and outward from volitions to events – is by now only to have been expected.

To the dark questions concerning the remnants upon execution of the philosophical subtractions, it is interesting to consider the radical answer that they equal zero: *nothing* is left over when we subtract the existence of *x* from the perception of *x*, or the happening from the doing of *b*. The first of these answers is due to Berkeley, for whom, since *to be* just is *to be perceived*, there is no room for something to occupy between existence and perceptedness. Berkeley sought to collapse the alleged space between reality and perception by assimilating the latter to the former: the external and internal world become, as it were, one, and hence the distinction between internal and external becomes meaningless. In logical parallel to this, to be done is just to happen, and *m*D*b* becomes one with *b*. It is in the spirit of this answer that, I believe, those philosophers who have stood in the long shadow of Wittgenstein have sought to eliminate the problem of the Internal Agent by collapsing actions into bodily movements and supposing the difference one of description only. For the Wittgensteinians,[21] the existence of covert inner events (volitions, say) was as odious as was the existence of covert *external* entities (material substrates, say) to Berkeley. So each collapsing strategy eliminates one class of dubious entities and renders meaningless one dubious distinction. Behaviorism is the counterpart in action theory to Phenomenalism in the theory of perception.

But then Behaviorism, like Phenomenalism, has to bear the responsibility of solving the problems to which each is a reductive response: to illusions in perception, and to the fact that '*m*D*b*' may be false though '*b*' is true in the theory of action. For not all bodily movements are actions, surely, and an arm-rise may be, after all, a tic. But there are natural, elegant, and parsimonious modes of handling these questions along lines of what we might term Coherentism, coherence playing the role here that correspondence does in Representational theories. In the theory of perception, thus, percepts are classed as veridical when they are not 'wild', when they are not, as it were, discrepant with a set of percepts regarded as normal. My experience, visually speaking, of an illusory dagger may be as such indiscriminable from my visual experience of a real one: but when I reach and my hands close on nothing, contrary to normal expectation, the visual experience is classed as illusory on grounds of inductive discrepancy. Our concept of reality thus grows apace with our inductive expectations, and any experience which is inductively deviant is unreal insofar as no better inductive principle can account for its occurrence consistently with beliefs already arrived at. Such strategies demand some philosophical care in their exact formulation, but my enterprise is only to indicate the *type* of strategy, and to propose for the Behaviorist an analogue for discriminating (mere) bodily movements from actions which *consist* in bodily movements. We may propose that they support different inductive expectations, and belong with disjoint classes of events. Let me now sketch the outlines of such a view.

If *b* is an action, then I am entitled to a class of predictions (and to a class of explanations) to which I would not be entitled were *b* a Mere Bodily Movement. Suppose I ask a question to the members of my class, and Isaac's arm rises. I am licensed *on the assumption that it is an action* not only to explain it as a response to my question, but to predict that Isaac will attempt an answer if I call upon him. *If* he does attempt an answer, then his arm-rise is retroactively describable as an action. Certainly I am not entitled to infer that Isaac knows the answer if his arm-rise were a mere tic! So, speaking loosely, *b* is an action if it coheres with other events of the sort we are entitled to expect on the assumption that it is one. And otherwise it is a mere bodily movement. This view, of course, is fraught with difficulties. Thus *b* may have been an action, but not a response to my question, Isaac having been distracted by the passing behind me of his comrade whom he is seeking to signal. In such a case it occurred coincidentally at a point in the institutional context which licensed expectations on my part which Isaac was woefully unable to sustain, as he happens not to have prepared his lesson. On the other hand, Isaac may have prepared his lesson and known the answer, but his arm went up involuntarily, a fortuitous tic read by me as the conventional sign of readiness to respond. And nothing in Isaac's subsequent behavior would enable me to know that *b* was not an action but a mere bodily movement.

These, the Coherentist may reply, are difficulties of the short run. Widening our horizon will ultimately reveal that certain occurrences of the sort *b* exemplifies were mere bodily movements coincidentally inserted into contexts in which they appeared as actions, and over the long run contexts will sort themselves out, and we will finally be able to say, with as much certitude as such matters admit of, which such occurrences are actions and which not. And, he may add, have *we* in fact a different way of proceeding?

To this challenge, there are, I believe, two replies. The first is that we may agree that we do ultimately decide, exactly as the Coherentist does, which events are bodily movements and which are actions, by seeing with what other events they fit, and allowing the differences to be a matter of contextual location. Moreover, we may concede that we proceed roughly in the same way in the domain of perception, much as the Phenomenalist proposes. But whereas our *evidence* that *b* is an action, or that it is a bodily movement, is accumulated and structured in this manner, this does not oblige us, unless we endorse the covert verificationism which animates the Phenomenalist and the Behaviorist alike, to *define* the difference between actions and bodily movements in terms of our evidence! But at this point, stripping off the mask of the Behaviorist, the Verificationist demands to know what further we can *mean* by an action than an event which coheres with a set of action-defining further events? Or at least, with the inevitable recourse to counterfactuals, with events which *would* have occurred were certain conditions to have been realized? This brings us to the second reply.

I do not believe we determine which of *our* bodily movements are actions and which are *mere* bodily movements in this way. I think that our knowledge of whether or not, for example, we are raising an arm or our arm is merely going up, is *not* something *we* determine retroactively and on the basis of evidence. It is as primitive a piece of knowledge as any we may have. It is something, I propose, that we know directly. The Behaviorist is thinking primarily of how we know in the case of *others*. If he is, then, a Verificationist, he will be obliged to distinguish two meanings of the term *action*, depending upon whether it is ascribed to ourselves or to others, if meaning is determined by the mode and content of verificatory procedures. Or, if the term is to be employed univocally, we either must know directly which events, in the case of others, are actions and which are bodily movements; or we must, in our own case, only know the difference between them by the indirection of Coherentist procedures.

It is not difficult to predict which of these courses will be the most attractive to Behaviorists. They will want to argue that I learn about my own behavior *exactly* as with others. This is not a view I shall wish wholly to endorse, however. I shall argue that such a term as 'doing' is one, the meaning of which we arrive at only through exemplifying it ourselves. To understand what *doing* is requires that we instantiate the predicate 'does ...' in much the same way as in understanding the predicates of perception, such as 'see ...', we must instantiate them ourselves. We then apply them to others only on the assumption that others are like ourselves. But the mode of instantiation in our own case is delicate, as might be seen by reflection, for a moment, upon the quandaries of Hume who failed to distinguish between *what* he perceived and his perceiving of it, and so felt constrained, by the outcome of a disturbing and reckless inquiry, to identify his *self* with his perceptual contents. But, of course, my perceiving something is not *amongst* the things that I perceive! Hence learning the meaning of 'perceives' is a different, I should say a more existential matter, than learning the meaning of such perceptual predicates as 'red' or 'smooth'. And similarly with our coming to understand the differences between 'doing' and *what* is done.

Both the Behaviorist and I, to be sure, have come to agree that *b* is neutral as between descriptions of it as a mere bodily movement – a bodily movement which is *not* an action – and an action. So the difference, at least with regard to others, is determined by factors external to *b*. The Behaviorist has an answer gratifying to his ideological tough-mindedness as to what these external factors may be. They are other events, no less observable than *b*, along with inductive and other verificatory procedures in terms of which all differences are to be defined. So he need countenance none of the inner events, volitions and percepts, for example, which the Representationists in the theories of perception and of action have appeared to require. And now the Behaviorist may ask what *my* program is, and whether I can give answers as elegant as he, without bringing in the discredited apparatus of Representationalism?

Well, we must not forget that it is not the case that Representationalism and Phenomenalism exhaust the field of theories of perception. There is a third form of theory, and, not surprisingly, a counterpart in the theory of action. What is called Direct Realism, for example, in the topic of perception regards perception as a direct cognitive relationship between a percipient, say *m*, and an object. It is not mediated *through* a representation. Rather, if *m* represents the object in question, say by believing that it is a certain way, then this may be explained *through* the fact that he directly perceives the object. Why then might not a basic action consist in a direct performative relationship between *m* and an event, say *b*? It is not mediated through a volition. But it may be that *m* does what he does *because* he intends that the event occur. This would be a Direct Realism of basic actions, parallel but appropriately inverse to a Direct Realism of basic perceptual cognitions.

Direct Realism allows us, of course, to distinguish between *b* happening without being done, just as it allows us to speak of an object existing though without being perceived. Indeed, it allows us to suppose it at least possible that *b* should be caused though the *doing* of *b* is not caused, much, or perhaps exactly, in the same way in which the causes of an object are not commonly amongst the causes of the perceiving of the object. And since we are not required to propose mediating entities, volitions or percepts, there is nothing except the question of how to give substance to these direct relations upon which the Behaviorist may fault us. Direct Realism of actions, then, might solve all the problems of the theory of basic actions we have touched upon in this chapter, and make plain what it is, in excess of *b*, '*mDb*' refers to if it is taken, as the Behaviorist and I equally suppose, as a non-basic description of *b*.

It is to this question that I now must turn. This requires that we divert our attention, for a moment, from *b*, which all may observe, and begin to enter, in the domains of perception and of action alike, the philosophically perplexing space *between* ourselves and what we perceive when we perceive directly, and what we do when we directly act. It is to the articulations of this space whose structure I mean now to begin to explore, that the verbs of perception and action refer. Meanwhile, it cannot but be gratifying, in view of our concern with structural parities between the concepts of knowledge and action, that there should be an array of positions in the theory of basic actions which map naturally onto a corresponding and familiar array of positions in the theory of basic cognitions. It may also be useful philosophical prophylaxis to recognize these similarities in structure and strategy, for it will induce caution in endorsing positions in either the theory of knowledge or of action, without appreciating the larger structural concerns which generate them. It is no longer useful to take an isolated stand on an isolated portion of the concept of action.

3

BASIC ACTIONS AND PHYSIOLOGICAL PROCESSES

I

A natural suggestion, when the question arises of the descriptive meaning of 'does' in sentences which ascribe *basic* actions, is that the man *m* *causes* an event *b* to happen. The suggestion is natural because '*m* does *b*' is somehow an explanation of the occurrence of *b*, and when explanatory contexts for events are invoked, reference to causation seems almost inescapable. If 'doing' then answers to a direct relation between *m* and *b*, as the final discussion of the preceding chapter permits us to suppose, perhaps the relation in question is just the causal relation itself. To be sure, it may appear a curious concept of causation to which appeal is here made, inasmuch as one seems more typically to explain one occurrence with reference to another – the *lighting* of a match with reference to the *striking* of that match, the *melting* of a piece of wax with reference to its having been *heated* – whereas here we appear to be explaining an occurrence only with reference to an agent. Still, philosophers have sometimes thought, there may be two species or perhaps two concepts of causation, one of which is routinely exemplified when events are explained through other events, while the other is exemplified, hardly less routinely, when we explain an event through an agent who directly caused it to happen, as in basic actions. Indeed, the scholastic distinction between *transeunt* and *immanent* causation has latterly been re-introduced[1] to provide some explicit nomenclature for marking the fact that we have, and commonly employ, two distinct and mutually irreducible concepts of causation, and accordingly two explanatory contexts for events.

Immanent, or *agent* causation, it has been argued, has been lost sight of, perhaps in consequence of some general acquiescence in the thesis that the concept of transeunt causation just *is* the concept of causation, a view we owe to Hume. For the concept which was famously dissected by him has the logical form of a law-entailing relationship between ordered pairs of events.[2] And so long as causation is thought of in these terms, then, it is contended, we shall never appreciate what doing *is* or what basic acting comes to. Agent causation not only has been obscured because of the glamour of Hume's theories, but it is the more fundamental,[3] the primordial, the more primitive concept of the two, and one we have to our immeasurable philosophical detriment simply allowed to lapse.

Hume, I believe, would have been quite unmoved by these considerations, since the notion of an *agent* would be viewed by him as a dark item of ontological furniture, and by no means to be reckoned as a final and unrefinable philosophical category. But then an adequate resolution of the agential concept might yield a resolution of agent causation into the framework of transeunt causation – or of causation as such, inasmuch as no contrast would any longer be forthcoming between transeunt causation and any other kind. Now Hume, of course, was constrained by an empiricist scrupulosity to regard the self as a mere bundle of fleeting particular events.[4] Certain of these might be found causally related to events not themselves part of the bundle, and certain others causally related to events themselves also part of the bundle that the self simply is. Indeed, the distinction between *internally* and *externally* related effects to causes which are themselves internal to the self almost exactly answers to one form of the traditional distinction between transeunt and immanent causation,[5] but since in either case the *relata* are events and causation then a relation between events, we are not really dealing with two sorts of causal concept after all. Hence causation might remain more or less as he had analyzed it. For Hume, an action is an event (transeuntly) caused by a volition.[6] Thus, when *m* does *b* as a basic action, this must for Hume be counted an episode of transeunt causation: there is an event, itself a volition and part of *m*, who himself is but a shower of events ontologically on a par with the volition in question, this volition causing *b* in the only sense of 'cause' we now need countenance. Not every action, of course, is of this sort, for experience instructs us that some events cannot be directly caused by volitions. Some are actions only because caused by events themselves caused by volitions, these being just what *we* have marked out as mediated actions. No event which is external to the set of events in which *m* consists can be a basic action of his (= caused by one of his volitions), and it may be counted then a necessary condition for an event to lie outside *m*'s boundaries that it be indifferent to the direct influence of *m*'s will (= the set of *m*-volitions). But the stream of

causation is homogeneous, showing nothing save episodes of transeuncy: with regard to it, the boundaries of selves, or of agents, are absolutely permeable. Such, I expect, would be his response to the charge
of conceptual negligence with regard to immanent causation.

It cannot be pretended that either Hume's radical dissolution of the
self or the concept of volition to which he appeals are in current high
favor amongst sharp or even deep philosophers. But it may be worth
noting that Hume's view of the self might easily protect him against
certain destructive arguments regarding volitions. Gilbert Ryle, for
example, has argued that if an action is a compound event in which one
event is caused by a volition, then volitions cannot themselves be actions.
For *they* then would have to be caused by volitions in order to be so, and
these by other volitions themselves caused by volitions, and on to
infinity.[7] If volitions are actions, there then can be no actions. But
nothing in Hume's account requires him to suppose that volitions are
actions. Some may be: a volition *might* cause another volition; but
none *need* be. And why, in order for an action to be an event caused by
a volition, need volitions themselves be actions? Ryle's intended
opponent perhaps called upon volition in explanation of doing, but
then left unresolved the relation in which we stand to volitions themselves: if we do not (and logically cannot) *do* volitions, what *is* our
relation to them? And if we cannot answer that, in what respect have
we really clarified the concept of doing? But for Hume, the question
carries no embarrassment whatever. Others, who have not carefully
thought through the notion of the self, may wonder how a self might
be related to a volition. But for Hume the relationship is only that of
part to whole: volitions are amongst the things we *are*: we are not
something to one side, which then has to make the volition happen. So
the argument is easily deflected.

But Ryle has another, perhaps more telling criticism, which is that
Hume's phenomenology is defective. If actions are as frequent as we
would commonly suppose, volitions could hardly be *less* frequent. But
if pressed to answer simple questions about volitions, we find ourselves
in straits. It is no great feat to individuate arm-rises, to say how many
times our arm goes up in a certain interval of time. But what of
volitions themselves? How many volitions do we require in order to
recite 'Little Miss Muffet'?[8] It may be replied that it is not yet clear
how many *actions* we perform in reciting 'Little Miss Muffet', it not
following from the fact that it is a simple poem that reciting it is a

simple *action*! But *do* we in fact introspectively note the occurrence of volitions even in admittedly simple cases, like raising arms? In introspective honesty *do* we observe volitions causing arm-rises? This question has a special pertinence to Hume.[9] For Hume's theory of causation requires that we not only note the two events called 'cause' and 'effect', but that we *frequently* note the co-occurrence of their peers: *x* causes *y* only if the *x*-like and the *y*-like have been found in frequent, constant conjunction. So to the extent that he is phenomenologically lax regarding volitions, to that extent is his analysis of action as an event transeuntly *caused* by a volition suspect. *Other* philosophers may propose that Hume's analysis of action stands, that volitions are theoretical entities invoked both to explain the occurrence of events designated actions and to distinguish them from other events which are not actions because not so caused.[10] This preserves transeuncy as the unique model of causation, since there is an event, distinct from *b*, which directly causes *b* if *b* is an action, even if we must postulate this event as a covert, theoretical happening. But this is not open to Hume. It is not open because of the uncompromising empiricism which initially led him to collapse the self onto the events in its available history. To allow unobserved volitions would be philosophically retrograde: one might just as well allow *spirits*, in the manner of Berkeley, and construe volitions as episodes of activity which we do not observe but of which we have 'notions'! So the crafty defense of transeuncy we have worked out for Hume founders upon an inadequately conducted description of the experience of action. Perhaps he merely believed in a para-mechanical model, which he carelessly supposed experience would support.

At this point, the advocates of immanent causation may assume the offensive, not so much against Hume whom they may regard temporarily as defeated, but against those who sought to preserve transeuncy and hence a univocal causal concept, by enlisting theoretical, sub-phenomenal occurrences like volitions. Explanation with reference to these, let us recall, was to mark off those events which are actions from those which are 'mere bodily movements'. To speak of them as *theoretical* is automatically to adopt the stance of an external observer, one for whom the problem arises of which events are actions and which are bodily movements but *not* actions. From that external point of view, perhaps (mere) bodily movements so resemble (basic) actions that discriminations between them is observationally impossible. Hence, if there is to be a difference between them at all, this *must* be by reference to covert occurrences, *in the light of which* certain bodily movements are redescribed because explained as actions. Yet what, save a compulsive prejudice in favor of transeunt explanatory contexts, really justifies this move? One would think that theoretical posits, like volitions, are executed in the name not so much of philosophy as of science. But the scientific literature on physiology is largely mute on the topic of volitions. And if we turn to the point of view of the agent himself, and away for a moment from that of the external observer, the gratuitousness of the posit becomes conspicuous. Philosophers seem almost naturally to take the stance of the outside, the judge, the observer.[11] But we *do* act, we are existentially engaged in action, we are changers as well as recorders of the world. And why not *look and see* what the *experience* of acting reveals?

From the agent's point of view, there is perhaps not a distinction which is experienced as more clear than that between doing something and something just happening without being done. Should my arm begin to rise without my raising it, I would be alarmed indeed; but I should notice directly, as directly as I notice that something is blue and not red, that this was happening. Nor is this a matter of mere irregularity, as someone might propose. What, they might ask, if my arm went up when and only when I would have wanted it to and never contrary to but only coincident with my will? Could I really tell that I was not doing it, but that it was happening? I am certain the answer is that I could tell. And there are experiences which bear this out. Consider the male erection, a bodily event externally quite like the raising of an arm. The normally responsive male achieves erection whenever he would have wished to, invariantly as to his 'will.' It remains the commonly received view that erection is *not* an action, and men invariably are aware that it is not something they do, that it is a response, something that happens to them. Later I shall treat this sort of case in some detail.[12] But here I enlist such phenomena on the side of the Immanentist, who employs them to make the point that whatever may be the case with an external observer, *I* at least (for every I) do not require reference to anything covert to account for a difference which instead is perfectly observable. So from a perspective available to all, volitions would be redundant were postulation of them not so obscurantist a move as to blind us to a mode of causation – *immanent* causation – with which each of us is intimate.

Finally, the Immanentist might draw attention to patterns of explanation from which reference to the self and its immediate relation to events are logically uneliminable. We all draw some sort of distinction between causing *b*, and causing *m* to *do b*: between causing *m*'s arm to rise and causing *m* to raise his arm. Consider, in this regard, a certain sort of sadist. He applies pain to *m* in order that *m* raise his arm in the gesture of submission. A mere elevated arm has as such no interest for him: he could, by applying brute force, cause the arm to go up, treating it as a *mere thing*. But this would be to circumvent rather than to enslave *m*'s will, and the effect he intends is not *b* but the doing of *b* by *m*. Or again, it is perhaps no great trick of ventriloquy to get words to come out of *m*'s mouth; but to cause the words to come out has no point if one wants a confession from *m*: then he must be caused to say the words, and the difference between causing *b* and causing *m* to do *b* is total. In both illustrations, what is required is that *m* stand in that relationship of immanence to the event in question which makes it particularly *his*.[13] But this ownership dissipates when we ponder mere transeunt causation, which accordingly is inadequate to account for a difference in explananda central in many ways to the entire enterprise of morality.

None of these arguments will finally be persuasive, but let us for the moment concede to the Immanentist. I shall now suppose, just as he insists, that there are episodes of immanent causation and that basic actions are examples of these. I shall speak of them as *complex* events,[14] to point a contrast with the kinds of events which *transeunt* causal episodes illustrate, and which I shall designate as *compound* events. A *compound* event is an event which consists of at least two distinct events externally related to each other, each of which could in principle occur on its own. By a guarded analogy with propositional logic, in which the *truth-value* of a compound proposition is a function of the *truth-values* of its component propositional parts, we might say that the *occurrence* of a compound event is a function of the *occurrence* of its component eventival parts. And indeed, if we think of single causal episodes as analyzed by Hume, this is exactly what we do find. To say that the event decsribed as '*b* caused *a*' occurred is only to say that *b* occurred and that *a* occurred, and *nothing more*. Or at least nothing other than *a* and *b* happen. The remaining content of causal description has reference to some organizing framework which is 'in the mind' say a 'habit of expectation'. Since all compound events are functions of their constituent eventival parts, all that *really happens* is the latter: the whole of history, as it were, is a mosaic of independent events bracketed together under an organizing framework, one element of which is the concept of transeunt causation. The Immanentist denies this analysis. For him, the doing of *b* by *m*, for example, is an event and it contains a component event, namely *b*, with which it is not identical. But when we subtract *b* from the doing of it by *m*, something is left over which is not an event in its own right: for there is no *mere* doing: doing always is *of* something. If, as Hume and others believe, basic actions were episodes of transeunt causation in which the event done were caused by a volition, subtracting *b* from the doing by *m* of *b* would leave another event, namely the volition, externally conjoined under transeunt causation to *b*. But there is, the Immanentist claims, no such event. Rather, there is just the original relationship between *m*, an agent, and *b*, an event which is *his*. So – since a complex event is not a function of its constituent evential parts, and more happens when *m* does *b* than just *b* itself – the Radical Atomism of events which transeuncy underwrites as an ontology of history is *false*. As must be any ontology which entails the non-primitivity of agents and of basic actions.

So far, apart from certain difficulties in the transeunt analysis of basic actions, the Immanentist has no real *argument* in favor of the irreducibility of complex events to compound ones except the suggestion that *doing* is not something which can occur on its own: there is no doing which is not the doing *of* something. So there is no separate event which 'doing' describes, and which stands to another event in the transeunt relationship. This is a curious notion, however, suggesting as it does that with basic actions we are somehow immune to failure. For we cannot do *b* without *b* happening. And this sounds ominously like the perceptual episodes which basic *sentences* were meant to express, and with regard to which we were again held to be immune to error: basic cognitions are *incorrigible*. But suppose that there were two ways to read 'of' in the slogan 'no doing without the doing *of* something'. One way is *intensionalistic*, the other way is *extensionalistic*. The first way permits us to say that we can think *of* something which does not exist, the second way requires us to say that we can only think *of* what does exist. Suppose a basic action involves both the intensionalist and extensionalist modes of construing 'of'. That is, '*m* does *b*' is a compound of '*m* does-*b*' and *b*! Then the former could occur without the latter occurring: one could do-*b* without *b* happening. And the latter could occur without the former: *b* could occur without 'doing-*b*' being true of *m*. Then 'doing-*b*' could be an event in its own right, and a basic action might then be an episode of transeunt causation between the doing-of-*b* and *b*, and hence a compound event rather than a complex one! The Immanentist would then have permitted the intensionalistic reading of 'of' to entail performative incorrigibility in the *extensionalist* sense.

Well, this may be or may not be. We have a long way to go yet before we can say. So let us continue, however uneasily, to countenance complex events and immanent causation as a fundamental mode of causation.

II

Let us now consider the ways in which complex events can relate to other events in the causal order.

To begin with, the complex event may itself and as a whole be the effect in an episode of transeunt causation. So much is already conceded by the pattern of explanation the Immanentist has cited, for in causing *m* to do *b*, it is not obvious that any notion other than transeunt causation is involved when the doing by *m* of *b* – an episode admittedly of immanent causation – is the *effect*. If causation is a law-entailing relationship between ordered pairs of events, the event in the effect position may be a complex event, in which case the law covers the cause together with the complex event; and if the latter is *m*'s doing of *b*, it is this event, and not *b* itself, which is covered by the law. If I throw a stone, causing *m* to raise his arm in a protective response, I have caused the occurrence of a complex event, but it is not at all clear that the throwing of a stone causes an arm to rise (save as part of a complex act); and without the assumption of such a context, it is probably false that throwing stones and rising arms are jointly covered by laws.

On the other hand, the component event may be caused transeuntly by some other event which does not cause the complex event containing it. A flexing triceps muscle, for example, transeuntly causes *m*'s arm to rise *without* it causing *m* to *raise* his arm. We may represent these various cases diagrammatically. Let *e* and *f* be events of whatever sort, let *m*D*b* be a complex event, and let *b* be the event contained in that complex event. The lines, which shows the direction and termini of transeunt causation, exhibit the relations we have been discussing:

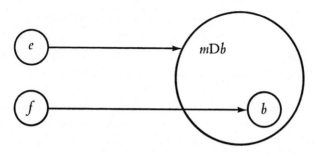

Here there are two episodes of transeunt and one episode of immanent causation. The throwing of the stone (*e*), say, causes *m* to raise his arm (but does not cause the rising of the arm itself). The rising of the arm is caused by the flexing of a triceps (*f*) which does not cause *m* to raise his arm. And *m* immediately causes *b*, which is interestingly overdetermined, at the crossroads of immanent and transeunt causation. I shall discuss transeunt causation with complex effects in the next chapter. But here I want to concentrate upon this order of overdetermination, which has some philosophically crucial aspects. We might note, in passing, that in the diagram, *m*D*b* has different causes from those *b* has, and by the plausible criterion that events are distinct when they have distinct causes (because identical only when thay have all the *same* causes),[15] the non-identity of *m*D*b* and *b* is patent. But perhaps this issue is no longer interestingly contestable.

I wish to make it quite plain, if it is not so already, that the concept of a basic action does not rule it out that *b* should be transeuntly caused if *m*D*b* is a basic action. Indeed, if *f* causes *b*, it is not even ruled out that *f* should itself be (permissibly redescribed as) an action. All that is ruled out by the concept is this: if *f* causes *b* and *m*D*f*, the latter cannot in any sense be a *component* of *m*D*b* if the latter is basic: for basic actions have no components which themselves are actions. Hence it is ruled out that *m* should directly do *b* *and* that he should do *b* *through* doing *f*. As we shall see, even this allows for anomalies of sorts, but at least in the case of most immediate interest to us, where our concern is with the physiological causes – with flexing muscles and nervous impulses and the firing of neurons – of things we do directly, it is plain that we do not, if we raise an arm directly, raise it through firing a neuron, say, if the latter is understood as action. It is independently arguable that firing a neuron cannot be a basic action, simply on the grounds that few of us have direct power over our neurons.

It *may* strike the reader that if *b* is caused it is difficult to see how *b* can be done, and certainly difficult to see how the basic action can be *free*. This latter reflection is too broad and ill-defined to be usefully glossed at this point, but we at least may emphasize that the causes of *b* are not typically if ever the causes of the *doing* of *b* by *m*, and that it is accordingly consistent with *b* being caused, even determined, that the *doing* of *b* should *not* be caused or determined. So the action could be free though the event which is done were determined. The alternative must surely be that if *b* is immanently caused it can have no *transeunt* causes. In this case there are no embodied agents: *either* we raise our arms as basic actions *or* our arms rise through transeunt causes, but overdetermination, as graphically represented above, is untenable. *If b were* an action, then, it would have to be a mediated one at best, its ultimate transeunt cause being an event which, since we immanently cause it, cannot itself, on the theory considered, *have* transeunt causes. And the question then arises as to what these events may be. It seems to me in part due to the demand that there be events, themselves causes of other events but which cannot themselves be effects, that one part of the theory of volitions may be accounted for: since volitions have precisely this quality. Volitions, indeed, are exactly counterpart through their asymmetric characterization to *percepts* in the theory of cognition, since these were meant to be knowable only directly though everything further were known through them: hence sentences about them could only be premisses and never conclusions. But at least in the theory of action the need for volitions dissipates somewhat when we surrender the theory of the complementarity of transeunt and immanent causation, which then allows us the sort of overdetermination of events we routinely expect to find in embodied agents. There may *be* events which can only be causes and never effects. But before acquiescing in their occurrence, we ought first to determine whether we have not invented them because we believed nothing can be simultaneously caused immanently and transeuntly. And this belief is false if the common belief is true that raising an arm exemplifies in the normal case an episode of immanent causation.

Suppose, now, that the complementarity theory is not compelling, that an event *f* transeuntly causes *b* when *mDb* is a basic action. The question then is what *m*'s relation to *f* is to be?

I want now to answer this question, but I must make clear what our ground rules are to be. First of all, I want to retain as essentially correct the phenomenology of action, the experience of normal agents to which I appeal for intuitions regarding basic actions: that when, for example, I raise an arm, there is nothing I do through which the arm rises: that raising an arm is not a mediated action. But secondly, I want to accept whatever science tells me is correct about how our bodies work. The problem is to fit these two pictures together. But thirdly, I do not want to postulate anomalous events, which I regard volitions to be, unless I am certain they are not merely a shadow cast by the intersection of the two pictures I believe it a philosophical obligation to render mutually coherent. I believe both pictures are correct, and I mean to endorse them both, denying neither phenomenology nor physiology.

III

The normal physiological account of what happens when we voluntarily raise an arm is that something happens in the brain which causes a flexing of the muscle which in turn causes the rising of the arm. *We*, of course, do not raise our arms by flexing our muscles. Some men might, the raising of the arm then being a mediated action done through the flexing of their muscles. But that it not how the common case occurs, and indeed most of us are impotent to flex our muscles, at least the relevant muscles, as basic actions. And this is unambiguously so with regard to occurrences in the *brain*: so far as we know, and our knowledge should be a controlling factor in this inquiry, we cannot do anything as a basic action within the brain. Rather, as writers on action have long pointed out, we flex our muscles *by* raising our arms, we fire neurons *by* moving our limbs. But we cannot let matters rest with this. For the question of how this 'by' is to be interpreted remains.

Do we wish, for example, to argue that firing a neuron – call this the event *n* – is a mediated action (we know it cannot be a basic one if it is done 'by' what is by hypothesis a basic action, namely raising an arm)? The immediate difficulty here is this. Our analysis of mediated actions is that, if *m*D*a* occurs, there is some event *b* such that *m* does *b* directly, and *b* causes *a*. Here, then, if *m* fires a neuron by raising his arm, the arm-rise would cause the event *n*. But *n* was that event in the brain which is invoked in the physiological explanation of the arm-rise (= *b*). Can *b* cause *n* and *n* cause *b*? Can causality run in two directions this way?

My own view is that bilateral causation is in general an unintelligible notion. It is *conspicuously* so in the present instance. For *n* and *b* are time-separated events. If the concept of causation requires that a cause temporally precede its effect, then *n* would have to precede *b* and *b* precede *n*, which, by the transitivity of precedence as a relation, would have *b* preceding itself, which is ruled out by the irreflexivity of the relation of precedence. Now it can of course be argued that the causal order need not be a temporal order, and that causes need not temporally precede (though they presumably cannot temporally succeed) their effects: but they can occur simultaneously with their effects. Philosophical thought appears to be divided on this question. For Whitehead the criterion of causal independence is contemporaneity, so that no two contemporary occurrences could have causal ties.[16] Hume, by contrast, has argued that causes must be contemporary with their effects, so that *non*-contemporaneity would be the criterion of causal independence.[17] Pending resolution of this metaphysical contest, common experience reveals cases in which causes may occur simultaneously with their effects or appear to: water boils *just when* it reaches 100° C;[18] the typewriter key is depressed *when* I depress it;[19] and more immediately appropriate, the arm rises just *when* the muscle flexes. I believe that bilateral causation is unintelligible even here. For if *b* is contemporary with an event which is at once the cause and the effect of *b*, then *b* is the cause of it and hence the cause or part of the cause of *itself*, since if *x* is cause of *y* and *y* is cause of *z*, *x* is part of the cause of *z*. But transeunt causation requires cause and effect to be distinct, even if not temporally distinct events: and *b* can hardly be distinct from itself. But even if this argument may strike the reader as too precious, we may retreat to the considerations of time to cope with cases in which, in the present sense of 'by', a man does what causes *n* 'by' doing *b*. Nervous impulses travel at a finite velocity (5 cm/sec to 100 m/sec), and so *n* occurs before its putative cause. And these considerations rule out, as well, the ingenious proposal that *n* is caused *not* by *b* but by the complex event in which *m does b* as a basic action (see page 63). Here *b* is caused by *n* but *n* is not caused by *b*: it rather is caused by *mDb*, and the law relates *mDb* and *n* in the relevant direction, rather than *b* and *n*. For *mDb*, whatever time it occupies, cannot have occurred until *b* occurs, and hence *n*, since earlier than *b*, is earlier than its putative cause, *mDb*. One may say, 'so much the worse for the concept of causality as you have so far glossed it'. But is a different concept of cause really available? Does one want to say that *mDb* causes *n* in a different sense of cause from that under which *n* is said to cause *b*? Have we *three* distinct causal concepts here? Immanent and transeunt and now this new kind?

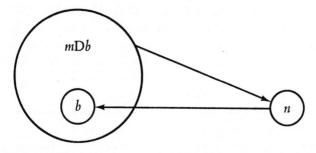

Something like this appears to be suggested by Professor Chisholm, who introduces the otherwise undefined expression 'makes happen'[20] to cover the troublesome case: *m* 'makes happen' *n* when *m* does *b* and *b* is caused by *n*. But since 'makes happen' only baptizes our conceptual ignorance without especially lightening it, and is introduced just to cover the case antecedently found puzzling, and finally would have to be counted a primitive explanatory concept, distinct from those we already have cited, a perhaps pardonable conceptual conservatism with regard to it is in order. I believe there is an available way of handling the problem which, though not without difficulties of its own, is at least already entrenched as a philosophical concept. This is the concept of *identity*.

What I propose is this. Call that series of events beginning with the brain event *n* and terminating in *b* the *n*-series. I shall claim that the complex event – the basic action *mDb* – is *identical with the n-series*. That is to say, we have here one and the same event. And now we might give a plain sense to the expression 'makes happen'. The agent *m* 'makes happen' that event which is the cause of what he does directly in the respect that the cause in question is part of a compound event with which his action is identical. It does not, of course, follow that *m does n*, except in the restricted sense that *n* is part of a series of events identical with his doing of *b*. A measure of confirmation for this may be found when we consider causes of *b* which lie outside the *n*-series. There are two cases to consider. (1) the cause of *b* is some internal physiological occurrence outside the *n*-series. Then *b* happens without *m* doing *b*, and thus an arm goes up without being raised by *m*. This would be a disordered body. (2) Something causes *b* which is external to *m*'s body, say a blow from someone else's arm, causing *m*'s arm to swing up without *m* swinging it. In both cases we get a causal series, terminating in *b*, with which *mDb* is *not* identical. It is identical only with normal physiological series.

I find this a philosophically attractive conjecture, and, strange as it may at first sight appear, I believe it is not difficult to reduce the strangeness in question; the following comments are an attempt at philosophical rhetoric: to make the identity thesis for actions palatable.

IV

Philosophers might like to say that if we assert an identity, what we must in effect be saying is that this is a relation which holds between two *descriptions* of the same thing: that '*n*-series' and 'basic action' then are co-referential descriptions. This is in some respects unexceptionable. But some condition in excess of mere co-referentiality is called for in the present instance. Suppose Jane loses a penny, which I then find. Then 'the penny Jane lost' and 'the penny I found' are descriptions of the very same bit of copper. Yet the *properties* of having been lost by Jane and having been found by me are altogether different properties, albeit of the same thing. The bird that makes the shrill clatter is the bird that sports the bright tail, and while I may *identify* the maker of the noise to someone who does not know birds by saying that it is the very same bird which has the bright tail, no one will suppose that having this tail and making this noise are one and the same property. But being the basic action and being the *n*-series *are* one and the same property. It would be of no philosophical interest that the same person who performs the basic action should also undergo the *n*-series, for these need have nothing to do with one another. Nor would it solve our problem if there were high correlations between having *n*-series take place in one's body and performing such basic actions as raising arms. So the only way we can capture the tightness we require in conventional semantical nomenclature is to say that it is the *very same property* which instantiates the two descriptions. If there is resistance to accepting this identification, it must be because, at the level of phenomenology, my experience of raising an arm seems not at all to be like the experience of something happening in my nervous system. But this, I think, is generally so when we identify, as it has become increasingly attractive to philosophers to do, mental states[21] with neurophysiological and especially brain states. If we think of the complicated mediating apparatus commonly required for us to observe anything happening in our brain, and then how differently what we finally do observe appears to be from what we experience when we have a feeling or a thought, that the two should in any instance be identical must seem radically implausible. It would greatly contribute to the plausibility of the identification, then, if some plausible explanation were available which accounted for its *implausibility* at the phenomenal level. So I shall concern myself with this, and not especially with the task of chivying the required form of identity-sentences into some canonical notation.

It is striking that very few philosophers of mind in the present period defend a position which is both a substantive one – a claim as to what mental phenomena *are* – and an Immaterialist one. Rather, there are Materialists on the one side and, on the other, philosophers who do not so much have a position to defend as one to attack, which is Materialism. So recent debate has had the form of an argument between a player and a referee – or between a man and his conscience – and the body of relevant literature has acquired in consequence a legalistic, casuistical tone. One learns what are the obstacles round which the Materialist must find his way, with very little if any attention paid to what the world would be like if he were wrong. So let us match the forthright Materialist view with an equally forthright contrary view, namely Idealism, and see whether some clearer picture of the issues does not emerge from their confrontation. I believe we can begin to get the argument we need from the dialectic between the two positions which it would be difficult to derive merely from considering Materialism in isolation, and in the rather paralyzing context of Verificationism which is the usual habitat of such scrutinies.

Speaking *grosso modo*, then, Materialists believe that thoughts are brain-states, and Idealists believe that brain-states are thoughts. Since each of these is an identity claim, and since identity is symmetrical, there is an ironic danger that each antagonist is saying the same thing, albeit it from an opposite direction. In order to keep the positions from collapsing ignobly into one another, Materialists slyly insist that not all brain-states are thoughts and the Idealist that not all thoughts are brain-states. It is this which enables them to go on to mount their generalized opposed claims that Matter and Mind are in general the substance of the single-substanced world. I propose, however, that these moves are irrelevant, since upon analysis it will appear that Idealists and Materialists are addressing themselves to something different in their respective claims. The Idealist, thus, is actually concerned with the *content* of thoughts, whereas the Materialist is concerned with thoughts as such. By the content of a thought I mean what the thought is *of* or *about*: I mean the representational property of thoughts in the sense logically identified in Chapter 1. As before, nothing follows from the content of a thought concerning its truth: the thought of St Sebastian is a St-Sebastian-thought whether there historically was or was not that oft-represented, oft-perforated martyr. It is to such properties as these the Idealist refers when he says that brain-states are thoughts. He means that there are thoughts of brain-states. And when he says that not all thoughts are brain-states, he means that there are thoughts of other things, of different content: thoughts of home, of fair ladies, of martyrs. So if it is an identity thesis the Idealist has advanced, it is that the content of (certain) thoughts is of brain-states, and that brain-states have no existence *save* as content: they lack, as the seventeenth-century philosopher would say, formal reality. Or: their formal reality is their objective reality.

Let us now furnish the Idealist with an argument, invented, I believe, by Berkeley. Try, he urges us, to think of a brain-state which is not a thought. Either this is self-defeating, since the brain-state one is thinking of *is* a thought, and to think of an unthought-of brain-state is, in Berkeley's words, 'a manifest repugnancy'. Or it will not be a brain-state one has succeeded in thinking of. It is on the basis chiefly of this curious argument that Berkeley concludes that the brain is in the mind. So, of course, must everything be, since we plainly cannot think of something without thinking of it. Translated into discourse about contents, the thesis of Materialism then sounds like the absurdly false claim that we think of nothing save brain-states. This may be so in the case of certain obsessively monomaniacal brain physiologists: but hardly of you and me. So it is easy to refute the Materialist once we transform his thesis so: but he obviously must resist the transformation. Certainly he would be mad to say that we really are (*au fond*) always, however it may appear, thinking of brain-states. For this was not his claim: it was that thoughts *are*, not that they are *of* brain-states. Idealists have the option of saying that thoughts are what they are of, which here must mean that thoughts just *are* their contents. I distinguish it from the famous, difficult view that things resolve into our thoughts about them: that St Sebastian, for example, is one with the set of St-Sebastian-thoughts. But we may hold off allowing him to exercise this option until we have listened to the Materialist's side.

The Materialist does not deny that there are thoughts: he would disappear if they disappeared, since he requires them (in two ways) just to have a position at all. Nor need he deny that thoughts have representational properties or 'contents'. To be sure, if thoughts are brain-states, then brain-states must have representational properties if thoughts do. If F is identical with G, anything which is a property of F is a property of G, and conversely. This claim must, of course, be carefully qualified, in part through deciding what it to be a property and what is not. Certain things, thus, may be true of something without being a property of it. This seems especially the case when certain cognitive things are true of objects, e.g. of Napoleon that I believe him to have existed: I balk at calling this a property of Napoleon. My reason for this is that permitting it would block almost any statement of identity. Thus Samuel Clemens could not be identical with Mark Twain if some-one somewhere believed, of Samuel Clemens, that he was not Mark Twain. So I shall suppose it not an argument against identification of F with G that someone might not believe of F that it is G, and hence I must refuse to regard a person's beliefs about something a property of that thing. Indeed, I think we must in general reject the way something is represented to be amongst its properties. Often, for example, representations of something will differ so drastically amongst themselves that no obvious resemblances will exist at all within the set of St-Sebastian-representations, for example. And when representations vary as much as they do, it will be easy for someone to believe that quite different things are being represented by them when in fact only one thing is. Identification of representations through their content, and identification of the two representations as 'of' the same thing, is a very complex matter, only slowly appreciated by philosophers. Certainly we cannot go to what, in the extensional sense, two representations may represent: for in the case of unicorn-representations, for overworked example, no such entity exists.

Rejecting as properties of them the way in which things are represented – and having beliefs about them *is* a way of representing things – we may deflect certain arguments, once thought stunning, that I know what thoughts are but know nothing about brains, so thoughts cannot be brain-states; such arguments are blankly irrelevant. My representations of thoughts may not be representations of brain-states, without it following that thoughts are not brain-states! Suppose I represented a thought as little words running through my head, and I represented a brain-state as a constellation of pink charges: surely as representations these are wildly different! And it is this which finally must inhibit the Idealist from saying that a thought just is its content.

For he also wants to say that a thing *x* is the set of *x*-thoughts. Do I want, then, to let the character of objects vary with the vagaries of thoughts about them? Must Nirvana be a cube because, when I happen to think of Nirvana, the thought is of a translucent cube? No, the Idealist as much as anyone has to distinguish correct from incorrect representations. But in any case we shall have to distinguish between what belongs *in* the content and what belongs *to* what has the content, whether we are concerned with thoughts or descriptions or pictures. And as so often in such discussions, the case of representational art is instructive enough to merit a glance.

A painting of a tree fails if it looks like anything save a painting of a tree. It fails as art if it looks, thus, like anything except art, e.g. if it induces the illusion that it *is* a tree. But it also fails as a painting of a tree if it looks like a painting of something else: Lloyd George, say (though trees may, like clouds, show profiles and the like). The first sort of failure generally requires that the object, which is the painting, should lack certain properties that the thing it is *of* would normally have, and it is no violation of the concept of identity that a painting of a tree should be identical with a piece of canvas, and yet the tree have leaves and the canvas none: what belongs to the represented object need not belong to the representation itself. These discrepancies, in some measure essential to representational art, have at times been vexatious to artists concerned to collapse the distance between reality and art; and these have come to adopt a program requiring the painting *per se* to have the properties of what it is a painting *of*. Artists have been ingenious in finding subjects which permitted this coincidence, e.g. a painting of a flag could *be* a flag; a painting of a target could *be* a target, etc. But this demands the subject be presented in a certain way: a square presented in perspective *is* not itself square; a flag painted as fluttering does not itself flutter, etc. So the square, if it is to be a square painting of a square, must be shown head on and in strict frontality. But even then, when coincidence has been achieved, it remains *of* a square though itself *is* a square, and the distinction between representational properties and ordinary properties remain. Let us attempt now to extend these notions to *thoughts*.

Pictures are perhaps a misleading case, because they can have the properties they also show, being and showing spatial objects; and because congruence between their intensional and non-intensional properties can become an artistic program. But it is not clear that thoughts actually can have the properties had by what they are thoughts *of*, unless they are thoughts *of* thoughts. Thus Chomsky's notorious example of a nonsense expression – 'Colorless green ideas...' – is not so lunatic as it appears: if 'green idea' refers to what an ideas is *of* when it is the idea of green, it is sensible to suppose the idea itself should be colorless. It would be necessary that it should be colorless if an idea were a modification of a *res cogitans*, as in Descartes, *res cogitans* being unspatial in a way in which colors could not be. But we plainly can have the ideas of spatial things, or things presupposing spatiality, when the ideas themselves are spaceless. If ideas are brain-states, they may be spatial and may even be colored, for all I know, but still they need not have the color they are of: any more than the word *green* need *be* green. Thoughts may be vague, ambiguous, self-contradictions, without it even being sensible to suppose that the thoughts as such have these properties. Some of the darkest sentences in our literature are presented in lines of print which are triumphs of graphic clarity. We thus can distinguish properties of what is thought of, as well as properties of the *way* this is *given* to thought, without any of this being true of the thought itself, as an entity. And thus we distinguish what goes on *in* my thoughts from what goes on *in* my brain, a distinction which holds even if the thoughts themselves are in the brain. For the 'in' is respectively intensional and extensional. The thought itself may be located a half-inch back from my forehead; but what is going on *in* the thought may have no, perhaps can have no spatial relation to my forehead (not even if it is my forehead I am thinking of). To confuse these 'ins' would be like opening *Anna Karenina* to page 267, where Anna and Vronsky consummate their love, hoping to surprise them in the act. There is no spatial relation between that page and the room in which the adultery transpires. Now the point of these remarks is that the last place one would look to see what thoughts are is to their content, to what they are of. There is nothing in the content of a thought which, at least typically, will tell you what the properties of the thought itself are. And since it is to their content that we commonly appeal when we refer to thoughts, and which we are primarily interested in when we *have* thoughts, it is not surprising that men who have had a great many thoughts should not know what thoughts are. There is no way of easily bringing what they are into what they are about. And this is generally true of mental phenomena, at least to the degree that intentionality is the mark of the mental. Meanwhile, this would explain why it would be difficult to tell from examining *brains* anything about what brain-states are *of* when they are thoughts. In the first place, when the brains are not ours, neither are the thoughts, and in the second place, even if we could examine our own brain from the outside *while* thinking, there would be no way in which I could get what I experience when I perceive the brain externally into the content of the thought I am having while simultaneously conducting the examination. Not unless I were thinking about brain-states. Now suppose I were. Suppose, indeed, my thought were an image, an image of a brain-state, indeed an exact image of the very brain-state in which the image consists, and which I examine from without! Then this would be like the square painting of a square, here intensional and extensional properties having become coincident. But the case is exactly exceptional enough to show why thoughts of things other than brain-states should show so little of what they are, if what they are is brain-states.

We may, I think, extend these notions to perception, though whether perception is intentional or not is perhaps moot. It is not moot on a Representationalist theory of perception, but then Representationalism itself is moot, and one would not wish here to prejudge the outcome of the philosophical controversy amongst theories of perception. But presumably there is no way of deciding on the basis of some internal differences in what we perceive whether this is a real object, a representation or what, and in any case we may regard *what* we perceive, however otherwise characterized, as the content of a perception. Suppose we are perceiving a tree. Then the tree would not be a brain-state: what at best might be a brain-state would be the perceiving of it: *noesis*, on Husserl's distinction, rather than *noema*. Since the act of perceiving is not commonly perceived, does not commonly enter as part of the content of perception, there is nothing in *what* we perceive which could tell us in what perceiving itself might consist. Nothing in the tree I perceive could tell me that my perceiving of it were something going on in my brain. And now suppose I take up the physiology of the brain, and actually begin to perceive perceivings: actually observe what goes on in people's brains when they perceive, say, trees. And suppose, as before, I begin observing my own brain in this manner: suppose I perceive what goes on in *my* brain when I perceive a tree. This requires that I have two perceptions, one of a brain-state and one of a tree, and of course, as far as content goes, I could hardly confuse the two, they are (one would think) so different. But what possibly could tell me that *what* I perceive, in the one case, is the same thing which takes place when I perceive the tree in the other case? I cannot combine these in a single content, I cannot bring the brain-content in with the tree-content. And this will apply even when I can perceive what happens when I perceive only the perceiving itself, viz. the brain-state in which perceiving consists. Nothing in what I perceive will here tell me that the same thing takes place when I perceive, say, a tree. So identification of perceivings with brain-states has to sound implausible when based upon the content of what we typically perceive. And the implausibility derives from exactly that distinction it is necessary to draw when making the sort of identification of perceiving with brain-states that the Materialist is interested in. We are identifying something which has intentional properties with something whose properties very seldom coincide with the properties of the thing represented. And it is made all the more difficult though the fact that most of us know so little about brain-states that we are very uncertain indeed, when we represent them, that the properties of *what* we represent are one with the representation itself, in case it *is* a brain-state; and through the further fact that most people throughout their lives almost never represent anything of the sort.

I, of course, have been concerned to identify basic actions with bodily processes here. My purpose in having digressed as far as I have into a general Materialism has chiefly been to dispel in advance any sense of implausibility my identification may induce, by attempting to make Materialism itself plausible. Of course nothing said *demonstrates* Materialism. What my argument may contribute to a general Materialism is rather this: it may be granted that a distinction is to be drawn between the properties of what we represent and the properties of the representation itself, without it following that representations in the case of thoughts and the like are brain-states or bodily processes of any sort. I have tried to show that unless we identify a basic action with a bodily process, we face anomalies which dissipate when the identification is made.

Before reverting to basic actions, I should like to note two consequences, of some philosophical import, which turn upon the general identificatory thesis which Materialism exemplifies.

(1) If an action is an *n*-series, we must not expect then to find actions *in* the *n*-series, as volitions say: for this would then leave begged the question of what *these* actions are. Actions have no place *in* the series

with which they are identical. And the point is perfectly general. If one identifies heat with the aggregate behavior of molecules in random motion, we must not expect to find heat *in* the molecules themselves: for then the question of what *this* heat is will have been begged. If perception is a physiological process, we must not expect to find perceptions *in* the processes, say as their termini. If, to take a grander topic, God is identical with the universe, we must not look for some special differentiating evidence for God *in* the universe: not even God can be a part of what he is identical with as a whole.

(2) If thoughts are brain-states, we cannot then speak of thoughts as being *caused* by the brain-states in question: for nothing causes itself. This does not mean that thoughts cannot be caused by other thoughts or, which comes to the same thing, that thoughts cannot be caused by brain-states distinct from the ones with which they are identical. But this may mean that brain-states enter as causes of other brain-states through the representational or intentional properties we predicate over thoughts. It would follow that one could not understand certain brain-processes if one did not appreciate the structure of the brain-states involved as given through their intentional properties. Neither associative phenomena in psychology nor the typically cited dynamisms of psycho-analytical theory could be explained in terms of brain-physiology except insofar as the latter were enriched by the assignment to the appropriate brain-processes and states of the relevant representational properties. But to explore *this* idea further here would take us well outside our subject, to which I accordingly return.

V

If the basic action which consists of *m* raising his arm is identical, as I have proposed it is, with a physiological series which terminates in *m*'s arm rising, then if the first exemplifies immanent and the second transeunt causation, we hardly can have *derived* our concept of transeunt causation from our experience of basic action. If basic action, thus, is a complex event and transeunt causation is exemplified in compound events, there is not, in the former, the required *pair* of events to be related under the concept of transeuncy. But are we indeed dealing with a complex event in the former case and hence with an example of immanent causation? Hume, we saw, believed we are not, and he disputes with an anonymous objector who appears to have claimed that we might derive the notion of necessary connection from the putatively internal relationship between ourselves and those parts of our bodies over which we have direct control.[22] Here, in the later, ironic words of Nietzsche, we credit ourselves with having caught causality in the act.[23] Hume denies that we are dealing with any special sort of causal episode. We are, rather, dealing with merely a routine case of transeunt causation.

'This influence of the will', Hume writes, 'we know by consciousness.' *What* we know, he claims, is that an act of will – a volition – causes an arm to rise or a leg to move. What we do not know is *how* this transpires, no more than we know, in any case of causation, *how* the effect is 'produced' by the cause: we know only that it is. In the present instance, Hume adopts a mocking piety, claiming that we have no real understanding of 'the mysterious union of soul with body, by which a supposed spiritual substance acquires such an influence over a material one, that the most refined thought is able to actuate the grossest matter'. The irony is due, in part, of course, to the fact that Hume's collapse of the self – of 'spiritual substance' – onto its percepts and of things onto their appearances and finally of percepts onto appearances, has flattened out completely the alleged metaphysical differences between spirit and matter; and in part it is due to the fact that even were he to give up his neutralized ontology, his view of causation, as a mere collating of like event with like event, cuts across all pretended ontological boundaries. No *different* concept is required to collate material with spiritual events, than material with material, or spiritual with spiritual ones, supposing these distinctions legitimate.

But Hume takes his physiology rather more seriously than this, and seems genuinely puzzled by the manner in which, on his account, we move our arms, for example. His puzzlement arises from the fact that he allows two sides of the processes I have identified to leak into each other. Thus, knowing, as he does, enough of physiology to appreciate that arms rise when muscles flex and that muscles flex when nerves transmit some energy to them, Hume supposes that *we* must somehow activate nervous impulses by means of volitions, so that our arms then rise as distant effects. And he did not know how we did activate nervous impulses as the theory required that we always do.[24] My account administers philosophical therapy to this puzzlement, for we do not, when we act, *enter* the physiological series with which our acting is *identical*, and there is accordingly good reason for our ignorance here, namely that there is nothing to know about at all. So if there *were* an act of will, which Hume confidently pretends to know of, this would be directly connected, as in any ultimate causal episode, with the rising of an arm, the two events then exhibiting the structure of transeuncy. And the question is whether there are two events, one an act of will and the other a bodily movement, or whether we instead have a single complex event which *contains* the bodily movement, but not another event to be related to it via transeuncy?

Well, if we subtract b from the n-series, leaving as it were the n-series minus b, we certainly, on the physiological side at least, have *some* events distinct from b. And what, then, is it that is part of the doing of b by m which is to be identified with this truncated series? After all, as we saw, the temporal boundaries of the basic action must be one with the temporal boundaries of the n-series, and the boundary events in the n-series are non-contemporary, so some *part* of the basic action occurs before b occurs. Indeed, *every* part of the basic action which is identical with that part of the n-series which occurs before b occurs, must itself occur before b does. If we decide that this cannot be an event, the question arises as to how we should justify the claim that it is not. And if, as seems plausible, it *is* an event, then why should not this event be related to b under the concept of transeuncy, so that *in fact* a basic action really exemplifies, after all, transeuncy rather than immanency? Then suppose that the doing of b by m, minus b, is what Hume would have meant by an act of will, and that the act of will then transeuntly causes b?

Perhaps there is an objection against designating it as an act of will. That does not greatly matter: call whatever it is which, being part of a basic action, is identical with the n-series minus b, anything you choose. The essential question of transeuncy remains. *I* shall designate it a *doing*. What if I now propose that a basic action is an episode in which a *doing*, which is one event, transeuntly causes another event? It is *doings*, then, which are identified with the physiological processes in question. I must quickly, however, expel certain immediate objections.

First, there is an objection, to which a response has already been sketched, that the verb 'does' is transitive, that there is hence no doing which is not the doing *of* something, and so one could not conceive of the event I speak of as a 'doing' without reference to what is *done*, and this is *not* the case with transeunt causation, where cause and effect can be formulated without reference to one another. The response to this, I believe, is that we might easily be able to give a neutral description of this event, that it may be redescribed as a *doing of* in the light of

74

its common effect, that even 'cause of' is a transitive expression, and that it, like 'does', might be regarded as a non-basic (re-)description of the event in question in terms of other events. As we shall subsequently note, it is not at all uncommon to redescribe events in terms of causes and effects in this way. So 'doing-of-b', while it descriptively straddles the gap between one event and another, does not entail a closer connection between the two events than Hume supposed is ever found in any pair of events held to be causally tethered.

This shift to a non-basic description yields some useful philosophical by-products. For, once the redescription has taken place, it is possible for the same sort of event to be redescribed as a doing-of-b even though b itself in fact does not occur. It is with reference to this, I should think, that we explain the phenomenon of phantom limbs, where a man might describe himself as raising his arm when he in fact no longer *has* an arm to raise. What happens is what ordinarily happens when his arm is caused to rise, only in this case the common effect is unavailable. Thus 'doing of b' becomes subtly transformed into an *intensional* description, allowing us to say that the basic action of raising an arm – of directly doing b – consists in two events, a *doing-of-b* plus b. And the conjunction of these is just the kind of conjunction typically found in transeunt causal episodes. There is, I believe, a clear analogy to this in the theory of perception. Perceiving x might naturally be treated as a conjunction of two events, x plus the perception-of-x, where the former causes the latter. And, because of the ordinary causal associations, the physiological events caused by x are redescribed in intentionalistic terms as a perceiving-of-x. The counterpart in the theory of perception to the case of the phantom limb no doubt is a perceiving-of-x which is not caused by x, which is a sort of illusion and predictably indiscernible as such from those perceivings-of-x which *are* caused by x.

Secondly, it may be objected that bringing causality into the discussion is inconsistent with the characterization I have given of basic actions or, for that matter, of basic cognitions, since an analogy with perception has again been noted. But in fact this will not do. A basic action is one where a man does b without doing something which causes b to happen. But in this case, surely, doing-b is not something which m does. *It is the doing itself!* What m does is b, not the *doing* of b. So that the doing-of-b can cause b and the entire compound event satisfy the criterion of a basic action. And similarly with the perceiving-

75

of-*x*. It *is* a perceiving, not something which is perceived. So *m* does not perceive *x* through perceiving something else, in this case through the perceiving of *x*. Far from that: he perceives *x* directly. And this causal theory is exactly consistent with our criterion of basic cognition.

Thirdly, it lies so far as we know within the competence of science to induce events in the brain through electrostimulation, and hence the event *n*, as first member of the *n*-series, may be caused to happen in this manner. But then, if *n* occurs, what is to prevent the entire *n*-series from occurring, and hence the basic action identical with the *n*-series? So by electrostimulation of the brain we can cause to occur a series of events identical with a basic action. I see no way to rule this out, and were it to occur to me, my experience would be of raising my arm 'for no reason' and I might, I suppose, wonder why I was doing it: or know that I was not doing it for any reason, nor as part of a mediated action. I would be like a marionette whose *will* was like a sort of limb, subject to external modulation. But the main problem here lies with the fact that electrostimulation, if open to anyone, is open in principle to me: and so *I* might cause the occurrence of a basic action of mine. And is this consistent with the concept of a basic action? I believe it is, though the case is not without anomalies. First, the action whereby I activate the electrostimulator is not a *component* of the basic action thus caused. What I have performed, rather, is a mediated action with a complex effect: it is a mediated action which has a basic action both as its starting point and terminus. And I should be like a marionette capable of activating his own mechanisms, tugging strings which move his members, inside and outside the apparatus at once. And by circuitous devices, I should be able to manipulate my will. The possibility is singular and schizophrenic, but I cannot see that it in any way subverts the concepts we have developed. It even helps confirm a thesis, namely that the event we might be prepared to call a 'doing' is one which can be an effect as well as a cause. That the cause should come from the physiological side, rather than from a quarter we should commonly look to for activation of the will – from a person's intentions – is only a curiosity. As is the entire case. It will prove in the end, however, to be a useful curiosity.

VI

We have now a theory that a basic action may be considered a compound event, with a doing-of-*b* on the one side, and *b* on the other, the pair connected in an episode of transeunt causalation. And I have enumerated the very considerable philosophical advantages and economies this theory may yield us. To these may be added another, suggested to me once by David Armstrong: a man may be struck immobile, like Lot's wife, just the instant when the doing-of-*b* is completed, so that *b* never occurs: between the doing and the deed falls a shadow. The theory that the action is a compound event allows logical space for the shadow to fall, since in uninterrupted instances there are two events. The Immanentist has no room, however, for this odd but possible contingency. There may be further advantages still. A philosophical analysis is satisfactory, at the most elementary level at least, when it captures all our intuitions and blocks all our counter-intuitions regarding the concept analyzed – just in the way a logical system is adequate if it permits all valid inferences and inhibits all invalid ones in the fragment of discourse it reconstructs.

It is not, in the end, an analysis I can finally accept, however. One reason for my resistance is that there is another account, equally compatible with our intuitions, namely that a basic action *mDb* is a complex event, and that what happens in *mDb* minus *b* may be described as a fragment of a whole, whose completing fragment then is *b*. Its being a fragment is obscured by the fact that other events, which resemble it exactly, may occur without being fragments of complex events: they may be integral occurrences, like arms going up. That the earlier fragment – what I have designated a *doing* – may be described in terms of the whole it forms a part of, and that it is accordingly susceptible of intensionalized construction, is underwritten by the rhetorical concept of metonymy, which we have in fact already exploited. And we may easily describe what happens when, in the case of the abrupt paralysis, the shadow falls between doing and deed, as follows: *an incomplete performance:* a truncated event, rather than an event in its own right. And one by one, I believe, we may accommodate to this analysis all those intuitions which seemed so well to support that reading of basic actions as compound events. Choice, then, of '*m* does' as designating an event or a fragment of an event must seem arbitrary were it not for an argument which seems to me to favor the latter analysis. The grounds for this argument are established only later in this book, but I must anticipate my account by introducing the conclusion here, without making any effort now to support it.

Having identified basic actions with physiological processes, I shall find myself later forced, willingly, as it happens, to identify *us* with our actions and hence with our bodily processes. We are our actions and one with the relevant reaches of our bodies. So there is not *m*, on the one side, and his actions on the other, with the problem of how they are to be connected: between *m* and his basic actions there is no gap to span. Now suppose the actional part of a basic action is *m*-does-*b*, with *b* as an external effect. Then the boundaries of the self appear to fall between the action and its effect: *we* are no more identical with that effect of a doing than we are with the movement of a hat we happen to throw. But suppose, as seems implicit in the facts, the doing itself is identical with a causal series. Then why should not some earlier event be the action, and the rest effect? The shadow of paralysis, thus, might fall between any pair of events in the normal series with as much justification as it falls between everything up to *b*, and *b*. So only the first event in the series seems immune, and accordingly we might just as well call this the action. This being an event in the brain, we are, if identical with our actions, identical with our brains. Perhaps we *are* the pineal glands Descartes mistakenly only supposed we were seated in! But now, having shrunk the boundaries of the self to this narrow cranial circumference, let us consider the events which take place within it. Surely these take time, however brief, and surely the shadow has temporal room at least to fall. What then should we use to describe whatever happened before it fell? I imagine we would say that it was a fragment of an action, an uncompleted action. Since we have at last to make this distinction, why not have made it sooner before we were driven by an inexorable logic away from the boundaries we may rightfully consider ours: those of the entirety of our bodies with which we actively perform?

So I shall reject, after all, separate acts of will which cause events, and count basic actions at last as complex events, identical with bodily processes which may themselves have now to be considered integral events in their own right rather than compounds of integral events. Immanent causation having dropped then from the picture, we may now consider transeunt causation – or causation *tout court* – in its own right. For it will be important for us to understand whether and how complex events – or basic actions – may enter as integral components of compound ones: as causes and effects.

4

CAUSALITY AND BASIC ACTIONS

Many terms, as we have seen, apply to the objects before us only on the assumption that they have a certain causal history, failing which the term is simply false of the object in question. A bit of observed behavior is the exercise of a habit only if it has been formed and reinforced by experience, and though nothing about the behavior would be observably different were this special history lacking, still it would not be the exercise of a *habit* if this were not its history. Something, again, is properly a scar if it has been caused by a wound, and should the thing in question have otherwise been caused – or not have been caused at all – it is not a scar, however strikingly it may resemble one. A footprint is a footprint only on condition that it was caused by a footstep, and should there be something in every observable respect like a footprint, but differently caused, it is not a footprint. Thus merely through the meanings of terms we very routinely employ in describing the objects before us, our language incorporates a considerable body of knowledge or what *passes* for knowledge of the world. And fragments of this knowledge figure amongst the application-conditions for terms which hold (which take the appropriate (+) semantical value) only if the former are correctly presupposed. *Causal* knowledge sufficiently penetrates the meanings of terms in the most ordinary employment, that our dictionaries incorporate a kind of encyclopedia as well.[1] And except by mastering the causal knowledge in question, ingesting the encyclopedia, one cannot truly be said to have mastered the meanings of these terms. To master a vocabulary is to master a causal picture of the world.

The terms we have been discussing are in consequence too rich by far to figure in what I have called *basic* descriptions of the objects before us: descriptions which make no implicit reference to anything outside the object of immediate experience, presupposing, indeed, the existence of nothing other than what we do in fact observe when we in fact observe it. When a causal history is entailed by the conditions for true application of a term, it very naturally follows that whether or not the term in question is true or false of an object at hand depends upon factors external to and largely independent of the experience delivered at the moment. It is not so much that our words are too coarse to reflect the subtle curvatures and colorations of the objects at hand, if phenomenological description is our aim, but the fact that most of the words we use carry implications and entailments which control the application of even the most commonplace descriptions, should we settle for phenomenology at some acceptable level of coarseness. A *strict* phenomenology demands either a neutralizing function on these terms – the introduction of some entailment-aborting suffix like '-oid' or '-ish' – or else an expurgation of vocabulary, leaving as our descriptive resources those terms only whose application-conditions may be seen as satisfied by observation of the object alone, with reference to nothing, observable or not, which lies outside the immediate field of scrutiny. Call the result of these purgative and neutralizing strategies the Φ-dictionary. And let us not concern ourselves unduly with spelling out the strategies by which the Φ-dictionary is attained. One thing certainly that its attainment requires is subtraction of the encyclopedia from the dictionary, leaving a residuum of pure descriptivity suited to the experience of someone innocent of anything save what meets the eye, since it will be consistent with any (and no) causal picture of the world.

Let us now designate as the Θ-vocabulary all terms now appearing in the dictionary save those which appear in the Φ-vocabulary. Prominent amongst Θ-terms are those we have just spoken of, which apply on condition that the objects described have certain causal histories. Now the two vocabularies are independent, or non-interdefinable, in *one* direction. No set of Φ-terms entails, or explicitly defines, any Θ-term which happens to apply to the same object as it. The reverse is false, I believe, within limits: any Θ-term entails that certain of a limited set of Φ-terms is true of the same object *it* is true of. But since the entailment does not go the other way, the Φ-terms can be true whether or not the Θ-term is true of that object, and so agreement on the Φ-description leaves undetermined the truth or falsity to the object of the Θ-term in issue. The Θ-term refers to what is presently observed only against a background of causal assumptions which do not bleed phenomenologically into present experience. So one can, everything remaining the same, call into question any Θ-description. But one cannot do this for Φ-terms, for if these should not apply, the experience itself would have to be different from that if they did apply. One might withdraw from one's experience of the world the descriptive resources of the Θ-vocabulary, and everything would *look* the same.

Hume argued that no observation of an object, however minute, will enable us to know its causal history. However minute our observations upon an object *o*, the results will be expressed in terms of the Φ-vocabulary alone. We may recast Hume's claim as follows: it is not part of the meaning of any term or set of terms in the Φ-vocabulary that any term of the Θ-vocabulary should be true of *o*. So the truth of the Φ-vocabulary is compatible with the falsity of any Θ-description of *o*. So, for all we can tell from the Φ-vocabulary's being true of *o*, *o* may have a different or no causal history. We learn, not through observation of *o*, but 'through experience', which Θ-terms are true of *o*, what *o*'s causal history must be. It is this experience which is enshrined, presumably, in our present Θ-contaminated dictionaries, and which permits those redescriptions of objects before us in encyclopedic terms.

If we indeed learn the causal histories of objects only 'through experience', it might stand to reason that the experiences themselves can be formulated in the idiom of the Φ-lexicon. We may grant at least this: if T is a member of Θ, and T is true of *o*, then no set of Φ-terms, also true of *o*, explicitly define and so serve to replace T. But does it follow that no set of Φ-terms whatever explicitly define and so serve to replace T? For example, might T not be defined in Φ-terms true not only of *o* but of other objects, and of relations between other objects and *o*? Such has been at least the claim of empiricism in modern times. *My* present concern is not with the general success of such a wholesale absorption of the encyclopedia by the dictionary, but only with the term 'causes'. Here we may allow that 'causes', since a relational predicate,[2] cannot be determined as holding by mere observation of an object said to have been caused to be in this state or that. The question is whether the relation that makes '...causes...' true when the terms are filled in can be seen to hold through experience of the sort to which the Φ-vocabulary is adequate. This is the problem before us, made all the more crucial by the claims that Radical Atomism has made, however modulated these may be by virtue of the existence of complex events.

II

Hume was firm and, I believe, correct in insisting that when we experience an episode, the true description of which is '*a* causes *b*', what we experience is *a* and *b* in suitable non-symmetric order, and *nothing more*. So whatever further than the non-symmetric happening of *a* and *b* may be entailed by '*a* causes *b*', it at least answers to nothing in the content of the experience so described.[3] That something further is entailed, however, may plainly be seen from the fact that the non-symmetric happening of *a* and *b* is compatible with the *falsity* of '*a* causes *b*', which accordingly has a truth-condition not *experienced* as satisfied in the episodes it describes.

To confirm this, let us turn for a moment from the admittedly stilted description, to rather more vernacular ones which merely presuppose it. Consider, indeed, Hume's celebrated example of colliding billiard-balls. There are, let us say, two events here: *a* = ball 1 *strikes* ball 2, and *b* = ball 2 begins to *move*. It is perhaps analytic to the concept of *striking* that nothing can be struck by a stationary object, so it follows from the description of *a* that ball 1 has been in motion. But let us merely concentrate on the events as described. Now only if *a causes b* – only if the striking of 2 by 1 is the *cause* of 2's movement – are we entitled to say that 1 *moved* 2. And since the conjoint occurrence of *a* and *b* is compatible with the falsity of '1 moved 2', something further than what we in fact experience when we experience *a* and *b* sequentially is entailed by '1 moved 2'. And the same may be said of an immense class of descriptions which employ transitive verbs, the subjects and objects of which may be described much along the same lines: 'destroys', 'burns', 'detonates', 'cleanses', 'lowers', 'sweetens', 'fertilizes', and vastly many more. All these are terms which apply only if the subject stands in *causal* relation with the object, and it is consistent with the falsity of these descriptions that the events in question should have occurred conjointly. The holding of the causal relationship is part of the truth-conditions of all sentences making descriptive use of these verbs. Yet in every instance, what we might be said to experience are the two events – and nothing more.

But it may be urged that this is false to the phenomenology of experience, that men describe *what they experienced* as '1 moved 2' or '3 scratched 4' or '5 cleansed 6'. These transitive verbs are *observational predicates*! But sympathetic as I am to this rejoinder, I must insist that so far as these verbs entail a causal ligature as a truth-condition of the sentences which employ them, they cannot strictly be observational without their causal implicandum being so: and to *what* in their experience does this correspond? So, though we may experience events *legato* and kinematically,[4] and though the *staccato* idiom enjoined by our strictures is insufferable, the fact remains that we can make the distinction within experience required by the latter, and that the description licensed by it could be true while the freer, cause-entailing description is false. And when *you* say you saw the fluid cleanse the metal, I always may say that you saw (really) only the fluid spread on the metal *and* the metal brighten. And this is so even if you want to say that you actually saw the fluid *brightening* the metal, passing to the participial form in order to be faithful to duration. It always may be insisted that you indeed saw the metal brightening and the fluid spreading. You only believed that the latter caused the former, when you rashly described your experience as you did.[5]

The advocate who corrects the witness's description by insisting that what he *really* witnessed was the entry of the victim by the knife and the subsequent expiration of the latter, that he did not really see the victim *killed* by the knife, would not be held to have discredited the witness, or to have shown him a careless recorder of the events within his purview. And the effort required to granulate experience into atomic constituents and to describe them as such would at the least demand a purgation of language, leaving us the descriptive resources solely of those predicates which apply to isolated particulars, and such relational vocabulary as entails no causal ligatures, e.g. purely geometrical predicates descriptive of contact and superposition. It is, just incidentally, the thesis of Radical Atomism that the world so described is the way the world *in esse* is: a heap of atomic events in various geometrical configurations. To adopt the vision of Radical Atomism would be of close phenomenological kin to the attempt to see things through the eyes of the aphasiac, able to make out in their proper order such words as 'Jane' and 'can' and 'cook' but unable to fuse them into the sentence 'Jane can cook.' And what, the aphasiac might wonder, *do* we see that *he does not*? Bonds between words to which he is blind by virtue of a quirky astigmatism? Or what? And the answer, while easily negative, leaves unanswered the matter of sentential ligature, the *x* which permits us to raise questions regarding a string of words such as whether *it* is true or false.

83

It is instructive that whatever further than the sequential occurrence of events is entailed by '...caused...' is not part of the content of our experience of causation, since this leaves the possibility that a sequential occurrence might be there *whether or not* '...caused...' were true, as though it were neutral to the difference, the difference itself being due to factors external to the co-ordinated occurrence of events. Thus neutralized, there is a striking philosophical similarity between this neutral sequence and that neutral core which, according to certain theories of perception, is what we *in fact* perceive whenever perception occurs, e.g. a sense-datum, or, in the older idiom, an *idée*. For, asked whether I really see a pig, I might, if concerned with the possibility of error and illusion, reply that at least I see a piggish expanse, which may or may not be a pig. And certainly the difference between its being or not being a pig is not a difference which answers to anything in the *content* of my experience if, indeed, the piggish expanse is to be neutral as to the difference between true pigs and their illusory counterparts. What we find, indeed, is that our experience would be the same in either case, for in retreating to this neutral core, we do not, so to speak, impoverish experience, the mooted differences not being like shapes or colors, which do answer to experience's content, and whose elimination would constitute a genuine impoverishment of the field. Pigs, then, cannot be identified completely with piggish expanses of the sort epistemologists traffic in, since 'I see a piggish expanse' may be true when 'I see a pig' is false. But since the further truth-condition seemingly entailed by the latter answers to nothing in the experience, nothing in the experience enables me to know whether I am seeing a piggish expanse and *nothing more*, or am seeing something solid, porcine and real. And at this point the skeptic has bagged us, making contact with the External World a hopeless enterprise. For it is essential to the skeptical pressure that experience should be just as it is, there being no way internal to itself for settling the questions which he raises. For all the content of experience might reveal, the world which seems to lie before us *is* a dream. And in just this same way, the world which seems to hold together in intelligible sequences is but a heap of atomic events in at best geometrical co-ordination.

The reason it is instructive to note these parallels is that the *sorts* of terms which are of critical moment in the traditional duel with Skepticism are in fact what I have designated *semantical* terms: as for example 'exists', 'true', 'false', 'fictitious', 'illusory', and the like, which the

Skeptic treats as though they were descriptive words instead, predicating mysteriously undetectable properties of things. I have dealt with this at length elsewhere, and I offer here only the barest mention of my thesis: semantic terms are not correctly predicable of things but only of semantical vehicles, so that to say, for example, that chairs *exist* or that tables are *real* (in the relevant sense of the latter) is not to ascribe properties such as existence or reality to chairs and tables respectively, but rather to say of the semantical vehicles 'chair' and 'table' that they have application, that they bear a positive semantical value. Now if the parallel with the concept of causality may be sustained in virtue of the seeming logical covertness of the causal nexus itself – a thing which would be as common an item of experience as any, considering the number of terms which presuppose causal ties – then the theory is irresistible that 'cause' *is of the same family as the semantical predicates themselves*, having to do, as I have argued, more with the relationship between language and the world than with the world (or with language) in itself and in isolation. Philosophers have often enough sought for causal connectives between events which are logically of the same order as those which hold between propositions, subtly converting events into semantical vehicles in the process, inasmuch as these are the only appropriate things capable of being so connected.[6] And Hume himself, after all, went to some pains to suggest that events do not *necessitate* one another, that it is always logically possible for the event we term the 'effect' to occur whether or not the event we term the 'cause' occurred, and vice versa – that it is at least not logically contradictory to suppose *a* should happen but not *b*, or that *b* should happen but not *a*. This, of course, since only sentences (or propositions) could conceivably be so related as to be logically incompatible, is to imply that those he criticized were in fact treating events as though they were sentential entities. And Hume himself, in saying of events that they are logically independent, one of another, may himself not have deviated from the very pattern, for after all, in the required sense, *only* sentences (or terms) can be independent. What perhaps he ought to have said is that terms like 'necessary' or 'independent' simply do not apply, events being, as we say, of the wrong logical type to be either logically dependent or logically independent. One may say that Hume was not really talking about events but of their descriptions. But then he was wrong, for if '*a* brightens *b*' is true, then it *is* logically impossible that *a* brighten *b* and *b* not be brightened, and the two events in question *are* of necessity connected, viz. through the very meaning of the terms. So perhaps Hume must have meant that descriptions of the two events may be given such that the rules of meaning permit the two descriptions to be independent. This I would grant, but from this nothing whatever follows concerning the relation between the events themselves. There are descriptions of me and of my wife from which it cannot be deduced that we are married, and there are descriptions of me and of my wife, the denial of which being contradictory would make of our marriage a logical necessity.

But let us not hasten past the point in issue, or treat it crudely. I have tendered the suggestion that 'causes' may possibly be treated as a semantical predicate of sorts, but so far only on the basis of some parallel skeptical options. Some further confirmation for my thesis may be gathered by examining the way in which philosophers have dealt with the dangling truth-condition of '*a* causes *b*' when we subtract, from the set of truth-conditions for the latter, that *a* and *b* occur with the appropriate non-symmetry. That strategy has been singularly of a piece with a counterpart strategy for handling semantical predicates.

III

The semantical predicates do not constitute part of the *meaning* of the vehicle to which they attach, nor again do they answer to anything in the content of those experiences they have been supposed to characterize. A 'veridical' experience bears no internal differentiating mark of its veridicality, and with regard to its content alone, is indiscernible from an illusory experience, much (or exactly) as a true sentence bears no *internal* mark through which it may, by inspection of it alone, be told apart from one which bears the negative semantical value. In view of this, it has sometimes occurred to philosophers that the semantical predicates might at least be defined in terms of the *processes of attachment*. That is to say, one first asks by what procedures one *establishes* that something exists (rather than is fictional or chimerical), that something is real (rather than illusory), that something is true (rather than false). Then 'exists', 'real', and 'true' are defined in terms of these procedures.

Imagine, thus, that I experience what, were I sure it were non-illusory, I would call a horse. Since, to follow the time-worn reflex of the epistemologist, I cannot tell from the 'content' of this experience whether or not it is illusory, what I experience is neutral with respect to that difference. But a *set* of such experiences might in fact confer upon the original one the favored semantical value (= reality). Thus I touch, palpate, smell; I look, probe, listen for characteristic noises; perhaps I mount and ride; I *test*. Should the tests prove severally positive, it was a real horse I experienced, and reality is then *defined* in terms of the tests being positive. Reality, in brief, forms no part of the content of any of the experiences in issue, but is a function over the whole, somehow, and is defined through the coherency of the set. This is a verificationist theory of reality.

Again, I understand a proposition, wondering only whether or not it is true, the answer to which mere analysis of meaning will not vouchsafe. I attempt, however, to test the sentence by seeking out evidence in its favor. The sentence will be true if the evidence is in its favor, and *true* is *defined* in terms of the processes of verification, and established through the coherency of the test sets.

In these cases, and in many more, philosophers have absorbed the semantical predicates, the predicates ascribing semantical values to the vehicles appropriate for sustaining them, into the processes of their ascription. They have, as it were, applied verificationist strategies to these terms. The Phenomenologist's analysis of existence;[7] the Pragmatist's theory of truth;[8] the Phenomenalist's, theory of reality, are all exemplifications of this strategy. The theories share as a common feature the view that the mooted terms have to do with the organization rather than the content of experience, and where no single experience or set of experiences is found to correspond to these terms, one makes what appears to be the most conservative next step in the view of those whose philosophical biases encourage them to look to experience for meaning. In so doing, it is tacitly acknowledged that the terms in question are not *descriptive*, or, if descriptive, then of the structure rather than the content of experience or of the world. It is now instructive to note that the analysis of *causation* has proceeded *exactly* along the same lines, from which it should be concluded that 'causes' is not descriptive either, referring instead to the organization of experience, and answering then to nothing in the elements organized. As with the semantical predicates, 'causes' attaches to an experienced conjunction retroactively, and on the basis of tests, and is to be defined in terms of the procedures of its attachment. Perhaps since Hume, an essentially verificationist account has been given of the concept of causality.

For Hume, we establish that 'causes' is predicable of the appropriately asymmetric conjunction of *a* with *b* by noting that conjunctions
of the *a*-like with the *b*-like recur. In Hume's case, we *first* note the
iterations, and then make the predication, but it could in principle have
gone the other way, and though we might not have *known* that in the
first instance, *a* was the cause of *b*, we retroactively assert this in view of
subsequent iterations. That Hume was concerned with the temporal
ordering of the evidence, that is, the noting of iterations, lies in the fact
that he believed repeated noticed conjunctions induce a habit of
expectation (and habits are *formed*),[9] so that whenever either of the
events is observed, we are led to anticipate the presence of the other.
It is this *felt* anticipation of *b* upon *presentation* of *a* which Hume felt
was projected by us onto the world, and read back as an objective
dynamism, in which *b* is somehow necessarily generated out of *a*. In
fact, he held, it is only a dynamism of the mind, an urgency of expectation. The habit answers to nothing we experience: it is not *descriptive*. It
is we who mistake it for something descriptive, and so suppose the
world contains ligatures, all the more mysterious since, by common
admission, no such ligatures are experienced, but only, so to speak, the
events allegedly tied.

If we put to one side, for the moment, the psychological factors
which Hume has introduced here, we find we have an essentially
verificationist analysis of 'cause'. Once more, 'cause' is not descriptive
of some feature in the conjunction we predicate it of, nor, for that
matter, in any of the resemblant conjunctions. It is just that we predicate
it of the conjunction *only* through the fact that there *are* resemblant
conjunctions: the term supervening then on each such conjunction by
virtue of the fact that it is a member of a sufficiently large set of like
such conjunctions. It is a curiosity of Hume's account that a single
conjunction of events, not elsewhere iterated, or better, uniterated
within experience, ought not bear the predicate 'causes'. We can modify
Hume's view, taking it beyond his somewhat subjectivist limitations, by
saying that it may be the case that *a* causes *b*, providing that there are in
fact, or even providing that there will in fact be iterated resemblant
conjunctions, whether we experience them or not, it being indifferent
to causation whether we *know* that *a* causes *b*. But this step in the direction of realism leaves intact the fact that 'causes' can *mean* nothing
further than constancy of conjunction, and moving now in the epistemological direction, we apply it only on the basis of *noted* conjunctions

88

And this is the path Hume took himself, leading to his precocious verificationistic analysis of '*causes*'.

It may plausibly be argued that Hume's description of the actual verificatory procedures involved are primitive and crude. There is a body of literature, beginning with Whewell and Mill, and running to the present, which involves an increasing refinement on the verificatory procedures Hume casually identified as the noting of constant conjunctions. But it is not his description of verification here which is so much of interest to me, as his identification of causation itself with its verificatory base. And this has some considerable practical importance for our own work. Unless we *accept* the verificationist program, which identifies meaning with evidence (or the gathering of it), we need concern ourselves *not at all*, if our interest is in *conceptual* analysis, with the refined but tangled questions of *how we establish* that *a* causes *b*. For these questions, of immense practical bearing and considerable theoretical interest, are not relevant to the *meaning* of '*a* causes *b*'. A parallel detachment of how we come to know which semantical predicate attaches to a semantical vehicle may similarly be effected. We may restrict ourselves, then, simply to the structure of the concept.

If this is so, then, in fact, we may drop out of consideration reference to constant conjunction, to iterated resemblant episodes, and the like. These bear on, and are merely a crude attempt to give an analysis of the concept of *induction*. And this brings us back to that dynamism which Hume's reference to habits was meant to explain. It is that we have a *right to expect* that *b* will occur when *a* does when (according to Hume) we have witnessed repeated episodes of their conjugacy. In fact, however, we may turn the tables on Hume, and suggest that it is not so much that the plain man has read his habits off as objective ligatures as that Hume has read logical ligatures off as habits, by psychologizing the essentially *inferential* ties between evidence and conclusion in the inductive procedures. Consider, now, a highly simplified statement of an induction, on Humean terms. We have a large sample, consisting of repeated resemblant conjunctions of events. We are presented with *one* member of the sort heretofore found coupled with an event of a sort we *now* expect *because* of the noted coupling. It is striking that in Hume those repeated conjunctions should at once be evidence *for* the anticipated event and the cause *of* the fact that we anticipate it, but in the latter role, they cannot be cited in justification, only in explanation of the expectation. Strictly speaking, we have a right to the anticipation only if we have a *rule* of inductive inference which carries us, as it were, from sample to population and thence to a fresh instance. But the crucial consideration for our purposes is this: there is nothing to distinguish Hume's account of causal ascription from Hume's account of inductive projection. Indeed, we may go further than this. Since the evidence for an inductive projection is just the evidence for causal ascription, and since we are supposing verificationism to be accepted, identifying the meaning of a concept with the evidence employed in its establishment, it virtually follows that the concept of causality and the concept of induction are *one*, in Hume at least and in those who have followed his strategy of analysis. As though there were no problems of conceptual analysis in the concept of cause beyond those problems involved in analyzing justifiable inductive procedures. For after all, what have the refinements on Hume been *except* refinements on inductive techniques? But how much further can one proceed in the direction of verificationizing the concept of causality than identifying it with induction?

If we eschew verificationism here, and attempt for once to address the concept of causation in isolation from the questions of how we set about establishing that causal propositions are true, then, as I have proposed, we may consider questions of evidence essentially irrelevant to our inquiry. We might not be able utterly to avoid questions of evidence, but at least we can prevent them from leaking into what must be an analysis of the structure of the concept.

IV

This prolonged approach to the topic of causation has not been without benefit of some logical insight we might not have been able to achieve without it. We have already acceded to the view that the logical form of causal proposition is relational, that '*a* causes *b*' asserts that the two events stand in a certain relation. We may, however, now proceed further in specifying the kind of relationship it is. We have enough parity of structure between the concept of causation and the concept of semantical values to suggest that 'causes', like 'true' or 'exists', is a semantical predicate, i.e., a value which attaches to a semantical vehicle on condition that a certain semantical relationship is satisfied. Let me now advance the conjecture that 'causes' *is* a semantical predicate. That is to say, while '*a* causes *b*' says, just as it appears to say, something about the world, it also and more crucially says something about the relationship between the world and language. If this conjecture is sound, as I shall attempt in the next several sections to show it to be, we shall have gone some distance in explaining the failure philosophers have sustained in their search for that *in* the world which answers to 'causes' when the latter is construed as a descriptive term. Such a quest would be of a piece with one which seeks for that in experience which answers to that in *a* which is described by '*a* exists', when the fact is that *nothing* answers to it because *existence* refers to the relationship of 'answering to' as satisfied. In just (or in much) this way, I want to claim that '*a* causes *b*' says nothing about that compound occurrence of *a* and *b* which satisfies a certain relationship with language except that it satisfies this relationship. It is *not* a further but empirically elusive feature of the compound event as such.

Let us begin with *singular causal ascriptions*. These are historical statements, referring in the simplest case to specific historical episodes, compound events consisting of the co-occurrence of two events. Let the events in question be *a* and *b*. Let, now, '*aCb*' be everything which describes the conjoint occurrence of *a* and *b* *except* the fact that they are causally related. So '*aCb*' says that *a* and *b* occur, that they occur in a certain order and at certain times, and so forth. I want '*aCb*' to cover everything in the compound event which would be true even if '*a* caused *b*' were false. Since the former can be true while the latter is false, it is plain that the two descriptions are not equivalent. I suppose that if '*a* causes *b*' is true, so is '*aCb*', but obviously not conversely. So we may say that '*a* causes *b*' equals '*aCb*' plus *x*. And the problem is to solve for *x*. What in *addition* to *aCb* does '*a* causes *b*' claim? Let us note that since *aCb* does not *alone* entail '*a* caused *b*', we may regard '*aCb*' as *neutral* with regard to whether or not *a* caused *b*. It is what we might retreat to if '*a* caused *b*' should prove to have been false. I shall assume that our experience of the compound event denoted by '*aCb*' is the same whether or not '*a* caused *b*' is true, and that the latter corresponds to nothing in our experience of that compound event. I thus assume that *x* refers to something outside the experience of *aCb*. And what I mean to claim is that what further than *aCb* is asserted by '*a* caused *b*' is that the former is *covered by a law*, that it *instantiates a law*. Now 'instantiation' and 'being covered by' are semantical relationships. And I contend that nothing about the (compound) event as such is described by '*a* caused *b*', but rather that a certain sort of description applies to it, namely a law. In other words, if *aCb*, then *a* causes *b* only if *aCb* falls under a law. Let me now try to establish this.

Let us first reflect upon what may be the most intuitive part of the concept of causality, the concept of *causal independence*. To say of *b* that it was causally independent of *a* is in effect to say that it would have happened whether *a* had happened or not. In this or in an analogous way, we say that Q is logically independent of P if, when Q is true, its being so does not presuppose that P either is true or is false: that Q's truth is consistent alike with the falsity or with the truth of P. This being so, the truth of P leaves the truth of Q undetermined, and likewise the occurrence of *a* leaves the occurrence of *b* undetermined. Its happening has 'nothing to do' with the happening of *b*. But plainly there is no way of telling this from *aCb* since *a* in fact *did* occur and *b* did so as well. Since the causal independence of *b* from *a* is wholly consistent with the occurrence of *aCb*, it hardly is to be expected that we could reject a claim either of causal dependence or causal independence on the basis of experiencing *aCb* alone. So far as this merely glosses Hume, I plainly am in agreement with him. And like him, I am committed to supposing that we must range afield from *aCb* in order to determine whether a causal ascription or a causal *independence* ascription holds. It seems on the surface that we cannot give much sense to the claim of causal independence without wandering into a subjunctive idiom, viz. that *b would* have happened whether or not *a* had. But then equally subjunctive dimensions appear to be entered with the causal ascription, which says that *b* would *not* have happened whether *a* had happened or not. Perhaps the first thing to do, then, is to give some sense to these subjunctive idioms. We can do so, I believe, only by moving to a level of generality higher than that on which singular causal ascriptions are made.

I shall now introduce a pair of event-descriptions α and β which are non-interdefinable and logically independent, and such that the events *a* and *b* respectively instantiate but do not *uniquely* instantiate α and β. Similarly, αCβ is a compound event-description, instantiated but not necessarily uniquely instantiated by *aCb*: *aCb* happens simply to fall within the extension of αCβ, much as *a* and *b* fall respectively under the extensions of α and β. Let us now say that α(+) means simply that α has an instance, and α(−) that it has no instance, viz. there has occurred no event satisfying the description α. Since we are dealing with two event types, we may work out the following exhibitive matrix which covers all the possibilities:

	α	β
(1)	+	+
(2)	+	−
(3)	−	+
(4)	−	−

If (1) is true, then αCβ(+). I shall now say that *b* is causally independent of *a* in case rows (1) and (3) are true. This means, of course, that there are at least two occasions on which β is instantiated but there is at least one less occasion on which α is instantiated than there are occasions on which β is, all background notions for the moment supposed constant (I shall advert to these subsequently). In sum, if (1) and (3) are true, we have adequate evidence that the singular causal ascription to *aCb* is *false*, that is, that *b* is causally independent of *a*. I do not, however, wish to define causal independence in terms of evidence, for this would be a concession to verificationism.

The problem with verificationism is that (1) may be true though (3) is never true; (1) may be amply instantiated though (3) is never instantiated, so that there are as many occurrences of α-instances as of β-instances; and yet it be true, though we have no evidence for it being so, that *b* is causally independent of *a*. It grows, no doubt, decreasingly probable with the increase in the number of instantiations of αCβ that *b* was causally independent of *a*, but that does not signify. If *b* was causally independent of *a*, (3) *can* be true though (1) is true, and this follows from the very meaning of causal independence. The truth of (1) and (3) is consistent with *b* being independent of *a*, even though in fact (3) is never and (1) is frequently true.

I shall now define *causal dependence* in terms of the simple denial of causal independence. That is, '*b* is causally dependent upon *a*' means that (3) *cannot* be true if (1) is true. So *aCb* entails that (3) must be false, if *b* is causally dependent upon *a*. Once more as regards *evidence*, it is possible that we shall have as much evidence for causal independence as for causal dependence. But my project is not to determine when we might be said to *know* that a particular causal ascription is true or false, but only to analyze what the notions of causal dependence and independence mean. And this I have sought to show by means of our matrix.

Now ascription of causal dependence of *b* upon *a* entails, of course, that it is *not* the case that both (1) and (3) are true: either that α and β are not both instantiated, or that β is not instantiated if α is. We deny, in brief, the following conjunction of conjunctions:

$$[\alpha(+) \text{ and } \beta(+)] \text{ and } [\alpha(-) \text{ and } \beta(+)].$$

But it is a simple matter of logic to transform this into

$$[\alpha(+) \text{ and } \beta(+)] \supset [\alpha(-) \supset \beta(-)].$$

In other words, if αCβ, then the instantiation of α is a necessary condition for the instantiation of β. Now since *aCb*, αCβ *is* instantiated. Hence, if *b* is causally dependent upon *a*, the instantiation of α is a necessary condition for the instantiation of β. And since *a* instantiates α and *b* instantiates β, it is only natural to speak derivatively of *a itself* as a necessary condition for *b*. Obviously, given the usual definition of necessary conditions, namely through implication and denial, it is strictly a mistake in category to speak of *events* as necessary conditions. I do so in fact only in a semantical respect, viz. as instantiating a description. But with adequate orientation, there is no harm in speaking thus.

Now a statement of a necessary condition, of the kind entailed by our definition of causal dependency, may be regarded as a law of sorts. And it is for me a striking fact that we should be able to deduce that *aCb* instantiates, or is covered by a law at least of necessary condition, if *b* is causally dependent upon *a*. Philosophers have often enough suggested that causal ascriptions presuppose laws, but we have, on the basis of fairly weak assumptions, actually *deduced* this. Of course causal dependency of *b* upon *a* never could have been determined on the basis of observing *aCb* alone. I am only drawing out what we are conceptually committed to in saying that *b* is causally dependent upon *a*. I am suggesting that the value of *x* in the formula *aCb* plus *x* equals *a* causes *b*. But we have a way yet to go, since we have only gotten an explication of causal dependency. Perhaps we may go further.

Thus far I have been noncommittal regarding row (2) of the matrix. Causal dependency does not seem to entail that (2) is *false*, although the usual or *Humean* analysis of causality as *constant conjunction* – α is never instantiated except β is instantiated – does entail the negation of row (2). I am allowing, however, that *b* may be causally dependent upon *a* even though there may be instantiations of α when there are none of β. And I believe this consonant with our intuitions. Suppose it the established fact that measles-virus is the cause of measles, or that coming down with measles is causally dependent upon having been attacked by measles virus. Plainly, this does *not* require that everyone attacked by measles virus in fact come down with measles. It requires only that no one come down with measles that has not been attacked by measles virus. We have serums and immunization procedures, in view of which the instantiation pattern of α(+) and β(−) is perfectly consistent with the causal dependency of *b* upon *a*. So causal dependency at best entails a law of necessary and not one of sufficient conditions.

I believe we are nevertheless entitled to a somewhat stronger inference than we so far have drawn from our analysis. Let us reflect upon a world vastly simpler than the one in which we live, wherein the only event-descriptions which are ever instantiated are α and β. Let me make explicit that when I say that β is not instantiated, I do *not* mean that not-β *is* instantiated, where the latter is taken as the description of a *negative event*, as one might regard it. I shall concern myself with negative events later, but here I stress that when I speak of a certain event *not* occurring, I shall mean the absence of an occurrence, not the occurrence of an absence. Imagine, then, that in this monotonous world, a given event *b* is declared causally dependent upon a given event *a*, in the respect that the instantiation pattern for causal dependency is affirmed. So there is no case in which β is instantiated and αCβ *not* instantiated: whenever β(+), then α(+). But it is now still possible that there are occasions on which α(+) without β(+). Now on the assumption that α and β exhaust this world's repertoire of events, and there is no third sort of event γ, then, I believe, the following is a plausible if a largely pragmatic argument. If, nothing else about the world being different, sometimes β is (+) when α is (+) and sometimes it is (−), then it must seem as though, β's instantiation has nothing really to do with α's, and that in any given instance, the occurrence of *b* has nothing to do with the occurrence of *a*, even though *aCb*. Something which remains constant while something else changes must clearly appear to have nothing to do with that change. Hence the world described must appear to be a strictly non-causal one, and we would, in the light of (2) and (3) being true, withdraw the claim of causal dependency of *b* upon *a*. So if, in such a world, *b* is to be held causally dependent upon *a*, (2) *cannot* be true, so that if α is instantiated, β must be as well. For this *simple* world, therefore, if *b* is causally dependent upon *a*, then *a* is a sufficient condition for *b* in the respect that if α is (+) then so is β. Or, which comes to the same thing, the truth of (2)

Analytical Philosophy of Action

would be adequate evidence that *b* is never causally dependent upon *a*.

But now I think we may export our argument from the event-impoverished world to our rich one. We may say that if *b* is causally dependent upon *a*, then, if α is (+) and β is (−), there must be some explanation of the latter: something must have *prevented* the instantiation of β. Or, which comes to the same thing, something was a sufficient condition for β(−). To speak in this vein, of course, begins to move us in the direction of rather explicitly speaking of negative events, but it is easy enough to handle this with our matrices. Thus, if *c* is the preventative event, and γ our general description for *c*, then to say that *c* is causally sufficient for not-*b* is to say that γCβ is always (−), and that the matrix for γ and β is such that (2) entails that (3) is false and that (3) entails that (2) is false. But for the moment, it is enough to get on without pragmatic notions of prevention and abortion, and to say that it follows from the claim that *b* is causally dependent upon *a* that

$$\alpha(+) \supset [\text{not-}(Ex)(x(+) \supset \beta(-)) \supset \beta(+)].$$

And hence that the causal dependency of *b* upon *a* entails what we may call a *law of conditional sufficiency*. So not simply is *a* by law a necessary condition, it is also conditionally sufficient for *b*.

I shall now propose that '*a* causes *b*' is to be analyzed as: *b* is causally dependent upon *a*. And since it does not follow from the fact that *a*C*b* that *a* does cause *b*, but rather that *a* causes *b* only *if b* is causally dependent upon *a*, this will perhaps make it clear why I regard *cause* as a semantical concept: it means that the occurrence of *a*C*b* is covered by laws of necessary and of conditionally sufficient conditions. This, of course, entails something about the entire description of history. But none of the latter belongs to the content of our experience when we experience *a*C*b*. And *that* experience would be the same whatever the description were of the entire rest of history. It is only when we ascribe the causal predicate here that we make a claim about how the rest of history must go. That a conjunction of events is covered by a description can hardly be determined, however, from our experience of *that* conjunction, and in this regard Hume was simply right when he argued that the concept of causation could not derive from our experience of *a*C*b*. But neither, I should think, could it derive from repeated experiences of events which resemble *a*C*b* in the respect of instantiating αCβ. Causality, like most terms – I would say all terms – which give

96

rise to philosophical perplexity applies to the relationship between language and the world.

V

Before applying these results to the topic of action, let us draw out certain general features of the concept of causation, if my analysis of it has been correct.

(1) Let us first sort out the transparencies and the opacities in the concept of causation. These, I believe, are exactly parallel to those we found in Chapter 1, in connection with the analyses of mediated actions and cognitions.

Suppose that *a* causes *b*. And suppose there is a description '*d*' of *a* so that $a = d$. Most people would allow that *d* then causes *b*, since *d* and *a* are the same event, albeit it under distinct descriptions. On the other hand, we have analyzed 'cause' in terms of causal dependency, and the latter in terms of laws which cover *aCb*. It may be that it is false that *aCb* is covered by a law in which the description '*d*' covers *a*. A law which covers a given pair of events need not cover them under all possible true descriptions of the events in question. Under the description '*d*' the event *a* may not be either necessary or sufficient for *b*, inasmuch as it need not follow from the matrix for *a* and *b* under the descriptions α and β that any further instance of α is covered by such a description as '*d*'. Only under certain of its descriptions is *b* causally dependent upon *a*, and indeed, it may be that *b* is causally dependent upon *a* without being causally dependent upon *d*, which should sound paradoxical, given that *a* and *d* are one. But it is not, inasmuch as the instantiation matrix for *d* and *b* may have *b* come out causally independent of *d*. And this might just as well have been expected when we realize that causal ascriptions make reference not just to conjunctions of *events*, which take place in the world, but also to representations, namely laws, which only *describe* the world. After all, 'causes' is a semantical mongrel, just as 'knows' and 'does' are semantical mongrel, referring, as they do, at once to the world and to a representation of it.

Philosophers have argued that singular causal ascriptions entail laws, and recently the claim has been made that this is so even if we do not know *which* law in fact is entailed by such ascriptions.[10] But this may be explained through the fact that we may not know under what *descrip-*

97

tion of *a* and *b* the latter is causally dependent upon the former. When we say *a* caused *b*, we indeed imply that a law covers their conjunction. We may, consistently with this, hesitate to specify under what law they stand in causal connection. But in effect, to say that there is *some* law is to say that there is *some* description.

It may elicit some surprise that the concept of cause, through its semi-transparency, should be in consequence semi-intensional. Perhaps the surprise is occasioned by the fact that intensionality has been closely associated (though not exclusively associated) with *mental* concepts, and the intensionalization of causality thus sounds dangerously like the mentalization of the causal order. I shall comment in a moment upon this metaphysically charged observation, but for now it is perhaps usefully disarming to emphasize that contemporary discussions of causality have unwittingly employed a para-intensionalistic notion already, specifically the concept of *relevancy*. It is generally agreed, for example, that something is a cause and something else an effect only in certain *relevant* respects. To say that *a* is the cause of *b* is to imply a respect in which it is that, and presumably not *every* respect is relevant. But then the quest for the relevant respects under which *a* is the cause of *b* is exactly the quest for those aspects under which the conjunction of *a* and *b* is covered by law. Indeed, relevancy may be defined, I believe, precisely in terms of laws, and hence so far as the concept of law is intensional, the contagion extends equally to the concept of relevancy.

But it seems to me unexceptionable that the causal concept should be quasi-intensional, and that it should be so through the concept of law which the causal concept entails. For there is a close tie between the concept of law and the concept of *understanding*, in the sense that understanding something entails bringing the latter under a law. Hence the world is understandable so far as its occurrences are covered by laws, and we *in fact* understand it just to the extent that we have the laws it instantiates. The concept of understanding and the concept of causation are internally related through the fact that each is internally related to the concept of law. Causation is a concept whose application implies a representation with respect to which the world is understandable. Hence it is understandable relative to a representation. And this must account for the intensionality of the concept of causation. For there is always a description under which the world is not understandable, and to which we may retreat when we give up our causal ascriptions, namely such descriptions as '*aCb*' typifies. Now *aCb* may be regarded merely as a conjunction of events. To suppose it intelligible that *a* and *b* should be conjoined is to suppose a law which covers their conjunction.

(II) In the light of this claim we might dilate for a moment on the concept of induction, all the more warranted in view of the long history in which the concepts of induction and causation were mere disguises of each other. Induction over events, presumably, consists in noting a heretofore constant conjunction of α-instances and β-instances, and inferring that a β will occur when an α next occurs. Presumably, this expectation is justified with an increase in the number of conjoinings, but it is a matter of some interest to inquire why even a *high* number of iterated conjunctions *should* justify the expectation of its own increase. Hume, of course, with his inveterate psychologizing, had a kind of answer: iterated *noted* conjunctions instil a *habit*. Without iteration there would be no habit, and without habit no (psychological) expectation. But the issues are very little psychological in fact: the question is whether expectation would be *justified*, and while iterated conjunctions might *cause* habits of expectation, the issue remains whether they justify them and why. And my own view is that we are justified here only if we believe the conjunctions to instantiate a *law*. If this is our belief, however, then the question is to what extent repetition entitles us to hold it. And my answer is that it gives no grounds at all.

A conjunction is *accidental* when the events conjoined are causally independent, that is, are *not* covered by law(s). Now, of course, the conjunction of *a* and *b* is invariant to the two cases in which their conjunction is accidental or non-accidental, and so one cannot refer to the conjunction *itself* to differentiate them. But to the degree that we believe the conjunction accidental, to that degree have we *no* grounds for believing the conjunction to recur, and this is so even if it does in fact recur. For repetition of accidentally conjoint events itself is accidental, and so long as we believe the conjunction accidental, we have, however large the number of repetitions, still no grounds for believing in its prolongation. We may, indeed, universalize the conjunction, and claim that it always will recur, but our claim is groundless if our only grounds are that it has been repeated many times. For it is consistent with the latter that the repetitions should be accidental. There is after all nothing logically impossible in a universalization of accidentals being true, the world never affording any exceptions. All this shows is that we have to distinguish laws from universalizations. For we are *licensed* to generalize from these instances only if we first

1.3219

believe their conjunction non-accidental. And since the law is required in order that the universalization be licit, a law has to be stronger than a universalization and hardly then can *consist* in a mere declaration of constant conjunction.

To these considerations, we may add this. So far as we believe the conjunction of a and b to be accidental, to that degree must we regard reference to a as of no explanatory value whatever in understanding b. And this is so even if α's and β's have been constantly conjoined and we believe, however groundlessly, that they will be moreover always conjoined. This is why, when asked why b happens when a does, it is of no explanatory value to say that it always does so happen, since the latter is compatible with a having no explanatory value whatever in regard to b. A universalization, since it can be merely accidental, is itself of no explanatory value, which is in some degree the reason that, since they fail adequately to distinguish (if they distinguish at all) between laws and universalizations, critics of the so-called Covering Law Model of explanation have found that model wanting.[11] The model is not defective, but rather what *is* defective is the assumption that a law just *is* a universalization when in fact the latter is licit only if licensed by a law.

If, as I have claimed, a law is what defines an intelligible process, the belief that a β will occur when an α does not is *unintelligible* if the conjunction of b with a is non-accidental. The reason a law affords understanding, and *a fortiori* an explanation of b, is just that failure of b when a occurs would be unintelligible, would violate that which defines an understandable process. Of course, it is possible that the world should be just as it is, with all the conjunctions its history has exhibited, in just the same number of instances as ideally might be chronicled. It is only that the world would be unintelligible if all its conjunctions were accidental. If this is so, then our analysis has afforded a striking confirmation of a view of Kant's. Since the world might be just the way it is but accidental rather than nomic, the existence of laws cannot be *deduced* from the way the world reveals itself to us. We saw this already, in a way, when we noticed that the conjunction of a and b is invariant to the difference between its being an accidental or a non-accidental conjunction.[12] In this regard, Hume himself was right in saying that we cannot from our experience of the world deduce that it is causally ordered. A causally ordered and an accidental world could *look just the same*. So it is consistent with the world looking just as it does that it should be understandable or intelligible. The principle of its intelligibility, then, is not derivable from the way the world looks and it is, in that regard, *a priori*.

(III) It does not follow, from the concept of a law, that it has any fixed number of instances, taking the latter to be *compound* events consisting of such conjunctions of events as *aCb* does. A law, as it were, defines a class of compound events, but does not entail any specified member- ship in that class. It may be argued that we would not speak of something as a law if its 'compliance-class'[13] were empty, and that the very concept of law entails a degree of existential import; and if we are verification- ists, as virtually all since Hume have been on this topic, nothing could count as a law unless there were a great many instances compliant with it. But I have a general argument against semantical vehicles entailing their own semantical values, and I see no reason to exempt the prin- ciple there from application here. It might be said that a law rules out any compound event *discompliant* with itself, but this does not by itself entail that it has any compliants, and I shall suppose that, as always in such matters, we must look externally to the law itself to find out whether it covers anything. This, incidentally, yields a benefit which might convince reluctant verificationists. Hume was in no position to think it even meaningful to suppose that a *unique* historical coupling of events should be related as cause to effect. This must be counted a defect in his analysis. But, since a law entails no definite number of com- pliant-instances, it is consistent with the existence of a law that it should have a single instance. It is inconsistent only that it should be logically *restricted* to a single instance. But it is equally inconsistent that it should be logically restricted to *any* definite number of instances.

The indeterminacy of compliant instances is what I should call the property of *generality* which pertains to laws. From what I have said, it follows from the fact that *a* causes *b* that there is a general law which covers the conjunction of *a* and *b*, even if, as a matter of what has to be a purely contingent fact, this conjunction is the sole compliant with the law in the whole of what proves to be history. Formally speaking, the traits of generality are commonly secured through the *terms* in which laws are expressed, and writers have supposed this to exclude, in the content of laws, terms such as proper names, from the rules of meaning of which it follows that they do have unique reference. This must not be taken to mean that there cannot be laws covering events in the

Solar system, or, for that matter, that there cannot be laws of French or of Napoleonic behavior. The class of compliants defined by a law consists of conjoint *events*. That amongst these should be Solar or Napoleonic events is not to the point. It could be a law of solar activity that sunspots appear when a certain temperature is reached, even if sunspots should appear once in the whole history of the Sun. It might be a law of Napoleonic behaviour that he would attempt an escape from captivity even if he were in captivity only once – even, indeed, if he *never* were in captivity.

(iv) Let us once more ponder, this time from the point of view of its truth-conditions, the claim that *a* caused *b*. By my analysis, '*a* caused *b*' is at least a conjunctive assertion to the effect that (1) the compound event, consisting of the conjunction of *a* and *b* took place, and (2) *b* is causally dependent on *a*. Obviously, these two sentences are independent of each other, in that (1) can be true though (2) is false, and (2), since it unpacks into a statement of law(s), does not entail the truth of (1), for laws do not entail the existence of any instances which they cover: it is consistent with something being a law that its class of compliant events should be empty. By the common rules governing conjunctions, '*a* caused *b*' is false if either of its conjuncts is false, but it is uninteresting to consider the case where it is false because the compound event failed to occur. Since we are concerned, after all, with the truth-conditions of '*a* caused *b*' apart from the fairly non-controversial condition that a conjunction of events must occur, let us in what follows simply suppose that (1) is true, (1) being exactly neutral with regard to the truth or falsity of '*a* caused *b*'. And let us ask under what conditions the latter *would* be false, supposing (1) true. This, in effect, reduces to the question of under what conditions (2) is false. And this is easy enough to answer in a general way.

We may say that '*a* caused *b*' is retroactively false if either of these descriptions should be true at *any* time: (3) $\alpha(-)$ and $\beta(+)$; and (4) $\alpha(+)$ and $\beta(-)$, though there is nothing *x* such that $x \supset \beta(-)$. Either of these descriptions, if true, entails the causal independence of *a* and *b*, and so (2) entails the *negations* of (3) and of (4). These negations, then, are the truth-conditions of '*a* causes *b*' over and above (1).

It seems conspicuously plain that it must be a great deal simpler to tell that '*a* causes *b*' is *false*, then, than to tell whether or not it is true. This much (*at least!*) must be said for Professor Popper's famous claim[14] that the issue in science is falsification far more than verification.

A single falsifying instance is enough to disestablish '*a* causes *b*', and it is exceedingly difficult to suppose that we could ever say with certainty that *a* caused *b* simply because (1) was frequently echoed by resemblant compound events, and (3) and (4) had never been so far found true. So to a very large extent there must seem a degree of indefiniteness in connection with assertion of '*a* causes *b*'.

On the other hand, there are mechanisms available for neutralizing any easy attempt to falsify (2) and hence the causal ascription itself. For one thing, there is always the possibility of *multiple causation* in the case of (3). That is to say, β-instances may have more than one sort of cause. Suppose, for instance, that *b* could be caused either by *a* or by *c*. Then (3) would not falsify '*a* caused *b*' in case, here, α(−) had a positive identification with *c*. With multiple causation of this sort, we might require laws with *disjunctive* necessary conditions (*weakly* disjunctive, in order to accommodate the possibility of overdetermination). Essentially, however, the possibility of such laws, or of such further necessary conditions, makes it possible to retain our original causal ascription through retaining (2) – the latter for whatever pragmatic reasons. And similarly, it is not difficult to neutralize (4), since there is *always* a clear possibility that something heretofore undetected served to prevent a β-instantiation, even though there were an α-instantiation. So, as many writers have pointed out, laws, and hence causal ascriptions, may be asserted in the face of seemingly adverse evidence, and falsification is not the simple knock-down matter that textbook simplicities seem at first to imply. The falsification-conditions have an inexpungeable openness and porosity about them after all, which permit all manner of adjustments and flexibilities.

Against the background of these factors, let us briefly gloss the concept of *necessity*, traditionally thought to attach to the concept of causation. Certainly (2) is not entailed by (1), and it is true in general that compound events do not entail their being covered by law. So it is not in *this* sense necessary that a conjunction be a causal conjunction. Nor are laws themselves necessary in that modal sense which requires that a sentence first be analytic in order that it be necessary. The falsehood of any law is *thinkable*, as we have just seen. It is logically possible, then, that the world should be covered by quite different laws than in fact cover it, and it is equally possible, logically speaking, that it should be covered by no laws at all. We find it *intelligible* that the world should have been *unintelligible*, and indeed, it might, as we have often noted now, exhibit all the same compound events in its history which it in fact exhibits, and be covered by *no* laws at all.

All of this we may accept. Yet I think there is one necessity left us, which is this. Though it is intelligible to suppose the world might be unintelligible, it is not intelligible that it should *both* be intelligible *and* all its events causally independent. And this is because intelligibility here just *means* seeing events as causally dependent. So, if we understand the world at all, it follows that we are constrained through the conditions of understanding as such to regard events as causally dependent. That is the main reason we might wish to retain a causal ascription in the face of seemingly contravening evidence, namely, that giving up the laws entails facing an unintelligibility. Understanding, of course, is not knowledge, and meaning is not truth. Perhaps a pragmatic argument may be made out to the effect that it is better to misunderstand a process than to regard it as unintelligible, simply because misunderstanding might, through investigation, generate its own rectifications whereas surrendering to unintelligibility leaves us always where we were.

Be this as it may, to regard the world as intelligible is necessarily to regard it as covered by laws, and events as causally dependent. Some stronger sense of necessity may be desired, but for the moment no stronger concept need be entertained, for surely we have as much as we need to provide us with the concept we are seeking. Necessity is not a *descriptive* concept, it is not part of the content of any description of the world. Rather, it attaches to the mode of description itself through the concept of intelligibility. And with this we may revert to the topic of action, from which we have been obliged to digress. The concept of cause plays too central a role in the topic of action for us to have left it unrefined.

VI

The question now before us may be phrased as follows: can an *action* be caused, in the precise respect we have defined in which it is causally dependent upon another event, so that the conjunction of the two is covered by law(s)? Let me, before going deeper into the matter, very quickly deflect one set of considerations. Suppose mDb and suppose moreover, that some event in the brain, say v, causes b. Then the conjunction of v and b will be covered by some law, presumably of physiology. Call this L. Now in virtue of mDb, b is redescribable, to the perpetual confusion of philosophers, as an *action*. But the conjunction of v and b, when the latter is taken as an action, is almost *certainly* not covered by L. Indeed, the physiological explanation of an event is in every likelihood no explanation of it whatsoever when that event is understood as an action, since its being an action entails its having relationships to other things than are covered by L. It then remains an open option, pending further analysis, that b should be an effect in a compound event covered by a law, *without* it following that mDb is an effect in a compound event covered by a law. It is even consistently thinkable that mDb should be uncaused though b is caused. The question, accordingly, takes us beyond the question of whether b should be caused to whether the complex event which *contains* b should be an effect, taken as a whole, of a cause.

There are, when we introduce complex events, *four* distinct kinds of episodes to consider. Traditionally, philosophers have confined their attention to episodes compounded of simple events. But that is simply *one* case:

(I)   Simple event causes simple event.
(II) Simple event causes complex event.
(III) Complex event causes simple event.
(IV) Complex event causes complex event.

(I) is exemplified by the familiar collision of billiard balls, and my concern is whether, without altering our analysis in any serious respect, we might extend it unequivocally to cover the other cases.

That we may sensitize ourselves to the issues, let us note that case (III), appearances to the contrary notwithstanding, is not exemplified by the typical mediated action. The latter, recall, has this structure: mDb and b causes a (with further factors which do not enter as relevant at this point in our analysis). Here, note that the causal line runs from b – which is only *embedded* in the complex event mDb – to a, and not from the complex event itself. So the law covering the conjunction of b and a in no sense varies if a should be embedded or not, and hence it is case (I) we are dealing with, namely, causality as holding between simple events. Only were the law to hold between a complex event and a simple one, and *not* between the simple event *embedded* in the complex event and another simple event, would we have a true example of case (III). Indeed, as we begin to see the sorts of factors which are involved in complex events being either effects or causes, we shall see reason for supposing case (III) to be unexemplifiable – an *impossible* case. But it little matters that it should be that, if, consonantly with a univocal causal concept, we might have ready to hand exemplifications of (II) and (IV). I believe we do have these exemplifications.

When an event *f* causes a complex event *mDb*, which is a basic action, I shall speak of the latter as a *response*. The following appears to me to be an exhaustive schedule of the possible sorts of response:

(I) *f* causes *mDb*, and there is no agent *x* such that *xDf*. Suppose a stone falls, and *m* raises his arm to shield his head. But nobody threw the stone: its falling was not an action.

(II) Again, *f* causes *mDb*, but there exists an agent *y* (*y* ≠ *x*), such that *yDf*. Here, *y* might throw the stone, whether to hit *m* or not, and *m* acts as in (i).

(III) Once more, *f* causes *mDb*, but there exists an agent *z*, such that *zDf* and *z* = *m*. Thus *m* throws a stone, inaccurately perhaps, and responds as in (i).

Let us represent these cases graphically.

(i)

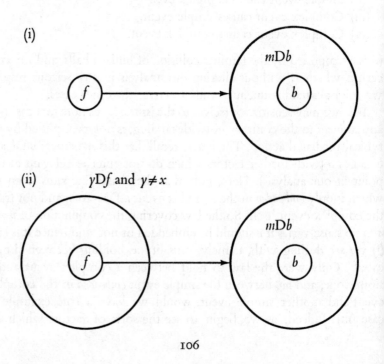

(ii)   *yDf* and *y* ≠ *x*

(iii) $z\mathrm{D}f$ and $z = m$

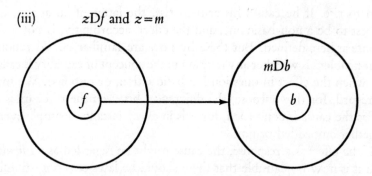

It cannot be overemphasized that the arrow, which marks the direction, provenance, and target of causality, runs in every case from the event f, invariably as to whether it is embedded or not in an action. And it terminates at the complex event $m\mathrm{D}b$ and *not* at the event b embedded in it. If it went from f to b in case (ii), we would be representing a non-basic action of y, rather than a response of m; and, in case (iii), we should be representing a non-basic action of m himself, which is *incompatible* with the effect in question being a basic action of his. All the cases, in brief, must be distinguished from this one

(iv)

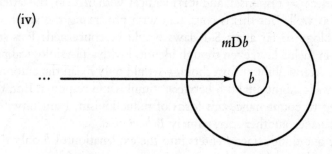

From our earlier results, this case is possible only when the cause in question is *not* an action, hence not an action of m. An action is basic only if there is no event distinct from the event embedded in that action, which causes the latter and is itself done by that agent. But this does not in any way entail that basic actions cannot be caused, even caused by the agent himself, if they are responses, and if it is the action which is the effect and not its component simple event. Case (iii), indeed, is a case of *m causing himself to do something*, in this case raise his arm, in contrast with his causing something to happen, viz. causing his arm to rise. If he causes his arm to rise, the latter, if an action, has at best to be a non-basic one, and the effect, accordingly, is not a response as here defined. But these by now are familiar considerations. Our problem is whether any revision in the concept of causality is called for when the effect in question is a basic action, or response. We may disregard, for this purpose, the differences between the three cases so far as the cause is concerned, for it is in every instance a simple event, whether embedded or not.

If the effect is a response, the cause might be regarded as a *stimulus*, and it is now implausible that there should be laws covering stimulus and response, of just the sort sought by psychology, without it following that these are not *causal* laws in just the sense we have been working with. Insofar as I am committed to the irreducibility of mDb to its component embedded simple event b, I suppose it must follow that I am committed to some thesis regarding the autonomy of psychology. I will accept this commitment, with some reservations. In Chapter 3 I was willing to endorse an identity theory for the action mDb and some physiological series $(n...b)$ of events, and it does not thus follow from the irreducibility of mDb to b that mDb cannot be identical with a causal series in which b is the terminal event. But then, insofar as mDb is an effect (= response), and it is identical with $(n...b)$, the latter is the effect as well. But this is consistent with preserving the autonomy of psychology so far as its S–R laws would be concerned: R is still the effect in such a law, even though identical with a physiological process. So the irreducibility of psychology would only mean the autonomy of the laws it might establish between stimulus and response. But, though willing to countenance this form of reductionism, I am unwilling to countenance another sort, namely *Behaviorism*.

For one thing, since f enters into the explanation of b only through the fact that m *does* b, there is an inexpungeable reference to m in the description. This is so even if, again, we should ultimately accept some identity theory through which it followed that m was identical with say, his body. There would still be an inexpungeable reference to m i the event to be explained were a response. It is *false*, thus, that f causes b *simpliciter*. It is not a law that falling stones, for example, cause arms to rise. Falling stones seem neither necessary nor, in the absence of preventing conditions, sufficient for an arm to rise. If the claim, then, were that f causes b, it would be false. What f causes at best is mDb: the falling stone *caused m to respond by raising his arm*. It seems almost certain that *b* and *mDb* are covered by disjoint classes of causal laws and hence have disjoint classes of simple events as causes. It is this fact, I believe, which makes psychology irreducible to some other, more basic science: its laws are autonomous to the extent that their effects are complex events themselves irreducible to their component simple events, which, in turn, are not covered by the same laws as, nor effects of the same causes as, the events which contain them.

Secondly, the inexpungeable reference to *m* implies a range of conditions, the *absence* of which would prevent *f* from being sufficient for *mDb*, i.e. *f* is sufficient *only* if these conditions hold. One such condition is this: unless *f* is perceived by *m* to be happening, then *f* will not cause *mDb*. A stone falling unperceived *m*-ward will plainly not cause *m* to raise his arm, and in general, if *f* occurs and *m fails* to perceive *f* and yet *mDb*, the latter must be explained with reference to some cause other than *f*. I am prepared, accordingly, to propose this thesis: an event causes a response, and hence is a stimulus, only if it is perceived by the respondent. This reference to perception I regard as a limit upon Behaviorism, even if a perception should, like an action, be identical with a physiological process.

It is, I believe, analytic to the concept of responses that they are *to* something, and I have claimed that *what* they are responses to must be events perceived by the respondents, it being the nature of stimuli that their *esse est percipi*. It is no accident that the archetypical stimulus – pain – was precisely the lever Berkeley was able to use to prise off the surface from reality, and show, amazingly, that in the end reality was nothing *but* surface. Reference to Berkeley at this juncture is somewhat ominous, as we shall see in a moment, but it is plain sense in the present case that in the class of responses, *unperceived* events cannot be their causes. If this is so, then it is plausible to suppose the event in question is a cause only so far as it is perceived, and that the causal law(s) hold between *perceived* events and responses. We may suppose that had he not perceived the falling stone, *m* would not have raised his arm, unless certain preventive conditions held, e.g. he does not know or care about the impact upon sensitive flesh of hard missiles, or is, through some internal or external factor, inhibited from the normal response under those conditions. I shall undertake clarification of those notions in a subsequent chapter, but just now I must take up a problem which is bound to arise in any context in which Berkeley's name is appropriate. For once we admit into our analysis a perceptual component, the lid is sprung on a boxful of philosophical monsters which must be charmed if we are to progress any further.

I have so far been concerned with epistemologically normal cases, where we have 'veridical' perceptions of the event constituted a stimulus through its perception as such. Now there are misperceptions and illusions and hallucinations which can occur. Would *m* not respond just as he would have done under the normal condition? If this is so, then the event *f* need not occur at all for the response to occur, and the response seems causally independent of its putative cause. What happens then to the causal laws our analysis requires? Ought they not to cover, instead of *f* and the response, the *perception* of *f* and the response? So that it is the *perception* which is the cause, invariantly as to whether or not it is veridical? After all, if I *dreamt* a stone were falling, I might *really* raise my arm!

I am grateful for the appearance here of illusions and dreams and the like, for they signalize the fact that we have moved a step upward in the scale of the universe: where there is the possibility of illusion, there is the possibility of knowledge and of truth, and we have entered upon the territory of intellect. But moreover, we have further reason for regarding reference to *m* as inexpungeable from the analysis and the explanation of responses, for it is *his* perception of *f* which constitutes it a stimulus and hence a cause *if* the perception is veridical. We have, however, the question of the causal independence of the response: the only dependency seems to be that of the response to the *perception* of *f*, whether veridical or not. And the latter may be independent of the occurrence of *f* if an impressive tradition in epistemology is to be credited.

The issues which arise here, which I shall treat somewhat exhaustively in connection with the topic of beliefs and feelings, do not so much cripple as complicate the application of the concept of causality to the case of responses. We may persist in saying that *f* causes *mDb* if *m* perceives *f* and the perception is veridical. But any event *x* which *m* perceives as *f*, even when not veridical, will equally cause *mDb*, *m*'s faulty perception here regularizing a class of externally dissimilar events and constituting them as causes because perceived *as f*. So it is virtually as though the law relating *f* to *mDb* holds because *m* acts as though it held, and it is only with reference to it that we could countenance a bird's passing shadow as the cause of *m*'s raising his arm: it was because *m* perceived it as a hard, threatening object in transit. But this enables us to take care of the hallucinatory case as well, where there *is* nothing which m perceives as f but it nevertheless occurs that he raises his arm because he believes he does perceive f. The law relating f to mDb is, so to speak, internalized by m, who acts as he does because he believes his is what we may term the epistemically normal situation. The law he internalizes is parasitic upon what holds in the case in which perception is veridical. The laws of stimulus and response accordingly hold against a background of assumed perceptual normalities, and m responds as he does only because he spontaneously supposes his perception to be normal. There is, to be sure, an element of reflexiveness in responses to objects which approach one as rapidly as a thrown stone would – which is fortunate as regards survival. But that does not mean that the response does not occur only because the man believes a stone is coming towards him.

It may be argued that if the law holds between perceiving f and doing b, then it holds between complex events and not between a simple event and a complex event. But the fact is that it is *as* a simple event that m perceives f, and his response to f is a response to what is perceived as simple. This brings us to the case in which he responds to what he perceives as a *complex* event, and this may serve to clarify the issue.

In the last sort of case I wish to consider, an event e is to be a cause of mDb only in case it is embedded in, and hence redescribable as an *action*. And the causal laws in question hold, again, only insofar as it is so embedded. When an event is a cause only if it is an action, we move to a scale of behavior, and to a range of laws which hold for that scale of behavior, which at last bear a truly human stamp. I shall wish to generate only sufficient of the structure of this case to suggest that our causal model applies to it easily and intactly, however philosophically fascinating details of this structure may be.

Once more, it is easiest to stick to the epistemologically straightforward case, noting merely that the possibility of epistemologically *deviant* cases entails the supervention of a perceptual factor, which is somewhat complicated in the present instance. It is enough that an event should be perceived as embedded in an action (= as an action, via redescription) for it to be a cause here, whether the event in fact is so embedded or not. A savage, thus, may hear a roll of thunder as a warning from the gods, and hence as an action; and though there *are* no gods, and rolls of thunder are *merely* rolls of thunder, his response will be appropriate to one who *believes* a warning has been issued. What is presupposed, in order that such a perception should occur, is that he who perceives should have certain *beliefs*, true or false, regarding the events which occur in his purview and, no less significant, that he should have the concept of *action*. What the savage just referred to believes is that rolls of thunder are *done*, and so must have the concept of action if he is to hold this belief. It is sometimes suggested that men primitively went through a period of animism, according to which *everything* was done, and only bit by bit gave this general belief up, e.g. in connection with rolls of thunder. Since '*mDb*' has truth-conditions in excess of '*b*', and since *b* can occur without it being true that *mDb*, '*b*' itself seems a more primitive description than *mDb*. But there is scant reason for supposing that primitive man began with primitive notions, and I see no logical reason to suppose animism could not have been the initial view of our predecessors. But this is by the way. What is crucial here is that the perception of *e* as an action can be the cause of a response, not only independently of whether *e* occurs (as in the case of illusion just canvassed) but also independently of whether *e* is an action, so long as it is *believed* to be one. So not only perception on the respondent's part, but also a set of beliefs and a certain conceptual sophistication must be regarded as entailed by the occurrence of responses of this order. An action which is a response to what its agent perceives as an action, I shall speak of as a *reaction*.

With responses, and even more strikingly with reactions, we are constrained to make reference to the interiors of agents. Not merely is reference to *m* entailed by the causal laws we should have to invoke – the effect, after all, is always an action of an agent, is always (say) *mDb* rather than *b simpliciter* – but reference to *m*'s perceptions and beliefs (at least) must be presupposed in the characterization of the cause, i.e. whether it is a stimulus or a provoking action. And this means that in order to understand *m*'s behavior, we must know how *he* perceives the world. Thus men do not commonly scream when they perceive feathers. But if they believe, abnormally and as part of their psychopathology, or normally and as part of their cultural inheritance, that feathers are omens of disaster, they could understandably respond by screaming. It is this essential reference to the beliefs of others which philosophers of the Continent have meant by their concept of *Verstehen*. *Verstehen* is understanding understanding. I do not believe that *Verstehen* is especially mysterious, and I certainly do not suppose it requires any empathic leap of identification across the barriers of the soul. Rather, it involves merely the ascription of such predicates as 'believes-that *-s*' to others, when such a predicate, if true of *m*, would explain the manner in which *m* reacts to a stimulus he perceives as an action. It is, incidentally, not at all required that the belief be a conscious one on *m*'s part or even that he formulate or be able to formulate it in other than the language it already exists in.

Whatever may be the case regarding the ontological status of beliefs and the epistemological facts in applying belief-predicates, it nevertheless remains that reference to others' beliefs and perceptions is implicit in almost any social act any of us perform. And it with this consideration that we recognize that we have entered the sphere of *communication*. Much of what I do, I count on as being perceived as an action,[15] and as the right sort of action, by others, and often my actions will lose their point entirely if they are not so perceived, or are unintelligible. Imagine that one were a god, seeking to communicate through natural events with a community of atheists! They would hear thunder rolls only, and never warnings: they would not perceive the world as Divine Visible Language. It hardly then is to be wondered that if we have a language at all, or any system of communication for the matter, we have a capacity for *understanding* actions exactly proportionate to our capacity for producing them. In the straightforward case, the performer antici-pates that another's understanding of his action is the same as his *own* understanding of it. This brings us to the topic of *interpretation*.

To perceive a stimulus as an action I shall regard as a case of inter-pretation. Interpretation is understanding the *meaning of an event*, i.e. first by locating it in an action and then by identifying the action it is located in. If a roll of thunder is *not* located in an action (= is not done), no interpretation is called for. But if it is, then the question arises of what it means, which, as I shall wish to argue, is to ask with what intention it was done.

Understanding is bringing under a rule, and the Understanding, in the quaint facultative idiom of Kant, is the Faculty of Rules. *Verstehen* then is mastering the rules under which other persons bring events which are *supposed* embedded in actions, whether done or only witnessed by those persons. I emphasize the word 'supposed' here, for *Verstehen* does *not* require that the beliefs and perceptions of others be correct. After all, the understanding of understanding can equally be the understanding of misunderstanding, which is failing to interpret what is an action, or interpreting as an action what is not one, or in correctly identifying something as an action but incorrectly identifying the action that it is.

I now wish to propose that my concept of causation is consistent with the concept of reactions. In acting, I have a right to expect that a reaction will occur in every instance and of a predictable sort *unless* something prevents it from occurring, e.g. the Other does not perceive it, or misunderstands it, or some other thing. This is conspicuously the case with socially conventional behavior. When a man smiles upon meeting a stranger, he expects the reaction to be a smile; and if the latter fails consistently to occur, it is often reasonable to suppose that one has entered another atmosphere of rules. In France, for example, the social smile is unknown, and the smiling American, entering a shop, looks like an idiot to a Frenchman who looks hostile to the American. In a *closed world* of conventions, a world in which Other Cultures have not entered, there would be no way of distinguishing between the laws of nature and the conventions and rules of society.

Be these fascinating questions as they may, your smiling, when in reaction to mine, is caused by my smiling through the mediation of your perceiving it, understanding it, and nothing being present which inhibits the proper response. It is, in brief, though somewhat more complex through the fact that spiritual factors have been introduced, covered by a model of causation which allows actions to be caused by actions. After all, *your* smile could have been causally independent of mine: you smiled *when* I smiled, but at some inner fond thought or some private wit or, for all I know, only seemed to smile through the mechanism of a facial tic. But much the same independence may be found, as we saw, in the world of causality whose terms are simple events. I shall regard my model, then, as univocally applicable to the world of actions and mere unembedded events alike.

We have been constrained by our analyses of responses and reactions to build m's representation of the world into our account of the causation of basic actions, to at least the degree that the laws which cover these actions *as* effects do so only relative to a specific perception and of beliefs held by m. The content of our laws is in a curious way derivative upon the content of m's own implicit theory of why he responds or reacts as he does. We are obliged, then, to invoke m's conception of the world and of his relationship to it in order to explain the way the world moves him to act. And this is all the more marked when we take into consideration the fact that it can happen that he acts in the light of incorrect perceptions and often in the light of false beliefs and mad reasons. The laws of nature cover men only to the degree that men cover themselves by laws, and our explanations of human actions must take a man's *own* explanation into account, however wild and devious. His explanation is part of *the* explanation, and his representation, thus, gets woven into the fabric of the universe. History will go one way rather than another as a function of the way men perceive themselves and their world.

To be sure, not all responses (though I believe all reactions) presuppose beliefs held by the agent. Behavior becomes more uniform and less culturally differentiated as the force of beliefs approaches zero, and hence as responses verge on reflexes. Thus men spontaneously, and without reference to their beliefs, withdraw their hands abruptly from hot irons. What keeps this a basic action and not a pure response is that it is capable of inhibition by a sufficiently determined person, concerned to show self-control or demonstrate innocence at a witch trial, whereas no such options are available with the pre-patellar reflex. Or again, men writhe when in pain, mainly to secure a different stimulus in order to reduce the intensity of the pain. It is thus that we bite our lips or dig our nails into our palms when about to suffer inoculation. These remain basic actions in connection with which mere perception without specific beliefs is sufficiently explanatory, together, of course, with those mechanisms of homeostasis and self-preservation whose operation is automatic and commonly unavailable to the interferences of the agent. My point in singling these cases out here is to stress that though reactions and high-order responses are not, as these are, mechanical and spontaneous, no different concept of *causation* is required for their explanation; and to make it plain that it is consistent with the concept of basic actions that they should be caused. So far, then, though it is still premature to treat the matter, nothing in our analysis of basic action entails a negative theory regarding the possibility of a universal Determinism. Indeed, it is analytical to the concept of response and reaction that, in at least the epistemically normal case, there be causes; and in the epistemically deviant case, that the agent *believe* there are causes for his action. Whether the fact that something is constituted a cause through an agent's beliefs has any bearing on Determinism as a theory I shall not here pause to consider, but postpone it until the end of our inquiry.

5

GIFTS

I

'We are not able to move all the organs of the body with like authority', Hume observes, 'though we cannot assign any reason besides experience, for so remarkable a difference between one and the other.'[1] 'As we are *now*', wrote St Augustine,[2] 'not only do our articulate members obey the will – our hands or feet or fingers – but even those that are moved only by small sinews and tendons we contract and turn as we list, as you may see in the voluntary motions of the mouth and face... and the lungs do serve a man's will entirely, like a pair of smith's or organist's bellows.' Like Hume, Augustine supposed it merely contingent that our 'authority' should be circumscribed as we find it to be, for there are men capable of doing odd things: 'We see some men's natures far different from others, acting those things strangely in their bodies which others neither do nor hardly will believe.' So we *could* have been framed with our authority differently seated: 'God could easily have made us with all our members subjected to the will', he writes, adding the possibility which obviously haunted him as a man, as we might recall from the *Confessions*, 'even those which *now* are moved by lust'. I italicize the word 'now', which occurs twice in this passage. For it was Augustine's curious view that Adam, in paradise, indeed was so framed that he could perform what I have termed basic actions with his sexual organ, and hence achieve the sexual act immune from the contaminations of sin. It is thus not sex but lust which is the root of sin, and hence the domination by the flesh of *us* rather than the domination by us over our bodies, which is the fallen state. Paradise accordingly is a condition we may get some glimpses of from our present powers of direct action, executing intentions without the concomitant torment of desire.[3]

I am not at all certain that it is a merely contingent matter that voluntary erection lies outside the boundaries of direct action. For curiously enough, a man who were able to erect at will might in fact be impotent in the received sense, which is an incapacity for genuine sexual *response*; where *response* implies precisely the absence of that order of control Augustine supposes our first parent to have exemplified. A man who had direct control, or who was obliged to exercise direct control, would be a man without *feeling*, erection being the common *expression* of male sexual feeling. And it is in some measure a logical truth that if erection were an action it would not be an expression, and the entire meaning of sexuality would be altered were tumescence something over which we had 'authority'. Hence feeling, or lust, if you will, is not so contingently related to erection as Augustine's argument implies.[4] But perhaps it is his claim that there would in fact have been no sexuality in paradise: a wry conjecture in the light of post-Freudian sexual romanticism.

Augustine's philosophy of action, at least here, is almost painfully illustrative of Nietzsche's view that philosophy *au fond* is only disguised autobiography.[5] It is ironic, if this is so, that Hume, who believed that reason is and ought to be the slave of passion, must apparently have been less the slave of passion than the saint who believed the opposite. But unless we read it deliberately in these terms, the section in which Hume discusses the contingent disposition of our powers is hardly transparently confessional. Rather, it offers just one further argument in Hume's arsenal of arguments against the claim that we might derive our idea of causal connection from the knowledge we have of our powers over our own body. If we had the purported knowledge, Hume points out, then we should *explain*, and not merely note the fact that 'the will has an influence over the tongue and finger, not over the heart or liver'. But in fact we only *find* that we can do things directly in certain regions of our body and not in others, and matters stand here as they do elsewhere in the causal order. We *discover* that things are connected one way rather than another without being able to say why this is so. Like the world at large, we could have been made differently. But we are as we are.

It is contingent that we are bounded as we are or at all, so far as direct action is concerned, exception being made in the cases of feelings and responses, perhaps, though even there it is contingent that the movements we read as expressions are in fact that. If there were voluntary lacrimation or voluntary laughter – if tears and laughter came in the same manner in which we raised our arms or turned our heads – then these would not be *expressions* of sorrow or enjoyment. Still, it is a contingent fact that we are unable to 'cry' and 'laugh' at will. Let us say that, made the way we are, these are things we are *impotent* to do, for they lie beyond the boundaries we find to be ours.

Let me emphasize that by 'impotency' here I do not mean an absolute incapacity to bring something about, but only an incapacity to bring something about directly, and as a matter of basic action. In cognition as well, as we should expect, there are things which, though not altogether beyond our cognitive reach and regarding which we are accordingly not absolutely ignorant, are nevertheless outside the reach of our basic cognitive capacities. So we might speak of *basic* impotency and *basic* ignorance. And these will in many cases be mitigated through the fact that we may know and do a great many things of which we are basically ignorant and impotent, providing only that we have access to that *through* which they may be known or done, as in the case of mediated cognitions and actions. There are, to be sure, other boundaries of considerable philosophical interest: boundaries which mark the absolute limits of our knowledge and power even when amplified by the resources of mediated action and cognition, hence things we can achieve neither basically nor through ulterior means; and boundaries of a curious order, marking things we can do and know *only* basically, so that if we are basically ignorant or basically impotent here, then we are absolutely ignorant and impotent, there being no avenue save the direct avenue. I, however, will be dominantly concerned with those apparently contingent limits on our basic powers, beyond which we are basically, whether in addition we are absolutely ignorant and impotent.

Impotency, like power itself, is a concept philosophers would prefer to avoid, if possible, if only because of the severe straits it puts us in when we ask what powers and impotencies *are*, and how we know when they are present or absent. The inborn verificationism of philosophers makes them comfortable mainly with concepts whose instances are, if only in principle, observable or manifest, or which are at least tied by acceptable ligatures of explicit definition or logical entailment to concepts of this epistemologically tractable order. Thus, utilizing as an analogue a mode of inference regarded as unexceptionable since medieval times, namely that from the existence to the possibility of something there is always a valid inference, we may suppose it valid to infer from performance to power. If a man *does b*, then he can (= has the power to) do *b*; or at least he had the power when he did *b* and has it still providing (= *ceteris paribus*) he is 'the same' as he was when he did it. This leaves the meaning, or the descriptive content or the concept of power (or ability) unanalyzed – to *what* exactly have we inferred when we go from *esse* to *posse*? – unless we take the verificationist route and identify the meaning of a concept with the mode of its verification. In which case, since it commonly does not follow from the fact that *m* does not do *b* that he is *impotent* to, or *cannot* do *b*, the question sharply arises as to how, in the absence of performance, we are to say that a claim either to power or to impotency on the part of *m* is true? It is not ordinarily regarded inconsistent to say that a man can do what he does not and has not done. Now with verificationism one automatically adopts the third-person stance, that of attributing powers and impotencies to others. But if we turn instead to the point of view of the agent himself, and look for a moment *within*, then it seems to me we have a very clear idea of what power and impotency must come to, and our knowledge in such matters cannot be inferential but must be direct. That is, though we may be impotent without knowing that we are, if we know that we are, our knowledge must be direct. The following remarks apply exclusively to those who have always lacked a given power, not to those who may have had and then lost a given power. The concept of impotency may fail to discriminate between those who never have had and those who have stopped having a given power, but the difference, as will become clear, is crucial for my argument.

The knowledge that *b* happened without my having done *b* only tells me that I did not, not that I cannot or that I am impotent to do *b*. And this is true no matter how many times an event instantiating the same basic description as *b* takes place without my having done that event. Nor can I learn that I am impotent to do *b* by, as it were, doing *b* without *b* happening: for it is precisely with respect to *doing b* that we are supposing impotency. It is the doing itself of *b* which lies beyond my powers, and upon which I cannot so much as make a *beginning*. I shall subsequently argue that there is an immediate experience of incapacity, a kind of encounter with nothingness, to which our conception of basic impotency corresponds. I *discover* not only that I cannot do *b* but, more importantly perhaps and at the same time, that I cannot really understand what doing *b*, or even what having the power to do *b means*. By analogy, I discover that I am blind not by seeing things that in fact are not there, but by a blank incapacity to see and even (in at least the case of the congenitally blind) to know what 'seeing' *means*. So the limits of my basic powers, either performative or cognitive, are the limits of my understanding what the concepts of the powers mean. By contrast, I learn what seeing and what doing are by seeing and doing. So these are, after all, if this argument is correct – and the bulk of the chapter to follow will spell out the details of it – descriptive rather than modal concepts we are dealing with, concepts the meaning of which, at least in our own case, we acquire by a mode of direct experience. It is this experience which then gives content to those inferences, in the case of others, to powers and incapacities based upon overt behavior. Let us, now, begin the long ascent to these conclusions, and beyond them to what they imply about *us*.

II

I shall now speak of a schedule or a repertoire R of basic powers. If *m* is not basically impotent to do *e*, then doing *e* lies in *m*'s repertoire. We may define a *normal* agent relative to some specific repertoire R by making the content of R explicit as follows: for every event *x* such that doing *x* lies in R, *m* is called a *normal agent* relative to R if (i) *m* is not basically impotent to do *x* and (ii) for every *y* such that doing *y* lies outside of R, *m is* basically impotent to do *y*. Regarding the content of that R which defines *our* normalities, we need not tarry: 'as we are now', to echo Augustine, raising an arm lies in R and erecting a penis lies outside R for such of us as are males. But abnormalities abound. Let us thus speak of a man *n* as *positively abnormal* when *n* is not basically impotent to do *z*, when doing *z* lies outside R; and as *negatively abnormal* when he is basically impotent to do *w* and doing *w* lies in R. Abnormalities of either sort are relative to repertoires: *we* should be at once positively and negatively abnormal relative to repertoires which defined as normal agents gelatinous spheroid agents whose schedule of basic powers reached just so far as the expansion and contraction of their surfaces. And most of what the positively abnormal, as determined by our repertoires, are able directly to do, we can do at least mediatedly. Thus by administering belladonna, we may cause our eyes to dilate in contrast with those who are not basically impotent, as I assume we are, to dilate our eyes. Felix Krull, Mann's confidence man, sought to master voluntary dilation in order, as he phrased it, to demonstrate the power of mind over matter.[6] But it is not plain that he was not merely the unwitting beneficiary of the mechanisms of the conditioned reflex. Men can, after all, be conditioned to dilate their eyes – or their eyes can be conditioned to dilate – by a signal which accompanies an abrupt diminution in light.[7] But then it is altogether feasible that the signal might be self-administered. By whispering 'Dilate!' for example, their eyes may indeed dilate, and the command may be issued in the silence of the soul. But this still leaves them, as it may have left Felix Krull, *basically* impotent to dilate eyes: for one must *do* something here in order that the eyes dilate, viz. silently voice the stimulus word; and dilation is accordingly a *mediated* rather than a basic action. And it contrasts acutely with the mode in which the arm is raised in basic action. Our arms do not rise in response to muttered imprecations to rise; and while we may *on occasion* raise them in response to a self-issued command – issued incidentally to ourselves and not Canute-fashion to our arms! – only the superstitious would suppose that there must *always* be commands, or that something like a command is ever required to fill in a place merely imposed by an inappropriate causal model of action. So dilation as a positive abnormality is directly done, without being brought about *through* some other thing.

Conditioning makes possible a degree of control we had not thought within our compass of mediated action. Men can be taught to control heart-rate and blood-pressure, kidney function and brain-waves.[8] But acquiring these mediated powers in no respect whatever increases their repertoires of *basic* actions. Augustine offers a catalogue of what he at least takes to be positive abnormalities, for unless they were that, they could not furnish him evidence for the possibility he argues to on their basis, viz. 'that the first man might have had his means and members of generation without lust':

There are those who can move their ears, one or both, as they please; there are those that can move all their hair toward their forehead, and back again, and never move their head. There are those that can swallow twenty things whole, and pressing their stomach lightly give everything up as a whole as if they had been put into a bag ... there are those who can break wind backward so artfully, that you would think they sung. I have seen one sweat whenever he list, and it is sure that some can weep as they list, and shed tears plentifully.

Our repertoire of mediated actions grows with our causal knowledge, and is a function of the causal forces we can turn into means and instruments. But it is not clear *what* we might do in order to increase our repertoire of *basic* powers.

In a way, our powers are *gifts*. It is analytical to the notion of a gift that it is not received because of something one has done: gifts are not, so to speak, *earned*.

We may better appreciate this if we observe that there are almost precisely analogous distinctions to be drawn in the domains of cognition. Thus we may speak of a repertoire or schedule of modes of basic cognition, and specify a repertoire which defines a normal cognizer. If R is such a repertoire, then *m* is normal if, for every *x* which lies in R, *m* is not *basically* ignorant, that is, is not incapable of *basically* knowing *x*; and for every *y* which lies outside R, *m* is basically ignorant, is incapable of basically knowing *y*. Obviously, *m* need not be totally only basically ignorant regarding *y*, his knowledge of *y* being necessarily inferential since it cannot, given the R-defining limitations upon him, be direct. R is composed of a schedule which answers to the traditional 'five senses'.[9] But the concept of a 'sixth sense' then corresponds to what we might term the positively abnormal cognizer, that is, one who knows or can know directly that which we know, if at all, only inferentially and regarding which we are *basically* ignorant. And the negatively abnormal then would be he who was constrained to know inferentially if at all what the normal cognizer *can* know directly. Hence the blind are negatively abnormal in the theory of knowledge as the paralytic is negatively abnormal in the theory of action, these having lost – or never, in the case of the congenital defect, having had – the gifts of sight and motion.

Consider, now, the *totally abnormal* relative to a repertoire R. He has a non-empty repertoire, but it has no elements in common with R, so that the set of his gifts is logically disjoint with the gift-set of the normal as defined by R – us, let's suppose. In every case in which *we* do something directly, that is something the totally abnormal must do as a mediated action if he can do it at all; and in every case in which we may know something directly, he must know that thing inferentially, again if at all. And similarly in the other direction. Yet it is conceivable that we and he can know and do most of the same things, albeit starting from very different positions in the causal and inferential orders. Or put it this way. Suppose there is an event of type B which is or can be caused by an event of type A. And suppose the normal can make happen an event of type B directly whereas the totally abnormal can make happen an event of type A directly. Then, where the normal can make happen an event of type B directly, and through a basic action, the totally abnormal can only make an event of type B happen indirectly and through a mediated action, providing he knows the law L of causal connection between events of the two types. Under L, an event of type A is transformed into a *means* for type-B events. L, in effect, is a *recipe* for the production of type-B events for someone incapable of making such events happen directly, whereas the normal need a recipe only as an alternative route, since *he* is capable of dispensing with recipes altogether. He is already *at* a point in the causal order which the totally abnormal must *reach* by instrumentation. But then we must reach, if we can, points at which the totally abnormal already *is*, by virtue of his singular repertoire of gifts.

In epistemology, of course, that which corresponds to this notion is that of the *given*, where what is given is that which we are not required to arrive at by dint of inferential enterprise. Thus, if P is given, no *proof* of P is demanded: P, rather, figures as a freely available beginning point in proofs of other propositions. Axioms in deductive systems are in this regard given, and distinguished insofar from theorems.[10] The earliest thinking on the matter of axiomatization required that axioms somehow be propositions which were *inherently* given, essentially underivable, and such that were they not given, they could not be gotten into the fund of knowledge at all. Hence if they are known they must be basically known, and if we are basically, then we are totally ignorant in their regard. So a man to whom they were not immediately and directly evident – who was blind to their truth – would be indefeasibly ignorant; and axioms – like the basic sentences of classical epistemology – would be absolute starting points in inferentiation. Self-evident truths, clear and distinct ideas, *simple* ideas, protocol sentences: these and others of close logical kin to them were all in this regard classed as completely primitive. They belonged by nature, so to speak, in the base and never in the superstructures of cognition: they were *the* foundation stones in *logischen Aufbauen*.

I have argued, in Chapter 2, that it does not follow from the fact that we must begin somewhere, that there *is* somewhere that we *must* begin. Hence it would not follow from the fact that something must be given if anything is to be proved, that there are things which, unless they are given, then nothing can be proved. So it is consistent with a distinction between *being given* and *being shown* that what is shown in one context might be given in another, and this suggests that we might by dint of inference arrive at what the totally abnormal is given, as he might similarly arrive at what instead is given to us, so that we may in the end achieve the same body of knowledge. On the other hand, this overlooks a certain intuition possessed by those who believed in a natural asymmetry between what is given and what is shown. There is a serious question as to whether that which must be arrived at because we are so built that it cannot be given us, can *mean* the same thing to us as to someone so built that it can be given to him. Suppose a man can know immediately certain mathematical truths at which the rest of us can only arrive by long calculation: he claims he *sees* immediately what we of course can check up on, and so certify as true what he already knew. Still, we want to know, *what* did he *see*? And the feeling remains that he has available to his experience, features of numbers of which we can form no true notion, even though we can verify every proposition he may claim as true. If this is so, then there are aspects or dimensions of numbers to which we might be blind, and numerical concepts cannot have exactly the same meaning for him as for us. There is a certain continuity between what is known and the way in which we know it, and if there are ways of knowing things available to some but not to others, there is a problem as to whether they know quite the same things. So it might be that though we and the totally abnormal had the same body of knowledge, we might never be able to *know* this to be the case.

Suppose a man boasts that he can know the thoughts of other persons. We are impressed enough to request him to exhibit his ability, whereupon he *asks* someone what he is thinking and is told. Well, *anyone* can do *that*, and the question is only why he believed he had something to boast of. In order to sustain his boast, he would have to do something like *tell* people what *they* were thinking, so that we might be able to discern from the startled looks on their faces that he had scored. But then we cannot understand *what* he does for we are cut off from that mode of reading thoughts and it is not clear, in consequence, that we even know what thoughts *are* to someone with his gifts. Suppose a personage boasts that *he* can get bushes to burst into flame. Again we are impressed enough to ask him to display his ability, whereupon he soaks a bush with benzine and sets fire to it with a match. Since anyone can do *that*, there is something mad about the boast (like a man boasting that he always remembers to put his shoes on *after* his socks)

The boast is justified only if the bush bursts into flame as its predecessor might have done in the time of Moses, without the mediation of 'means'. Miracles consist not in what is done – we all can burn bushes, we can in principle divide the sea (with enormous wind-machines) – but in the *mode* of doing it, gods doing as basic actions what mere mortals must do as mediated ones. Now a miracle is something unintelligible if done through a mode of direct action outside the repertoire within which we are confined as agents. And there is a sense in which if we cannot understand the way in which something is done, we do not know *what* is done, in the same way in which he who does it directly understands it. The limits of our powers are in a way the limits of our understanding, and it may after all be true that *where* we begin is not someplace at which *we* might instead have arrived. And this is the deeper sense of the given. The given is not merely where we *do* but where we *must* begin, in the respect that if we were not there already, we could not arrive there at all. We might, of course, arrive at some-place similar, but there is a chasm of incomprehension, if this line of thought has any cogency, between ourselves and the totally ab-normal, which cannot be bridged. It is not that we live differently in the world: we virtually live in different worlds. So our argument must be qualified. It does not indeed follow from the fact that we must begin somewhere, that there are *places* at which we *must* begin. But there are, even so, places at which *we* ('– being made as we are') must begin.

It is with this concept of the gift that I want now seriously to occupy myself. The gift, as I understand it, partially defines *us* while partially defining our *world*.

III

A distinction structurally parallel to those just framed may be found drawn upon some of the most famous pages of philosophy, although under the topic of *understanding* rather than under either knowledge or action. Certain things, it is claimed, are, or at least in principle may be, understood through understanding other things of the same type as themselves – *ideas*, say – whereas ultimately there must be things which, *however* they are understood, at least cannot be under-stood through other things of the same type as themselves. Locke, for notorious example, distinguished compound from simple ideas much along these lines. He supposed that we may (though we do not need always to) understand a compound idea through understanding its component ideas together with the principle of composition (an architectonic definition of sorts), whereas we cannot understand a simple idea along those lines since a *simple* idea is such through the fact that it has no components and is, in the sense of definition which applies to compound ideas, indefinable. So it is trivial that mastery of it cannot be arrived at through the medium of definition, and some principle of understanding other than the avenue of definition must be invoked in order to explain how *these* are understood. Various theories, of course, are possible. The ideas could be self-defining, in the manner in which the axioms of Euclid were thought to be self-evident. Or we could say we simply *do* understand them (as we simply *know*, or simply *do* structurally comparable things in the theories of knowledge and action). Or we may invoke the mechanisms of causation, by saying that we understand them in consequence of being *caused* to understand by experience, or learning, or ostension, or whatever. It was consistent with the simplicity of such ideas that they should have a history of acquisition, simplicity ruling out only a *certain* acquisitional history, namely that they should have been learned through learning to understand other ideas which formed portions of their meaning: for there were no such. But it is easy to appreciate the immense possibilities such theories opened up for transcendental arguments of the most ambitious dimension, arguments which proceeded from the fact that a given idea was (i) understood and (ii) indefinable, to the conclusion that certain things conveniently correspondent to the idea in question *must* exist: for if they did not, one could not understand (could not *have*) the idea, contrary to hypothesis (i). Thus Descartes argues to the existence from the idea of God in the great Third Meditation. Thus Moore argues to the existence from the idea of Good in *Principia Ethica*. And so forth.

With the details of these celebrated theories we need not especially tarry. Nor does it greatly matter whether we doff the pseudo-psychology of ideas and adopt the pseudo-linguistics of *terms*, and speak of terms which we may in principle come to understand through understanding terms which explicitly define them, in contrast with terms which cannot be understood that way because, if they are definable, they at least are not so through other things (i.e. terms) of the same sort as they. Whatever the vehicle of comprehension, we might speak in obvious analogy to the distinctions here laid out of *basic* and *mediated* understanding. And with only the slightest distortions in our concept, we might speak of a repertoire R of *modes of basic understanding*. Normalities may be specified through R as elsewhere: if x lies in R and y lies outside R, then for all x and y m is normal if he is able basically to understand x and is basically incomprehending with regard to y. It is natural to suggest that basic incomprehension does not as such entail *total* incomprehension, inasmuch as room has been allowed for mediated understanding; and y may be amongst the comprehensibilia which may be understood through other things co-generic with itself. Early theorists of the understanding supposed that for compound ideas, two modes of understanding were available: we could learn the meaning of 'horse' by much the same means of causal acquisition as we learn the meaning of 'red' – by acquaintance, for example. But we might understand by purely definitional mechanisms in the former where this is ruled out in the latter case. But if y were *itself simple* and lay outside R, the normal understanding, since basically incomprehending, would also be totally incomprehending with regard to y, for the mode of understanding required for y would be unavailable. Thus, for the normal, y would be *absolutely unintelligible*. It was in this respect that 'red' was held to be absolutely unintelligible to the blind, or 'God' absolutely unintelligible to the graceless.

We may now bring the structure of understanding and the structure of cognition into perfect alignment by simply identifying the repertoires of direct cognition and the repertoires of basic understanding, a strategy which almost exactly yields classical empiricism. Classical empiricism was the theory that, if i is a simple idea, then m understands (as 'has') i only if m basically knew that to which i refers. Now m may not in fact understand i without being basically ignorant, simply because he is not basically incomprehending: the mode of understanding – or the mode of cognition – is in his repertoire, but he simply has not had the fortune to have it actualized in an episode of direct cognition. A man otherwise normal may not understand 'red' simply because his experience has been abnormal: he has never known red. He is ignorant but not indefeasibly so: his mind simply requires enrichment: he does not understand because he has not understood. His case contrasts with that of the *modally* abnormal, who does not understand *because he cannot know*. A mode of understanding or cognition is a gift, the lack of which cannot be remedied by any of the mechanisms which make for mediated understanding. Modal deficiency, which is the impotency of the intellect, is what, without being more definite as to which are the modes of basic understanding, I now wish to explore.

Consider, then, the congenitally blind reputed impotent to understand 'red', chiefly because he has not known, and this because he cannot know red. But there is, if this claim of armchair learning theory is correct, an incapacity of comprehension we may lay to the blind man which goes beyond anything which refers to what lies in the field of vision. *He cannot understand the term which refers to the mode of comprehension itself.* And since he does not know what *seeing* is, there is a sense in which he does not know what blindness is (what 'blindness' means) either. His is the condition of those in Plato's cave, regarding whom the chief philosophical problem was to explain that a cave was what they were in. For the condition of their imprisonment was such that there was no way of making them understand, save through actual release, that theirs was a condition of imprisonment.[11] In effect, to understand that they were imprisoned would be impossible, for the moment it were understood it would no longer hold, given the conditions alone under which understanding was regarded possible. So in a way, only the sighted understand what blindness is. There is no experience of blindness, but only the lack of the experience of sightedness, and being blind exactly disqualifies one from experiencing the lack. The truth, as Spinoza once said,[12] illuminates at once itself and falsehood. Falsehood, by implication, is simply the blank lack of illumination, rather than the experience of blackness.

'Seeing' does not, of course, refer to anything seen: it denotes nothing *in* the visual field; and this is true in general for modal terms. So we do not learn their meaning as we learn the meaning (on the implied theory) of terms which *do* denote elements in the field. And yet we learn the meaning of 'seeing' by seeing things in the visual field, or in general the meaning of modal terms by actualizing the mode in question. Let us say that our understanding of modal concepts is in this respect *existential*. That is, these are concepts we master only through *undergoing* what they denote. Modal incapacity, accordingly, is a limit on existence. We need not, of course, exist in all the modes available to us. A man kept in the dark his whole life through has not understood 'red' any better than the blind. He has a talent which external circumstance has prevented him from using and hence from knowing that he has it. Intermediate between his case and the case of someone who happens merely not to have encountered a specific color, is that the latter, while he may not understand the term which refers to that color, at least finds the concept of *seeing* that color intelligible, for he has after all seen colors. Hume supposed that in special circumstances I might be able in fact to imagine a color I had not actually experienced – by filling in a gap in a continuous color-band[13] – but the differences I am interested in are those between modalities rather than between the elements in a field which a given modality opens one up to. There is a difference between a defective (or a merely unexercised) gift and a deficiency consisting in not having that gift to begin with. Thus there is a difference between being unable to detect very high sounds, or colors like ultra-violet and infra-red, on the one hand, and being unable, say, to see or to smell on the other.

Suppose the norm-defining R were such that possession of the sense of smell were a positive abnormality. Imagine then encountering someone who possessed this gift. He would almost certainly strike us as having *uncanny* cognitive powers. Standing in the vestibule he would know immediately – 'by sniffing' – that there was lamb for supper, or that the house had been painted, or that his host had not bathed. He could tell that something was burning without actually seeing smoke! And of course he would always be right. For we could check up on him. We could in a sense know what he knew, but we could not understand *how* he knew it. Indeed the normal suspiciousness would lead us to suppose that he had 'inside' information: the butcher had told him what had been ordered, the painter had let slip that he had been there, *he had been spying*. Or we wait for a Holmesian deduction, based upon 'elementary' clues *he* happened to notice. But of course he does not know what he does know deductively, or inferentially: smelling paint or cooking lamb or fetid flesh is as directly cognitive as seeing is. And how is he to explain what smelling *is* (*we* can draw air in through our nostrils). A blind friend thought that seeing consists in having the outlines of things picked out on one's eyeballs, and assimilated blindness to numbness in confusing sight with touch. *He*, of course, could confirm by touch a great many of the things I, on the basis of sight, claimed to be true: that some piece of fruit was ripe, that something was soft, that a box lay in his path. In this regard he stood to me in something like the relationship I have imagined we would stand in were we normal and the odor-receptive man were positively abnormal. And not only – which is the point I am concerned to make – is there modal nescience, but the terms which refer to objects *we* can know as well as (albeit it through a different mode than) he must mean something different. Modal deprivation affects *the entire vocabulary of experience*, and it is in this respect that the blind live in different worlds from ours, and the totally abnormal would live in a *totally* different world.

It has been objected, against such views as these, that if a blind man understands how to use color terms in sentences, then he understands these terms, understands 'red' as well as we. Presupposed in such an argument, of course, is the theory that meaning and use are one. Thus if a blind man grasped the analogies between visual and thermal terms, for example, then he would be said to understand color terms with sufficient mastery. Red, for example, is spread all over surfaces, the way warmth is.[14] But I think that explaining this similarity to a blind man would only compound his confusion. Imagine trying to understand what, in addition to being warm, a surface *is* all over itself when it is also warm. Surfaces cannot at once be all over red and all over green, nor all over warm and all over cold: so how can they be all over red and warm? Where is the *space* even for two such seemingly exclusive properties? Mrs Stanley, a Jackson, Michigan, housewife who could tell colors by feel, reports in terms inaccessible to *my* understanding: 'The light colors are smoother or thinner or lighter in weight. The dark colors are thicker or rougher or heavier. Red, blue, and green just feel like red, blue, and green.'[15] And the maddening question is *how* red, blue, and green *feel*? My *eyes* cannot tell me this.

To be sure, there may be a common grammar for modal terms, and the blind may plausibly grasp that the term 'sight' plays a role and fills a structure parallel to that of a term like 'feeling'; and he may infer as well that terms like 'red' correspond to such terms as 'warm' (or 'blaring' to cite Locke's famous blind man). But understanding the family to which the terms belong does not entail understanding the terms themselves, and my argument is that such terms as 'sees red' are terms a man *must instantiate himself*[16] as a necessary condition for finding them intelligible. In fact there is evidence available to support the claim that unless a man has instantiated a modal term, he sometimes cannot even find it intelligible that the term can be instantiated. We may illustrate this from the topic of the imagination.

A philosophical example, used over and over again in seventeenth-century writings, concerned not an inability but a difficulty in imagining, or being certain one had imagined, a thousand-sided figure, in contrast with imagining a three-sided figure;[17] whereas we in fact understand the concept of a regular chiliagon as well as we understand the concept of a regular triangle. The illustration was meant to enforce a distinction between images and ideas, hence imagination and understanding, and to a degree it echoes a famous invidiousness drawn by the Eleatics between reason and sense. Nevertheless, it is hardly surprising that I should encounter the difficulty, since I encounter it even in drawing, or in recognizing a drawing of a regular chiliagon, whereas a glance informs me that the drawing before me is a triangle. So the difficulty is invariant to a distinction we may draw between pencil-picturing and mental-picturing. There are those, however, who cannot acknowledge the latter difference simply because mental picturing is unintelligible to them. One of Galton's correspondents, in response to a question concerning mental (specifically memory) images, attempted to reject the question as based upon some 'initial fallacy', which consisted in taking literally what was 'only a figure of speech'.[18] A comparable if more sophisticated response along exactly the same lines has been advanced by Gilbert Ryle in his chapter on the imagination in *The Concept of Mind*, viz. that reference to mental picturing is a miscarriage of common usage.[19] Nevertheless, there is empirical evidence, derived from the science of encephalography,[20] that certain persons *do not in fact* think pictorially, and (while the conjecture is at this point merely that) this constitutes some evidence that such writers as Galton's critic and Ryle do not instantiate the predicate 'pictures a triangle' in the literal sense picture-thinkers (like myself) find purely descriptive.[21] And so they find merely metaphorical, when not 'misleading', the language of imagination, much as the blind finds the language of vision to be a metaphor for the tactile.

IV

That there should be modes of cognition and hence avenues for basic understanding other than those which compose our *de facto* repertoires is intelligible, even if what it is to actualize such modes is unintelligible in existential terms. So one can imagine that there are aspects of the world to which we are opaque, although we can give no *genuine* content to these. A man can imagine that ultra-violet looks like deep purple, or can imagine (if he is negatively abnormal relative to our repertoire) that smelling consists in having the outlines of forms picked out on the nasal membranes. But this is a sense of 'imagine' which is synonymous with 'falsely believe' – as when the queen imagines that there are burglars in the dairy – and has nothing to do with that impotency of the imagination the classical empiricists had in mind when they claimed that we could imagine *compound* ideas, instances under which we had not experienced, but not *simple* ideas uncaused by instances of themselves.[22] It is a haunting thought that there might in fact be fields and modes we know nothing of, faces of the world which lie undetected and undetectable to such as ourselves, as are the colors of stones to the blindworm who responds only to their heat. It is surely this which is the major philosophical incentive in taking hallucinogenic drugs and provides the major promise of the mystical experience. Mystics are notorious for their incapacity literally to describe what they experience or how, and for whatever it may be worth in reducing the unintelligibility of their claims, we may observe that the unintelligibility is intelligible as such if we reflect upon exactly parallel difficulties which arise when we seek to communicate to those negatively abnormal relative to ourselves, or when we seek to understand the positively abnormal relative to repertoires we have exemplified. At either stage in communication, the language which is literal under one mode must appear metaphorical or rubbish to one who lacks that mode.

Now I mean to claim that just the same incomprehensions face us when confronted by a *mode of action* regarding which we are basically impotent. Indeed, we may observe this as having already been established if we consider imagination as an action, in that sense of the term that Hume had in mind when he speaks of 'raising an idea in the fancy',[23] and which Ryle is only the latest to regard as a misuse of the term in question. But a more tractable because more overt example might be any positively abnormal basic action (see St Augustine), or any normal basic action from the optics of the negatively abnormal: the paralytic, say. He can, let us suppose, lift his arm *by* doing something, e.g. swinging his body so his arm goes up, or activating a mechanism which is battery-powered and lifts his arm like a crane, or merely by picking his limp arm up with a string attached by pulleys to his feet. But in each of these cases he operates externally upon his arm, and achieves at best a mediated success. He sees the normally gifted *raise their arms* without any of the gear which mediates between himself and his arm, and might, in perfect analogy to the odor-insensate in the examples above, want to know *how* – meaning *by what hidden mechanism* – the normal raise their arms, when the fact is that normality here is defined through the absence of a mediating mechanism between their arms and themselves. There is, for the normal, *no* answer to the question of what *steps* they take to raise their arms: raising their arms is something done without steps; or *it* is a first step in the achievement of mediated successes. He does not understand not merely in the sense that understanding for him is structured by a model which has no application, but because he lives differently in his body from the normal, has never himself instantiated the description of basic action for arm-raising. Of course, it is not as though he had a *null* repertoire: there has to be *something* he does directly. But it will not especially help by saying we move our arms the way he moves his toe, say. That would be like the man with the gift of smell saying that he can tell 'the way we can when we see'. This merely deepens the mysteriousness of the claim. The best it does is to emphasize that it is intelligible to make such claims, even though the claim itself is con-strained to be unintelligible to those who lack the appropriate gifts.

I believe the fatality of gifts runs very deeply, so deeply, indeed, that when an action or a cognition lies outside one's repertoire, one cannot seriously even *try* to have the experience which alone is the necessary condition for understanding. Indeed, lacking understanding is exactly what makes trying itself unintelligible. Of course, there is that sense of 'trying' according to which a man may be held capable of trying *anything*: he may not succeed, but he at least 'can always try'. But my argument here will be that we can only try to do what we *can* do, what we are not basically impotent to do. An analogical but perhaps not otherwise helpful claim would be that for at least certain proposi-tions, one can believe them only if one is not incapable of knowing them to be true. It is said that a man might believe *anything*, that belief is not objectively determined the way in which knowledge is, so that being *right* is not presupposed by a belief. Well, what would it be for a blind man to believe that the object he touches is red? He could, of course, believe that the object is 'red' in some use or sense of the term other than the use or sense the term has for the sighted in describing the colors they recognize. He could believe that it is red in the sense, say, of giving off a certain buzz when placed before a spectroscope, or that it would solicit the noise 'red' when placed before non-blind English-speaking honest informants who are asked what color it is. But otherwise he lacks the concept required to form the belief, and so is impotent to believe *this* proposition. So though the proposition itself is 'credible', we must not confuse the claim that any *proposition* can be believed with the claim that *anyone* can believe any proposition. We cannot believe propositions we cannot, as it were, *form*. If, as I have argued, believing is representing, then there are modes of representation inaccessible save outside a man's repertoire, and hence there are beliefs that *he* cannot have. But let us concentrate on impotency of *effort*.

The question has rather more philosophical importance than might first appear, for there are philosophical theories to the effect that the word 'can' – and hence the concept of power – in such sentences as '*m can do b*' – may plausibly be parsed as '*m* will do *b* if he *tries*'. The contrapositive of this, incidentally (adjusting for tense) is this: 'If *m* has not moved his arm, then he has not *tried*.' It is perhaps this which gives hope to the paralytic, and encourages him to believe that he has somehow not made sufficient effort, when it is my argument that he cannot make any effort in consequence of his being paralyzed. Hence his is not a *moral* failure, if the latter implies *can* and this is ruled out in his case. But it is not here that the philosophical importance of paraphrasing 'can' into 'will. . .if tries', presumably without loss of meaning, lies. For since all that the latter appears to refer to are overt performances, or performances together with outcomes, the concepts yield to epistemologically more accessible and presumably less compromising notions than those of powers and incapacities which *I* have held are denoted by 'can' in the relevant sense. But then if 'try' in fact presupposes exactly this notion of 'can', any gain in philosophical perspicuity is illusory, for the question is whether *m can* try. And to say 'he will if he tries. . .' just engenders an infinite regression, as we shall see.

There is, Austin wrote,[24] some plausibility ('plausibility but no more') in the tendered paraphrase. For if '*m* can. . .' is equivalent in truth to '*m* will. . .if *m* tries', then it must be false if *m* tries and fails (That it is trivially true in case *m* never tries is perhaps less vexing, since it is a commonplace *malheur* of material implication.) For it seems plain that a man might insist on ability in the face of failure, even continued failure, and often a later try which does succeed vindicates a retrospective inference to '*m* could' when in fact *m* tried and failed. Or he might do so assuming all relevant conditions *constant*: the fact that I shall have tried and succeeded in analyzing basic actions does not mean that I *could* have done so twenty years ago: for I may have developed in philosophical ability and the subject itself became more clearly structured in the interim. But, making adjustments in these background assumptions, is there not perhaps more than mere plausibility to the suggested analysis?

It has been proposed that '*m* can do *b*' might submit to a philosophical reformulation in which reference to powers were translated out, if it were parsed thus:

> There is something *x*, such that if *m* tried *x*, then *m* would do *b*.[25]

This permits 'can' to stand in the fact of failure, if, for example, *m* tried *y* and *y* were other than *x*, collapsing only if there is no value of *x* for *m* to have tried. The pitfalls of material implication no doubt require a more fastidiously tooled formula, and a distinction plainly has to be drawn between a man not trying anything and there being nothing *x* for him to try, but there is little point in pursuing these lines if, as I believe, the resultant formula would at best provide an analysis of the 'can' of mediated actions. For the difference I am insisting upon is, so to speak, between a variable which has no values – there being nothing to try – and there being no variable to take values – there being no *room* for trying. And this is just the difference between the models of mediated and of basic action.

How, in the suggested formula, are we to understand trying? I expect it must be appreciated as *doing x* with the intention that *b* happen, and that the formula must best be read as follows:

> There is something *x* such that, if *m* did *x*, then *m* would do *b*.

Here, the occurrence of *b* crowns the doing of *x* with success, as the non-occurrence of *b* crowns it (if that is the term) with failure. But doing *x* is invariant as between success and failure, it being up to the universe, so to speak, whether *b* takes place or not. Thus I may in this sense try to phone S. This consists in dialing S's number. *I* do the same whether I reach S or not, but my reaching him or not then depends upon matters beyond my immediate control: upon whether he is in, the lines are working, and the rest. It will always be true, however, that I *tried*, whether I succeeded or failed, *trying* being a redescription of doing in the light of what one meant to accomplish. And to read 'can' in these terms merely means that there is a road to success, such that were I to have taken *that* road, I would by appropriate stages have reached my intended destination. This is less a matter of saying that *I* can do something than that something can be done; less a description of me than of the world. And hence a characterization of the mediated action. But with *basic* action there *is* nothing x, not because there are no means, no route available through the absence of which b cannot be done, but because if there were one and it were taken, the result would not be a basic action. The only *way* to do b as a basic action is – to do b itself. And hence trying and doing are one. And hence if you cannot do, you cannot try.

It is a philosophical curiosity that, with basic actions, there is no room for failure. They are logically immune to failure in the respect that there is nothing other than themselves through which they are done. The curiosity of the fact is partly due to the rather striking echoes, more than once noted, which this sets up with a correspondent claim in the theory of knowledge that basic cognitions are immune to failure, or are 'incorrigible'. And the reason is more or less the same, that there is nothing through which I know that s if I know that s directly, hence there is no piece of cognition invariant as to the difference between success and failure, to which I may always retreat in the latter's light.[26] Or, as we might put it, there is no room for cognitive effort here, no room for attempting to know something through something else, e.g. through finding evidence. For basic cognition is non-evidential.

It may, nevertheless, appear paradoxical to say that we cannot try to perform a basic action, and I should like, before drawing out the philosophical implications I believe are sustained by my theses, to attempt to reduce this paradoxicality by a few degrees at least. There *is* a sense of 'trying' in which a man may try to perform basic actions, but this is more an adverbial form, parasitic thus upon an original verb, than a verb in its own right, descriptive of an action of the sort the formula just rejected must require. A man may, for example, try to move his arm in the sense that there are obstacles or impediments to free movement. A man may have himself bound tightly in order to prove his liberating dexterities, and in order to satisfy himself that the bonds are *tight enough*, he may try to move his arms. But here trying consists exactly in *moving his arms* – against the confining chains. So moving his arms is not the outcome of an episode of trying: trying, rather, just is moving one's arms to see how far one can move them. So trying here entails doing exactly what trying itself consists in, in marked contrast to the case where a man may try to move a heavy stone, which certainly does not entail that he moves *it*. Moving one's arms freely is just another modality of the same basic action as moving one's arms restrainedly, or *effortfully*. If there is a metaphysical respect in which basic actions as such are free, that is, purely spontaneous – a thesis I have not as yet paused to ponder – this is so in a sense which contrasts markedly with any adverbial sense of 'free'. For the latter consistently alternates with 'unfree'. If basic actions *as such* were either free or unfree in the metaphysical sense, their existence (or occurrence) would be neutral to any thesis of determinism. But my point only is that the sense of 'trying' which is appropriate here, and which may give rise to the sense of paradox, entails doing, so that there is no trying *without* doing.

Analogously, a man may see with difficulty, either because of external conditions like poor light or internal conditions like myopia, but in either case the injunction makes sense that he *try* to see, for he can after all see – seeing with effort *is* seeing. But the blind cannot even make the effort. And this holds across the entire repertoire of basic modalities a person is excluded from by the absence of a gift. But the analogies may be drawn by this time by anyone who has appreciated the structures we have developed. So let us ponder some heuristic cases.

(1) I am a normal person who, participating in an experiment, has taken a drug known to render one gradually, though temporarily, paralyzed, inducing, as it were, an interim negative abnormality. From time to time I am asked to move my arm, to test the drug's progress, and I find that it has become increasingly difficult to move it: as though it were increasingly resistant to my efforts: as though it were made of *another substance than mine*. And now the drug has taken its full effect, and I cannot move my arm when asked. I am now asked to *try*. But what am I to do? I suppose I may make an effort which consists in moving what muscles remain under the sway of my will, say in the shoulders. But this is trying in the sense in which, by doing (flexing my shoulder-muscles), my arm might move. Which is a confession of basic impotency, for the possibility of failure implies that I have entered the space of mediated action.

(2) A friend supposes it would be nice to be able to retract and extend his finger-nails as a cat does. A devotee of positive thinking, he thinks that all we need to do is try *hard* enough. Well, in what will trying consist? I suppose he can shake his finger violently, or tense his finger-muscles, or send a prayer in the direction of his finger-tips. These may be construed perhaps as magical efforts to be *transformed into a cat-like creature* – like a man who tries to go back to Imperial Rome by wearing togas and praying in classical Latin; but this would be like a blind man undertaking an operation in the hopes that it will restore his sight. And the formula for this, perhaps, is doing something through which one will be able to perform basic actions or have basic cognitions. Which incidentally does not eliminate the 'can' since it must appear in the translation itself. But otherwise, it is not trying but trying's parody

(3) I am a normal man, asked to move a normal stone, which I do by the routine strategems of stress and strain. I am now told that this is not what was meant: I was being asked, rather, to move the stone 'the way I move my arm'. How am I to comply with this challenge? The challenger asks me to try. Well, my view of the matter is that though I can *do* things I might *call* trying, these will be matters of a piece with what was called trying in cases (1) and (2), viz. it will be a matter of either mediated effort (and who knows what causal routes there may be to moving stones?) or else of self-transformation. And what is interesting is that I stand at much the same remove from the stone here as I did from my arm and my ambitious friend stands from his finger-nails in those two cases. Which means, not unsurprisingly but surely interestingly, that when I cannot move my arms or nails or *whatever* as a basic action, I am separated from these by the same dense, impenetrable barriers of nothingness that separate me from mere *stones*. But the importance of *this* observation lies in the fact that if it is correct, *I* am ontologically alien to whatever lies outside my repertoire of basic action. The *limits* of my repertoire are *my* limits or better, are the limits of *me*.

v

Picture at this juncture the aspiring telekineticist. He confronts some suitably crass object, say a commonplace, unspiritualized hat. He means to fill the space between himself and it by will, and claims thus that he is trying to move that hat, a claim radically discrepant with the immediate image which comes to mind of a man trying to move a hat, viz. by manhandling, or otherwise wrestling with an abnormally heavy or embarrassingly tight homburg. Our ordinary advice to him would be: place your hand against it and *shove*. Odd advice, like telling a man in our society to be sure to wear clothes when he goes out: hardly needed, one would think.

This man, however, finds such advice laughably inapposite. *He* means to move the hat 'the way he moves his arm'. Well, how does he think he does move his arm? By some discharge of psychic energy across whatever gap sunders him from his body? Since, after all, he is no more sundered from the hat than he is (on such a theory) from his arm, it seems genuinely possible that a hat might be moved thus, and merely puzzling that psychic energy cannot be coaxed across wider gaps. For by rendering his arm a theoretically alien entity, the hat is at least no *more* alien in principle but only in degree. To him we reply that if he in fact so much as moved his arm the way he hopes to move his hat, the *deep* thesis he holds would be established, and the moving of a hat would be a minor extension of dark, amazing powers. If psychic energy can raise arms, why indeed not hats? But in fact this is not the way we raise arms: between ourselves and our arms there is no distance across which a mediating link of force is required, like gravity between sun and planet, to act. To pun against another concept of action, *basic* action is not at a distance. I am in this respect at one with my arm, seamlessly,[27] when I move it as a basic action. The telekineticist has swallowed for basic actions the structure of mediated ones, which lends immediate plausibility to his project at the price of making his view of how he moves his arm at logical odds with the facts.

So were he to move his hat the way he *in fact* moves his arm, it would be false to see him and the hat facing one another across the gap he sees psychic energy as hopefully bridging: rather, there would be a single entity, a hat-man with some striking topological properties: a sort of hole between one of his parts and the rest (like West Germany *cum* Berlin). So it would not be your common-or-garden hat he would move. It would belong to the man not in the sense of legally trans-ferable haberdashery, but in the obscure metaphysical respect in which my pains and my obsessions are intransferably mine. It would not be so much his hat that he would be moving as *himself*.

Now it is philosophically obligatory at least to attempt an unraveling of the dark genitive intended here by *his* arm or *his* hat. So let us replace the misguided telekineticist, hopelessly normal in his repertoire, with a hat-man, positively abnormal in the respect that he may raise his hat the way he raises his arm. Coming upon his abnormality for the first time, we would observe the unsettling sight of a seemingly routine hat describe a polite arc and then fit accurately back upon the head, the man's hands being otherwise occupied. (It would be common decency for the man to let his hand follow the hat, so that to outward, unoffended appearances his hat-raising were an unremarkable mediated action.) As matters stand, we could no more tolerate this discrepancy with normal behavior than those deprived of the sense of smell could, save as a last resort, tolerate with conceptual equanimity the cognitive feats of one correspondingly gifted. Just as they, in order to make intelligible to themselves the fact that he should know such things, must attempt to normalize his cognitions by hypothesizing intervening inferential routes of the sort *we* would use in order to reach seemingly identical goals, so must we suspect an intervening mechanism surreptitiously activated: a column of air, wires, hidden springs, or one or another of ultimately banal implementations of the cheap prestidigitator. That he should do it directly, as a basic action, is exactly unintelligible to the ungifted, and they must finally acquiesce in this unintelligibility so long as they remain negatively abnormal when the norm is defined through him.

Now there may, of course, as is true when we raise our arms, be a causal mechanism through which the hat gets caused to rise when the hat-man raises his hat. Finding this would indeed make it physiologically intelligible how the hat gets raised, just as we know with a fair measure of confidence how arms are caused to rise when normal agents raise them as basic actions. But this still leaves the way in which *he* raises his hat as unintelligible as it was before. For certainly he does not raise it by activating this causal mechanism as a 'means'. Any more than, as we saw, we raise our arms by activating at one end what at the other is a risen arm. So the physiological illumination leaves us quite as blank as ever regarding what we are entitled, by our prior argument, to regard as the action side of a process identical with the physiological side we have come to understand. Unless, indeed, we ourselves are hat-men, *living* those actions as *he* does: as we live those of our actions which are basic; and know how they are done through the fact that we have done their like, at one with our hats as we are with our arms when moving those is compassed in our repertoires of basic powers.

I claim that I am one with what I stand at no distance from, which means only that that of my body with which I perform basic actions is me. My repertoire defines in this respect the limits of my self, although unfortunately this is not one with the limits of my *entire* body, as Augustine gloomily remarked. Much takes place in my body which is not identical with any action done by me, although (if Augustine is right) this would not have been the case with Adam, whose congruence with his body was entire. I am (certain parts of) my body in the sense of identity I introduced earlier, in speaking of a basic action as identical with a causal process terminating in the event which we describe from the vantage-point of the optics of action as having been *done*. One then with my arm, I am one with a crass object insofar as my arm is a crass object. But just at this point we encounter a philosophical problem which may serve to lighten the seeming pretentiousness of this claim.

My arm, as a crass object, lies in the world of crass objects of which my hat is a convenient exemplar. Nobody, and least of all I, may move my hat unless by causing it (transeuntly) to move. Everyone is basically impotent, barring philosophical freaks like the hat-man, to move my hat in any mode save mediatedly. My arm, though ontologically co-located with other crass objects, is again something everyone, myself included, may move transeuntly, again by mediated action. Others, however, are basically impotent to move my arm for the following philosophical reason: I can move my arm, am thus identical with my arm, and others are not identical with *me*. So privacy, as the philosophical concept which licenses the genitive alluded to above, has application after all to crass objects (Other Bodies) as to non-crass ones (Other Minds), in that only *I* am basically potent to move my arm. For no one who is distinct from me can, on the principle of the transitivity of identity, be one with my arm, and his basic impotency to move it is thus unmysteriously accounted for through the fact that he is not me and hence not it.

Of course, part of my body with which I am not identical might, after all, be identical with some person other than me. But then I would be impotent, basically, to act with those parts of my body (if they moved, it would be as though I were *possessed*). Suppose one of your arms (and hence part of you) were attached to my shoulder.[28] And suppose one of my arms (hence part of me) is attached to yours. Each of us has an alien object attached at a part of his body which normal persons are one with in their own cases. Until we found one another, in an Aristophanic encounter, we would be afflicted with strange 'involuntary' movements of 'our' arms, which medical science was unable to fathom. But now we may co-operate in harmony. I can learn to use *my* arm, adventitiously attached to *your* shoulder, in concert with *your* arm, adventitiously attached to mine. So we could button our shirts as an exercise of abnormal teamwork, the work being done by distinct selves, though an uninformed outsider coming into the tiring room would see nothing out of the ordinary. It would look like two plain men, each buttoning his shirt with his own good arms, rather than two monsters metaphysically locked by mutual accident like Siamese twins!

You cannot, then, move my arm as a basic action (for it would then not be my arm). You only can cause it to move, or cause me to move it. And my arm, however crass, is exactly as private to me as are my thoughts, however refined their substance, are alleged to be in those philosophical views of thought which give rise to the Problem of Other Minds. We cannot think one another's thoughts nor feel one another's feelings because we are not one another. Indeed, the distinction between what belongs to action and what does not cuts at right angles across whatever distinction philosophers may wish to make, if they wish to make any, between the mental and the physical.

Consider, for example, imagination, taken once more in that contested sense of standing in a certain relationship to a mental picture. Now imagining in this sense may be counted paradigmatically a mental event, and may even be taken as constituting a class of thoughts, when we reflect that in the classical empiricists at least, thoughts were often exactly assimilated to imagination.[29] But just as we mark a distinction between our arm rising without our raising it, on the one hand, and our arm rising because we (directly) raise it, on the other, so may we mark the exact distinction in the topic of imagination between a mental picture occurring when *we* do not make it occur as an action, and a mental picture occurring which we *do* directly make happen as a basic action. I can, without difficulty, and without doing anything through which it happens, imagine – 'form the image of' – (say) the Niccolini–Cowper *Madonna*. Or St Ivo. But the image of the Niccolini–Cowper *Madonna* (or St Ivo) may also spontaneously appear in my imagination, *without* this being an action of mine. A man may be *haunted* by an image *he* has not spontaneously produced, but which happens to possess him, much in the way in which a diseased arm, which goes up contrary to our will, may be said to possess us.

So imagination may be an action, quite as much as raising an arm is. And in fact, if it may be so construed, an interesting consequence follows. For picturing, now, is an activity of the mind which is either something we do, or something which happens to us, the difference between the two being as ultimately discernible as I have argued to be the difference between raising our arm and our arm rising. But if picturing is in this regard an action, there need be no mental pictures: only the activity of picturing as such. Descartes thought of imagination as being related to a mental picture much in that relationship of contemplation in which I stand to the tempera reality of the Niccolini-Cowper *Madonna* in the National Gallery when I gaze upon that sublime work. But this may radically misconstrue what imagination consists in if it is an action consisting in picturing. But then one problem which has obsessed epistemologists may be resolved. Pictures-of-*x* might in principle so resemble their originals that it becomes logically impossible to tell, from viewing what they have in common (form), which one is real and which is merely imagined, and hence whether *I* am imagining something or actually perceiving it. Philosophers, such as Hume and Russell, have sought always to find some differentiating feature, e.g. 'vivacity' which the one has and the other lacks, a largely unavailing strategy. But if imagining is an action, there should be no more or greater difficulty in telling whether I am doing it than there is with whether I am raising my arm or it is rising without me.[30]

But let us not wander in the weed-patches of Skepticism. The reason I cannot imagine your imaginings is not that imagination is mental but that you are you and I am I. Not even God could imagine your imaginings. Not unless you and God were one. But then he could not imagine my imaginings, because then God and I, hence *you* and I, would be one.

VI

I once heard an anecdote about J. L. Austin. Pestered by a student who insisted, in the face of whatever argument Austin's ingenuity could furnish to the contrary, that we can move backwards in time, Austin struck at last like a Zen viper and told the student to *go ahead and try,* leaving him to claw at the void. The awareness of vacuity which comes when one realizes that it is the first step that cannot be taken is what I mean by the experience of basic impotency. It is a descriptive concept we master existentially by encountering spaces into which we cannot live, and whose unintelligibility partially defines the boundaries of our powers. *We* are what is given, and we discover what are our limits by our radical incapacity to try to go beyond them. Our basic powers are ourselves, and the limits of the will are also the limits on the sort of understanding I have endeavored to characterize here.

Descriptive negativity and the limits of our repertoires of powers are central concepts for the philosophical theory of action. I shall now attempt to develop our comprehension of them in connection with things we can understand but apparently could not understand as *actions,* namely our beliefs and our feelings.

6

FEELINGS AND FORBEARANCES

I

We commonly are credited with a degree of control over the expression of a feeling we are presumed not to have over the feeling itself. Processes of socialization in part consist in mastering the show of emotion by inhibition or modification, so that, constancy of feeling presupposed, Homeric heroes weep operatically where cowboys affect stony, calvinistical faces. Regarding the feelings themselves, however, we hold ourselves impotent to have feelings we lack or to annihilate feelings we have, except by external means; so that feeling cannot be a basic action. A man may know about himself that driving at high speeds will cause him to feel fear; that watching women disrobe will cause him to feel sexual excitement; that witnessing a military parade will cause in him feelings of hatred or of pride. So having this knowledge means that having these feelings lies indirectly within his power. And similarly, avoiding these feelings is within his power by avoiding those conditions under which the feelings are predictably caused. But, Hume writes, 'It is certain that we can naturally no more change our sentiments than the motion of the heavens.'[1] The context makes it clear that Hume meant: change our sentiments or the motion of the heavens 'by an act of will'. It is sensible to suppose that altering the motion of the heavens might lie within the repertoire of a being whose powers and composition differ vastly from our own. *How* he might do this as a basic action escapes the limits of our understanding, as must anything positively abnormal relative to us (though we know, of course, how one might *cause* the heavens' motion to change). It is not plain, though we can cause feelings in ourselves, that it is even sensible to suppose someone might have that sort of power in his repertoire, and *fear*, say, as a basic action. That is, we find that it is intelligible to suppose someone might have cognitive or performative powers which *we*, restricted as we are, find unintelligible as such. So perhaps do we find *feelings* which lie outside our affective repertoires to be unintelligible. But the proposal that someone might feel at will, even if the

145

feeling itself is one we existentially understand, is itself, I claim, not a coherent proposal. It is a matter of brute fact that we are able to perform basic actions with our arms but not our pancreases; that we are made with arms and legs rather than as gelatinous spheroids whose repertoire consists exclusively in dimpling one's surfaces like golf-balls; that we are basically unable to shift the paths of planets slyly, to confound the parallactic expectations of astronomers. And it is perhaps a brute fact as well that we have the gamut of feelings we do have and not feelings of another order we cannot any better imagine than scrooges, who are emotional cripples, can imagine compassion or love. But is it a brute fact that we cannot feel at will, cannot 'the way we raise our arms' have what feelings we might wish? I believe the powers in question are *conceptually* excluded; and, concerned now with the limits of the will, I can hardly forbear wondering why. If feeling cannot be a basic action, events occur which cannot be directly done, and *any* agent (including God) is confined by horizons of power which are not the horizons of reality itself.

A comparable and possibly instructive limit holds with regard to *beliefs*. This is reflected in the fact that, in asking *why* a man believes something, we do not expect in answer a citation of motive, viz. something he expects to achieve *through* his believing the things in question, and because of which he believes. Certainly there are cases where *saying* one believes something answers to a purpose, e.g. aborting the incendiary fate of the heretic. What I find inconceivable rather is that a man might say 'in his heart' that he believes when he also believes he so says 'in order not to be burnt'. I employ a dramatic case because the man who is in it must be under immense prudential pressures, and if he is unable to yield, this dramatizes the impotency to believe something for a reason, however urgent or compelling a reason. One may wish to believe something, thus, for the great peace of mind it would bring him, and find he has this peace of mind when he has the belief; but he cannot suppose that he has the belief only because he wanted the peace of mind, though this may have motivated his seeking out grounds for the belief: it is with reference to the grounds and not the motive that he justifies a belief which is admittedly 'worth having' if it can be had decently.[2]

If believing for a reason is conceptually ruled out, believing cannot be a first step in a mediated action, that is, an action where something is brought about through believing. This holds even in the case where a man believes something only because he wants to, with nothing ulterior intended, for 'because I want to' is a motive in the sense that believing satisfies it. And so would it be a motive were a man to try to believe something for no reason other than to see if he could do so. With its overtones of caprice, 'for no reason' is enough of a reason to disqualify believing because of it, if the applicability of reasons is inconsistent with the fact of belief. So if we could believe at will, this would be a singularly useless gift, as we could do nothing 'by means' of the believing. But this is not yet an argument. There might be basic actions which could play no role in mediated action, as there might be basic cognitions which were inert so far as facilitation of further cognition were concerned. And believing might be one of these.

James, whose celebrated concept of the *will to believe* suggests a measure of doxastic voluntariness, was concerned only with beliefs one already has, the question being whether one has a right to go on holding them when there is no evidence for their being true; or no better evidence for their being true than false. At such junctures, he appears to say, considerations of motive seem relevant: I have a right to hold a belief if it seems to me that the world would go unendurably flat were I to give it up, the suggestion being that continuing to believe is now a matter of resolve. In fact I think we can no more stop than start believing something at will, but I also think we never quite exhaust the evidence in favor of holding a belief, even in the cases which absorbed James. I shall rather perversely hold that the mere fact that one *has* a belief is already, at least for the believer, *some* evidence in its favor, and hence one can justify believing something by appealing to the fact that one believes it, all the more so when, as James's case requires, there really is no compelling contrary evidence. This sounds as though every belief entails, through the psychological fact of its being had, an ontological argument in favor of its truth. I want to spell out the basis for this claim, hoping that by doing so I can explain why belief as an action is ruled out.

There is a theory, a version of which is exemplified in the Third Meditation of Descartes, that having the belief in the existence of God is a mark of grace, there being no way save through the mediation of grace that believing in God can be accounted for: it is a gift. Those who reject the belief will hardly look benignly upon this explanation of its provenance, but the intuition implicitly invoked by the theory is largely sound, since it links the *causes* of having a belief with the conditions which make the belief true. It is a commonplace that he who believes that *s* believes that *s* is true. But I think it ought equally to be a commonplace that he who believes that *s* is committed to believe that his believing is explained with reference to whatever makes the belief a true one. In view of such a theory, believing that *s* is already some evidence that *s* is true. Or it is so for the believer himself. We appreciate that unlike knowledge, belief does not entail the truth of its own content, so that the falsity of *s* is plainly consistent with the belief that *s* is true. But this is not to take the point of view of the believer, who cannot coherently combine the belief that *s* with the belief that *s* is false. Neither can he combine the belief that *s* with the belief that the causes of his believing *s* are independent of whatever makes *s* true. Of course a man may not be able, frequently is unable to explain how in fact he came by his beliefs. I claim only that he cannot hold himself justified in believing that *s* if he believes either that *s* is false or that his believing *s* is to be explained with reference to something having nothing to do with *s*'s being true. This is so even if the man credits himself with a special clairvoyancy, an uncanny knack of being blindly right. He must believe that he is wired into the causal stream of the universe in a way which makes for surprising doxastic successes. None of this, to repeat, means that beliefs cannot flow into one's soul from a source having nothing to do with the sources for the belief's truth, but only that the believer cannot believe this consistently with holding his beliefs to begin with.

So from the believer's point of view, beliefs of his are not merely inert furnishing of his soul, isolated introspectable interior decorations. Beliefs spontaneously refer their holder beyond themselves to what makes them true, and equally locate him in a causal history originating in the latter. But it is exactly this which is inconsistent with believing that we have our beliefs through the fact that we enacted them. For this explanation of our believing is wholly independent, save in cases too rare to affect the general point, of anything which might make for the truth of the beliefs in question. To believe that we have 'done' our beliefs is radically incoherent with the point of having beliefs to begin with. For how shall a man trust his beliefs to guide him through life – or to provide him reasons for further action – if he believes that he has the beliefs only because he decided to have them? For he now knows that his having the beliefs he has, has nothing to do with their being true, if they are true.

Counter-instances abound. A major class of these may be voided by adopting the possibility that the same thing which causes us to believe *s* causes that to happen which also makes *s* true, without the latter causing the belief itself. But it is of less importance to enact the ritual task of philosophical journeymanship – plugging holes in leaking conceptual vessels – than to ponder whether *this* vessel will serve our purpose even if sound. For it may be said that from these considerations it will not follow that beliefs cannot be basic actions, done only because we have decided upon which beliefs to have. All that might follow is that *in our own case* we could not both have a belief and believe we have it only because we 'did' it; but that we cannot believe the latter does not make it true. We know from the records of psychoanalysis any number of cases where men hold beliefs for reasons having nothing to do with whatever might make their beliefs true, if they were by chance in fact to be true; and this might always be the case with any belief *we* hold. Still, this remains an external possibility, not an internal one, for the moment we internalize such a belief we must sustain a curious paralysis, the belief to which it applies being automatically neutralized as a possible guide to action. To believe it; and to continue to believe it true is to discount the psychoanalytical explanation as uniquely determinative of the fact that we hold it. It is an interesting logical fact regarding beliefs that there should be a difference, which is connected with the role they play in practice, between the beliefs I may hold about my own beliefs, and the beliefs I hold about the beliefs of others. It has been pointed out quite often, for example, that while I cannot say that I believe what is false, I can without breath of paradox say that *another* believes what is false. Similarly, I can believe that your beliefs may be explained in ways which constrain nothing so far as concerns their truth, while I cannot believe this of my own. So *your* beliefs are not available to me for ontological arguments.

Thus the objection is less to be met than merely granted: all my beliefs may *be* actions. But under penalty of a radical alienation as believer and agent, I cannot believe this true of them. Each in his own case cannot believe other than that his beliefs are caused in ways which excludes their having been done for a reason or done for no reason at all. Whatever final differences between causes and purposes there may be, there is a sense in which causes are entailed while purposes are rejected by the concept of belief, at least from the viewpoint of the believer. And for the moment, only that viewpoint is required. It will,

I hope, give us the argument we need for the parallel case of feelings, to which I now proceed.

Of course, a great many of our feelings have a certain cognitive dimension, and are had only against a background of beliefs, so that if the beliefs they presuppose are altered, it is difficult to suppose that the feelings themselves can endure. I cannot continue to fear what I believed was a snake when I discover it to have been a piece of rope instead, and if I do continue to fear, it clearly could not have been the *snake* I feared in the first place, for the 'snake' has been sublated. I cannot rejoice at having found a piece of silver when what I took as silver is but mother-of-pearl; and if my rejoicing survives this discovery, it cannot have been due to any fact in which the fortuitous possession of silver is a component, for that component has evaporated in the harsh light of reality.[3] And these considerations are general. So to some degree, our basic impotency with regard to our feelings may be logically derivative from our basic impotency regarding the beliefs they presuppose. But I do not think this can be the entire story.

Nor do I think the rest of the story is to be told by reference to certain trivial facts of usage. Let us undertake to imagine a man who claims that he can 'go into fear' whenever he wishes to, directly, without doing anything which causes himself to be afraid. Let us, indeed, imagine that he does it every five minutes, for about two minutes of uninterrupted phobic anxiety: after all, I can raise my arm every five minutes. I don't believe we would credit his claim, and I don't think that this is because the fear is hidden. True, I can hardly doubt the claim of a man who vaunts a positive abnormality in which his face may be blotched by him whenever he wishes: the coming and going of blotches is impressive evidence that his claim is true. Suppose the abnormal fearer indeed manifests the regularly associated signs of fear: shallow breathing, perspiring palms, shudders, and the rest? I think I would be unpersuaded even so that *fear* was being expressed. Rather, I would be inclined to suppose something like this: that he was positively abnormal in respect of breathing, perspiration, and the like, and perhaps thinks that fear consists in these. Or something *linguistically* odd: for in the end we want to say something Wittgensteinian, or at least Malcolmian to the effect that if he thinks he can 'go into fear' basically, he does not have *our* concept of fear. Whatever it is he is going into, it is not *fear* Fear is one of a class of states of ourselves such that we know we are in them only because we *find* we are in them. And even when we cause ourselves to be afraid, when the taste of death appears in our mouths, *we* are powerless to remove it until *it* goes away. This is true when we in fact know what will cause it to go away and are not impotent to co-opt the causes in question. But is this a *mere* fact of usage?[4] If a man were to say that, similarly, weather is something we find ourselves in, that rain comes when *it* will, and there is nothing we can do about it directly, though some day men may be, at least causally, no longer impotent regarding the rain, would we say that he is reporting a mere fact of usage? That a man who said, for whatever weird reasons, that we might not be basically impotent regarding the rain, would simply not have 'our concept' of rain? *Is* it part of our concept of rain that we are basically impotent regarding it? Anyway, I would like to have a better answer than this. Embarrassment, sadness, pride, joy, fear, and the like seem to be states of ourselves over which we have very little direct power, and this acknowledged impotency is *reflected*, perhaps, in language. But I would not want to try then to derive this impotency from the language. So I still press for something deeper.

II

Let us for the moment endorse our intuitions, and agree that whatever may be the reason, the will is (which means that *we* are) impotent to *do* our feelings: we are in *their* grip (slaves to passion), and though we may dissolve them or induce them through causes, and so attain a degree of indirect mastery over them, we are, basically impotent to have or not to have them. And let us further agree that we have, in addition to our causal powers over our feelings, some power over their expression. With the former power, which is emotional engineering, I shall be very little concerned here, crucial as this topic is in terms of human felicity: how magnificent were we able to tune out anxiety and depression! With the latter power I shall be rather more concerned, however little *human* utility the matter may afford. Conceptually, I think, it is the richer case.

Consider, then, *laughter* as the expression of an emotion. There is perhaps no emotion of which laughter is the *unique* expression, and in some of its occurrences laughter is not the expression of any emotion at all. Let us, indeed, mark out two cases in which it is not. The first is where laughter is caused, or where *m* is caused to laugh, through mechanical means – tickling, perhaps, or exposure to nitrous oxide. Laughter here is like tears induced by onions or tear gas; or erections caused by aphrodisiacs. Such tears plainly do not express sadness, and the erection does not express desire (but the absence of it and perhaps a *desire* to desire), and neither does the laughter express a feeling, say merriment. I distinguish this case from that in which tears, laughter, or the erection are caused through causing a feeling they may express: through telling bad news, or a joke, or administering a philtre (which actually causes a feeling of love). The mechanical or chemical means I have in mind circumvent the mediation of feeling, and their effect is thence not the expression of one. The second case is where a man is positively abnormal, and able to laugh (or weep, or erect) at will. Here there is perhaps a cause of his laughing, as there may, in basic actions generally, be causes of whatever is done; but these causes do not cause *him* to laugh, which is what makes this a basic action. Though nothing causes him to laugh (or whatever), neither is his laughter here the expression of an emotion.

It will be obvious enough that these cases admit of quite different explanatory patterns, which the invariant presence of laughter (tears, erections) perhaps disguises. It will be useful to run through a number of cases from this point of view.

(1) Something causes *m* to laugh, but not through causing in *m* a feeling which the laughter expresses. The cause may have been inhalation of nitrous oxide. Whatever the case, while we can explain, through reference to causes, the fact of his laughing, we cannot legitimately ask what he is laughing *at*. His laughter is an absolute condition, much as a flushed face is an absolute condition when caused, say, by an excess of cognac. He is not *blushing* in such a case, hence not blushing *at* anything. 'Why are you laughing?', which seeks an explanation through reference to an *object* of laughter, is logically inappropriate when *m* is caused to laugh but his laughter expresses no feeling. It is not, I am certain, that the concept of cause *as such* rules out explanation by reference to an object. It is that there is no object when there is no feeling which the laughter expresses. It is caused by something which is not the object of its effect, the effect having no object because it is not the expression of a feeling. I shall call this *mechanical laughter*.

(2) This case is just like the one considered above, with the following difference only. It is *m* himself who *causes himself to laugh* by deliberately sniffing nitrous oxide, and his laughing may accordingly be regarded

here as a candidate for a non-basic action. Thus, he may *want* to laugh. And he may know that sniffing nitrous oxide causes him to laugh. And he applies this knowledge *by* sniffing, and the laughter follows as effect. Once more, his laughter expresses no feeling. And it has, accordingly, no object. Perhaps *m* causes himself to laugh because he thinks it is good for the circulation, just as Hobbes sang thinking it good for the wind. There is method in his laughter, and his behavior has a *purpose*. But that does not give it an object. Indeed, typically, when laughter expresses an *emotion*, it has *no* purpose. It is almost as though purpose and passion are at logical odds.

(3) Let us now introduce an admittedly contrived case where *m* causes himself to laugh, in the mechanical manner of (1) and (2), but where *in a sense* the laughter has an object, even though it expresses no feeling. Imagine that *m* 'lacks a sense of humor', that is, nothing makes him laugh. But *m* recognizes that others laugh at certain things, say jokes. Hearing jokes never causes him to laugh, and he feels ostracized by his seeming dourness. So he learns inductively which are the jokes, and whenever he hears one in appropriate company, he steals a whiff from a private cartridge of nitrous oxide. The mechanics are as they were before. But it is only in a sense that the laughter has an object. For *m* is able to say what he wants to 'laugh at', viz. *that* joke. But what in truth occurs is this: *m* laughs in the presence of the joke, not at the joke. A precondition for laughing *at* the joke is that *it* cause him to laugh by causing him to feel whatever merriment laughter is the conventional expression of. Since there is no feeling in *m*'s case, the joke is really not the object of his laughter at all. He indeed has a purpose in laughing, namely 'not to appear dour'. But this of course exactly presupposes that he *is* dour, and it is this absence of *affect* which *m*'s mechanical laughter conceals, however successfully. I am not clear that *m* necessarily even understands his condition as numbness of the soul, never having really *been* amused: his is virtually a case of blindness (hence *sense* of humor), of the sort we have been at pains to elaborate in the preceding chapter. He is a logically co-specific with those who never feel sad, or never feel sexual desire, and may resort to clumsy mechanical equivalents of their normally expected expressions. If *sneezing* were the expression of an emotion (and who knows if in some affectively abnormal persons it is not one?), pepper would be a comparable crutch, inducing, as it does, mechanical ka-choos. Of course, it is not clear that there is other than mechanical sneezing.

(4) The clumsiness of *m* under case (3) is no problem for the man we may consider here, who is able to laugh as a basic action, and so need not revert to causes in order to conceal his numbness. This does not, however, make his laughter genuine, if we reserve genuineness for the expression of an emotion. So when it has an object, it will be in the crippled sense of (3): laughter at an object which is, so to speak, the occasion rather than the cause, for an *object* of laughter is a cause of laughter only when it acts through an emotion which it causes, and which the laughter then expresses. This plainly alters the quality of laughter in the eyes of someone who may know the conditions of its production. A woman may be the object of an erotic manifestation, but if she is not the *cause* of it, that is, by causing the feeling it is the normal expression of, she may not respond to it at all, or at least may respond to it differently. I think we would feel uneasy about a person who was able to produce tears 'at' something which did not cause the feeling tears are an expression of: he would be a curiously empty and to that degree inhuman sort of individual. We might blame him for heartlessness, if affect *were* the sort of thing men were able to do something about, but we can blame him in fact only for hypocrisy, for shedding crocodile tears, for *pretending* to express feelings he lacks. Indeed, we blame him for laughing or weeping *for some purpose*. Having a reason for laughter (or for anything which is normally read as the expression of a feeling) is reprehensible. For it is in effect pretending to be something other than one is, since the *feeling* in question is not had: it is a form of lying. And given the importance in the economy of human life which is ordinarily attached to feelings (sentiments), traducements of this order are properly regarded as manipulative (though there are 'white lies' here as elsewhere). They are manipulative because he in whose presence the manifestation occurs, if he is the *object* of the manifestation, must also be the cause: and so stands in a very complicated position of responsibility regarding one whose feelings he takes it are being expressed. But of course he is in no position of responsibility if, though the object, he is not the cause (through a feeling) of the laughter (or whatever). So he is being manipulated, is being put in a false position, when the behavior does not express a feeling *he* has caused.

(5) Let us conclude with the normal case of laughter, which is normal through the fact that it has an object, and its object causes the feeling it expresses. Asked *why* he is laughing, the laugher refers to that in the

object which causes the *feeling*. To be sure, this does not quite answer the further question of why he is expressing the feeling so caused. After all, it is normal to express a feeling one has, unless there is reason not to. So, as we shall see, the question does not arise unless there is reason for it to arise, that is, unless there is reason for a man *not* to laugh, or not to express a feeling which has been caused. Roughly, he laughed when he was caused to be amused by something, because he did not inhibit the laughter.

I shall revert to the case of genuine laughter in a moment, for it brings forward some matters which logically pertain to our topic. But I think we are now in a somewhat better position to explicate, or at least reduce a further portion of the obscurity of the question of our basic impotency regarding feelings.

In case (5), which is the normal case, *m* laughs *at* what he is amused *by*, the object of the laughter coinciding with the object of the feeling. And so again, a person weeps *at* whatever *makes* him sad. Briefly, expressions of feelings have exactly the objects which the feelings they express have. But I have argued that laughter is the expression of a feeling when and only when its object is the feeling's *cause*. Cause and object coincide in genuine laughter (and in the general case of expressions).

By 'object', of course, one means *intentional* object, the *content* of the emotion, viz. what a man feels sad or happy or amused *about*. It is only latterly, I believe, that the representational nature of feelings has begun to be philosophically appreciated; and, as in the case of belief, where there is no belief which is not the belief *of* (or better, belief *that*) something, so, in at least a great many cases (all those cases where, in fact, the expression of a feeling has an object), there is no feeling which is not the feeling 'of' something, e.g. of the bitterness of life, or the crookedness of destiny, or the beauty of a woman; and as a man can hardly be in a believing way without being able to say *what* he believes, neither, in these cases, can he be in a feeling way without being able to say what the feeling is about: what its object and hence what its cause must be. Indeed, since the object is the cause, to be ignorant of the cause is to be ignorant of the object, and hence to be ignorant of the feeling. Let me make it plain that it does *not* follow that a man need be able to say *why* something amuses him, or saddens or even arouses or frightens him. Men have odd tastes and odder responses; a child may be frightened by feathers or a man aroused by shoes, and to *explain* why *these* things should cause *those* feelings would exact a toll in psychoanalytical therapy. But even so, these things do cause those feelings.

If cause and object were identical, and if the object, read as intentional object, were *part* of the feeling in question – just in the way in which the content of a belief is part of the belief – then it would be curiously true that the feeling is logically dependent upon its cause. Since, moreover, one cannot identify the feeling without identifying the object and hence the cause, we appear to have encountered what Miss Anscombe[5] has written of as *mental* causation, a kind of causation she regards as radically distinct from whatever cases the Humean analysis is meant to fit. I think this is very largely true, at a certain gross level of analysis. If what frightens me is a face appearing at the window, the latter is the *content* of the fear; and if it is the cause of it as well, then the effect cannot logically be identified save with logical reference to its cause. But it was an essential part of the Humean program that cause and effect are logically distinguishable, which is why, of course, he refused to suppose they *could* be connected by necessity. Here, by contrast, there is a necessary connection, since if it had a different content (cause), it would be a different feeling. Before abandoning Hume, however, we had better make a few careful distinctions.

It is possible, in cases of mental causation, to sustain illusions of a certain sort. Suppose I am made suddenly happy by reading that the number of my lottery ticket is the winning number. It is clearly correct to say that seeing that mine was the winning number is what caused me to be happy. But suppose I misread the number. Then it can hardly be true that seeing that the winning number is mine is what caused me to feel happy, since the winning number *isn't* mine. Or again, I laugh at a man who has fallen on the ice, and it turns out that no man really fell, but that I was taken in by a shadow of some sort, which is not a matter to laugh at, only causing *me* to laugh because I perceived it as something it was not. Now, since I would have laughed whether a man fell or not, so long as I *believed* a man fell, it is difficult to say that the laughter is logically dependent upon its cause when the cause is taken to be the *actual* event of a man falling. Indeed, we encounter here exactly a case of what we identified as *causal independence*!

What we have, then, is perhaps this. Let F be a feeling and *o* be the content or object of the feeling, so that F(*o*) represents such things as 'happy that my number is the winning number', or 'frightened by the face in the window', and the like. Here, of course, o represents what he who has the feeling considers to be some state of affairs in the world, which we may call e if o bears the $(+)$ semantical value appropriate to it, and this is conferred by e. Now in what we term the *epistemologically normal case*, when e makes o $(+)$, e causes F(o). But of course, F(o) is logically independent of e, though not logically independent of o, since, after all, o stands to F(o) as part to whole. But now, I think, the man of whom 'F(o)' is true cannot both be in that state of feeling which it describes, and at the same time believe that o is $(-)$. To be frightened by something is to believe that the content of our fright is $(+)$. And I believe, indeed, that there is a kind of entailment, not from o being $(-)$ to F(o) being $(-)$ – for then there would be none of the illusions we have been concerned with – but from the *belief* that o is $(-)$ to F(o) being $(-)$. In other words, when we believe that what we are frightened at is not really there, we (allowing for visceral lag) stop being frightened. The reason o may be counted a (mental) cause is that o is really believed to be what he who has the feeling represents it as being, namely e; as it is in the epistemologically normal case.

This begins to explain why we are impotent regarding feelings. We are so because, in order to have a feeling, we must believe that it is caused; and even if we ourselves *are* the cause, e.g. even if I laugh at something I do, or am frightened by something I do, still, the feeling is caused and cannot be believed by me to be a basic action of mine. Does this mean that it *cannot* be one? The answer, I think is that even if it can be, *we* cannot believe it can. We cannot, in part because of the structure of the concept of feeling, as we have analyzed it, and partly because of our impotency regarding beliefs. And I think this is borne out by our ordinary practice in dealing with feelings. With a frightened child, for example, we often try to change the child's beliefs, convincing him, for instance, that there is really nothing to fear. And often this is so with sadness as well: we endeavor to tell the sad person things which modify the belief he has, e.g. not that the belief is false that the cat is dead, but that 'it is for the best'. And so on.

Ultimately more important, I think, we may count ourselves entitled to regard mental causation as no great exception to Humean causation after all. In the case considered, e is the cause and the effect is F(o); which is to say that the event e causes men to be frightened by o – it being believed by them, of course, that e *is* $(=)$ o. But the law in question covers, as the effect in question, the feeling *with* its content (or 'mental cause' if you wish). Obviously, the laws have perhaps rather complex riders and qualifiers attached to them, and reference to beliefs is logically co-implicated in ascribing feelings to people. But for all that, it is not surprising that more or less the same things make most of us happy or sad or frightened, and that the laws which govern our feelings are more or less a definition of our common humanity.

It may be objected that in at least certain conspicuous cases, this analysis will not work. It will not because the feelings in these cases have no objects and their expressions accordingly have none either. Pain must certainly be the paradigm of this. Crying is paradigmatically an expression of pain, and while we may in a sense say that the pain itself is what the crying is about, the pain is not about something because pains have no objects. They have, of course, causes, but these cannot be identical with their objects if they have none. But neither, in the crucial cases, are there beliefs upon which physical suffering depends: it is absolute in this respect, and no alteration in belief will dissolve it. The Buddha, who sought to dissolve suffering by radically altering our beliefs regarding the world, cannot seriously have had in mind *physical* suffering. *This* does not depend upon the non-illusoriness of the world: it is as insistent to quite the same degree whether it happens to be due to illusory causes or to be uncaused. Nevertheless, we are commonly regarded as incapable of *hurting* at will: of 'going into pain' whenever we wish, as a basic action. As before, we are commonly accorded a degree of control over the *expression* of pain. Part of socialization, as with expression generally, here consists in learning whether and how to express pain, which is the germ of truth in Wittgenstein's claim that the sentence 'I am in pain' is less a statement than a sophisticated wince. Or we are allowed to have this socialization up to certain limits of toleration, the trespassing of which is the pleasure of the sadist, whose objective is to increase pain to the point where the victim loses control, or loses his power to control, and hence loses his dignity as a human being, since human dignity is defined through the internalization of social norms. His aim is degradation and humiliation, unlike the routine torture-master, just concerned to do his job; and causing shame is an ingredient in the sadist's pleasure, since the victim is reduced to his bodily reflexes, futilely seeking through his writhes and groans a relieving stimulus. Shame is caused when the victim is rendered thus incontinent, no longer able to apply to himself the socialized inhibitions upon emissions of whatever sort, and so stands indecent in his own eyes. Sadism, and masochism as well, are cognitively complex appetites, for the masochist is not merely a consumer of pain, but of pain administered in degrading fashion, his circumstance and behavior then underscoring his own worthlessness. And I suppose a sense of his own worthlessness must drive the sadist as well: he *needs* to degrade others in order to upgrade himself; and these are correctly regarded as sides of the same pathological coin.

I am not, to return to the objection, as certain as I should like to be of how it is to be dealt with, except to point out that pain lies on a borderline between feeling ('sentiment') and sensation, and *sensations* have traditionally been reckoned beyond the power of the will in philosophy. It was precisely because of our impotency in their regard that Descartes, for example, supposes that they are indices to reality, with the implications reality has of constraint upon our powers.[6] Now sensations serve as signals at a highly automatic level of behavior. Thus pain is a signal to withdraw a hand, for example, and the latter is reflexive and virtually mechanical under principles of feedback (withdrawing a hand is not an *expression* of pain). Kinaesthetic sensations are signals the response to which is to adjust one's equilibrium, and so forth. So in general sensations are as it were wired into a complex system in which (felicitously) we have very little power of direct entry. Now to the extent that we may believe the explanation of a sensation to be that we *did* it, to that extent does it lose its status as a signal, even though the system itself is so constructed that the body will respond as though it were. Nevertheless, it would be stupid of *us* to respond as though it were, e.g. if a man *does* his pains, he would be insane to go to the doctor for their remission, or to treat them as though they were signals. That his body continues to behave as though they were does not mean that he needs to, and the fact that he does them locates them outside the system of true signals – they are false alarms – and hence, if sensations are signals, these are not really sensations. And so *sensations* cannot be done. To be sure, there would be no way to tell, from the thing itself, whether it were a sensation in this sense or not: one would have only the knowledge that it was done to distinguish it from its fellows, its neutrality between these two being exactly the basis upon which sensations were travestied as sense-data in the disastrous history of epistemology. Of course, most of us have no such knowledge, and moreover act as though we did not do our pains, since disjoint patterns of *rational* action are called for depending upon whether or not they are done. If pain is a sensation, insulation from its cause is the rational course. If it is an action, then the rational course is desisting. Now the point of this all is that if it is a sensation, pain has causes and not objects, and so is not a feeling. And at this point it becomes delicate to determine whether cries and groans are really in that case expressions or only symptoms. That we should be expected to control these socially is consistent with the latter: flatulence, for example, is a symptom but hardly an expression of over-indulgence.

There are other, less tractable cases which may be treated much along these lines, which we encounter as we ascend from physical pain, which seems clearly to be a form of signal, to more abstract suffering, as in depression and anxiety. I have specifically in mind those cases where a person is not depressed *by* or anxious *about* some specific thing, and hence where the feeling lacks an object as its presumed cause. These feelings tinge the whole world for the sufferer (so does confidence or free-floating ebullience), but must be distinguished, even so, from philosophical postures in which depression or anxiety have as objects the whole of reality, taken as absurd or empty or fearful. Hence they verge more on true pathology than on Continental metaphysics, and become logically open to straightforward medical treatment (tranquilizers, shock, surgery, and the like), rather than to the rectification of beliefs, as in deep therapy: since they presuppose no beliefs.

III

I do not wish to probe the topic of laughter so deeply that this chapter assumes the shape of a discourse on *le rire*, but the example has logical merits enough to justify continuing with it. The expression '*m* does something which causes him(self) to laugh' is ambiguous as between mechanical and genuine laughter. Thus he may satisfy the description through taking nitrous oxide, or through going to a predictably amusing comedy. Only in the latter case is the laughter genuine through the fact that it expresses a feeling which its object causes; mechanical laughter – *les cris aigus des filles chatouillées* – expresses none, at least not as such, and has no object. Only the former, I believe, exemplifies what Hobbes defined as 'sudden glory', and I believe the differences run deep.

Imagine being a normally risible person, watching a favorite comedian, say Fields. *Cognoscenti* know more or less exactly where in Fields's films they will laugh, so suppose you are on the threshold of a comic crux. Suppose, moreover, that nitrous oxide could be handled with a great deal more precision than it in fact admits of, and that an expert gasser releases unbeknownst a dose which makes you laugh at just the moment one would laugh *at* something done by Fields. Instead of the appreciative expression of amusement, an alien laugh forces itself through one, issuing into public hahas which in an important sense *are not yours*. Fellow *cognoscenti* will not notice the difference, the mechanical laughter having been timed to coincide with the expected genuine laughter. Now suppose this goes on, all through the film: what will be one's mental state? Well, I am not certain I could sit through an entire séance of this, but in the event I did, then my apprehension would be nightmarish that I would be seized by laughter at the *wrong moment*. Wild laughter when there is no conspicuous object to occasion it would cast me like a lunatic into the surrounding consciousness. Such nightmares are not of course restricted to laughter. Imagine, as we have done before, one's arm going up without one lifting it, as though again it were not yours, describing a salute when everyone is supposed to be at rigid attention. If this happened so much as once, there would be the fear it might happen again. Mechanical behavior which has the outward form of genuine behavior would drive a man mad, even if in fact it occurred when and only when genuine behavior was appropriate.

The nightmarishness stems only in part from the lack of direct control on the erstwhile agent's part. It stems equally from the fact that arm-rises and laughter are socialized to a high degree, such socialization in fact presupposing the control in question. So lack of control places one in an awkward social position, virtually the position of the infant or the idiot or the incontinent. It is because he appears controllable but in fact is not, since the behavior is mechanical, that he who is 'possessed' by it must feel adrift in events, subject to sanctions automatically applied to violations of social expectations. Or he will feel this if he has sufficiently internalized the pattern of sanctions and expectation to know what others must think and applies them to himself. So the nightmarishness does not arise in connection with, say, nosebleeding, which is not highly socialized, if at all, since the presuppositions of control over nosebleeding are satisfied, if at all, by the positively abnormal only. No sanctions attach to nosebleeding at the wrong time because there is no *right* time at which nosebleeding is either tolerated or *de rigueur*. There are doubtless socially awkward times for nosebleeding, e.g. at one's wedding, but people, save those with ruthlessly psychosomatical biases, are prepared to understand.

Mechanical laughter, like nosebleeding, is not susceptible to easy socialization, even though it is against the background of socialized laughter that we must appreciate those who, as in our case (3), must resort to mechanical substitutes since they cannot laugh when it is expected that they will. A man with subtle control over his nitrous oxide cartridge may very well laugh his way unnoticed through a dinner party, providing his inductive knowledge of the 'right places to laugh' is all it should be. But at its best, it is mechanical behavior masquerading as genuine behavior, and, as no feeling is being expressed, it is by way of making good some spiritual deficiency.

By introducing socialization, we have established a bridgehead for moving from metaphysical to social questions, much in the manner in we did so in connection with reactions in Chapter 4. I shall use questions of socialization, however, merely as a refractive device, for the better appreciation of the inner structure of expressions as a class. Genuine laughter is associated with two distinct offences: laughing when laughter is inapplicable, and not laughing when it is enjoined. For the moment, let us consider only the former. Such laughter is subject to a variety of rules. Socialization specifies when and how to express feelings, but also (to a degree) what are to be regarded as suitable objects, and hence causes, of laughter. So the social laughter will be one who has mastered a fairly complicated etiquette. He knows where laughter is enjoined, and where tolerated and where prohibited. He is apt to be amused by what amuses those who have internalized the same rules as he has, and to express his amusement in more or less the same modes and intensities. Obviously there are deviations and variations, both between and within societies as defined by sets of rules, and consistently with what we have said, we expect nothing less where the feelings are concerned. Bushmen find wildly amusing the death movements of wounded beasts, while we, where not indifferent, will respond to these with pity and queasiness. But even should one of our co-culturals be so inhumane as to respond as a bushman would, we would suppose him sufficiently considerate – or at least sufficiently prudent – not to express his amuse-ment with the bushman's easy spontaneity. We expect he would apply those controls whose abeyance automatically brings down sanctions, viz. to be explicitly *labelled* 'inhumane'. If a person laughs, then, where this exhibits breach of taste, the best moral light to put on it is that he is ignorant of the rules governing expression where offense is predictable. The anticipated sanctions of society must be expected to serve as automatic abortants of public hilarity when even private, or unexpressed hilarity is morally impugnable, e.g. where a man is amused by what his co-culturals have learnt to be horrified by: say, fatal accidents.

Consider, in this context, a man who knows the rules but laughs anyway, though he knows he should not, and faces, perhaps because he is indifferent or engaged in an oblique form of civil disobedience, sanctions he is indifferent to or believes ought to be repealed. So his laughter has a kind of purpose, or at least qualifies as an action of sorts. Even so, I believe, we would hesitate to say flatly that he had laughed 'on purpose'. And this brings us back to our theoretical concerns. Intuitively, I believe, we lack a degree of freedom in connection with laughing which is unhesitatingly accorded us with moving an arm. We can move an arm, discounting irrelevant external impediments, more or less whenever we want. But we do not in the same way seem able to *laugh* whenever we want. Perhaps this is because genuine laughter expresses an emotion, and we have argued that we cannot have a feeling whenever we want, that we are dependent upon external causes for being in this state or that, relative to which expression is relevant. I shall now attempt to characterize this restriction, which brings the concept of laughing into logical conflict with the concept of doing something on purpose, but which nevertheless acknowledges the aspect under which we want to say that a man who *has* laughed under the conditions just described has *somehow* performed an action.

Let me propose, then, what we might designate a First Law of Expression. If F is a feeling and e is the natural expression of F, then whenever m has F, m expresses F through e unless he has reason to inhibit e, that is to say, has reason not to express F. Beings who have feelings but are unsocialized never in this sense have reasons to inhibit expression, and may be supposed then to express whatever feelings they may have. They are spontaneous.

I employ the studied phrase 'natural expression' to mark a class of expressions in regard to which socialization enters only as an inhibiting factor. Hence I suppose them to be universal and pre-social, as tail-wagging is amongst dogs or purring amongst cats. Smiles and laughter, as pre- or non-verbal displays are almost certainly continuous between men and monkeys, and though the range of causes and objects of these primitive displays may be immeasurably amplified and varied by socialization, the mode of expression is largely unsocialized. I mean to contrast 'natural expressions' with those which, though they have objects coincident with the feelings they express, are also socially differentiated. Thus I express gratitude by means of flowers, affection by means of valentines, contempt by spitting rudely, concern by pointed inquiries (to show that I am interested more than to gather information). With these, we move further and further away from spontaneity and enter the territory of taste, tact, and conventions. Such expressions are gestures meant to be read *as* the messengers of sentiments and feelings; and often they serve merely as a kind of currency of politeness, with no backing in affect at all. These have no remarkable philosophical interest here, and seem to be only actions, in a way in which natural expressions are not. For the First Law – what we might think of as the Principle of Spontaneity – strongly suggests that expression is not an action whereas inhibition of expression is.

We do not laugh on purpose, but we can inhibit laughing on purpose, we can *forbear* laughing. So by an act of will, so to speak, a man may abort what under permissive or natural circumstances would automatically issue into public space as expression. When a man exercises control over expression, we might say that what he *does* is *not* laugh. Obviously, the negative predication holds of anyone throughout his sober moments, but in general it is not something we *do* unless there is an expression to abort through forbearancy. So, when a man laughs in spite of the rules, which he knows and defies, the thing we accuse him of is *not* not-laughing, of *not* forbearing.

The double negative here is striking. As is typically the case, not-not-*x* is equivalent to *x*: nothing would sound more like a record of a man laughing than a record of a man not not-laughing. But the equivalence holds in only one direction: whereas it is true that a man who not-not-laughs, laughs, the equivalence does not run the other way. For the question of forbearance only arises where there is reason to inhibit expression and the individual knows this. Otherwise, he is simply conforming to the First Law of Expression, and is not performing a defiant act of not forbearing: as is the case with most of us when we laugh under socially permissive circumstances. So the negativity here at least appears to be unexpungeable: as though with the appearance of forbearance in our scheme, *l'Être* first becomes infected with *le Néant*.

We might pause at this auspicious moment, and reflect on negativity. It has always been a problem how ontology is to deal with nihility, whether it is to be treated, so to speak, as the absence of something or the presence of nothing; or again, in an ontology of events, whether we are to countenance negative events as those in which nothing succeeds in happening, in contrast with something failing to take place. In some way, it is the former view, involving a very cautious endorsement of a kind of positive or real negativity, that we appear to be verging upon when we treat forbearance as we have, namely where it is not-laughing which a man *does* when he forbears to laugh. And, in the case of the complex event, it again sounds almost as though *not* doing *not*-laughing is what the defiant laughter is charged with, when he offends against the properties. We had better, then, proceed with circumspection. Even our formal intuitions regarding negativity are feeble, and until we have strengthened them somewhat, precipitous ontological stake-claiming in the name of Nothingness is severely counter-indicated.

IV

The case of expression is in some degree anomalous if we suppose that our powers here are largely restricted to forbearance from expression, so that the main sense in which we act, when we express, is to forbear from forbearance, letting the Principle of Spontaneity do its work. It is anomalous in the sense that we ordinarily cannot be said to forbear from *a* if we are impotent in the first place to *do a*, so that a man can hardly desist from raising an arm he is to begin with powerless to raise. So if it can be established that I lack the power to do *a*, the fact that I do *not* do *a* does not ordinarily count in my moral credit or discredit, for not doing *a* is not something I can be said to have *done*. In fact, of course, something like this is to be found in the common wisdom regarding the feelings and their normal expressions. A man gets no moral credit for self-control when there is nothing *to* control. No one can seriously be considered chaste who is sexually incapable;[7] or anaesthetic; no one who is by nature phlegmatic gets credit for keeping his temper in rein; nobody, to take a Socratic example of weakness of will, who is blind can claim the moral strength not to 'feast his eyes' on a pile of decaying corpses.[8] The *virtues*, in classical moral theory, seem typically to have this pattern. Thrift, for example, is a virtue only the funded may exercise, in that you can hardly desist from squandering money you do not have. More guardedly, honesty is a virtue available only to those capable of deception, the lobotomized being incapable of falsehood, not counting then as morally honest through the fact that they say only what the truth is, like thermometers.[9] The logic of virtue – and forbearance seems presupposed by most exercises of virtue – merits some comment.

Consider the negative attribution that I did not pass yesterday into Nirvana. True as an attribution, it at least does not ascribe to me something *I* did. For I did not forbear transferring to the nirvanic state, since such transfer does not lie within my present powers. Such powers are commonly assigned to, and indeed they define, the Boddhisattva. But the case of the Boddhisattva raises some curious questions regarding the logical presumption that forbearancy presupposes power: that *does not* presupposes *can*. Mahayana doctrine teaches that in contrast with the selfish conduct of the Elders, who sought salvation for themselves alone, passing one at a time into Nirvana, the Boddhisattva postpones his own bliss until *all* may be saved. This is the theory of the Greater Vehicle, as it is called, entailing a mass and total transfer of creaturedom. The ordinary assumption is that the Boddhisattva *can* nirvanize himself; having purified himself of karma, he is fully enlightened. The question now is whether in fact the Boddhisattva could pass into Nirvana after all. Suppose he decided to. Then surely he must be selfish, seeking his own bliss while countless others suffer. How can such a being be said to be fully enlightened? And if not fully enlightened, how has he the power to pass into Nirvana? He can only do this if he is sufficiently enlightened, and if he *is* sufficiently enlightened he cannot. We might call this the Boddhisattva Paradox, remarking *en passant* that it *logically* guarantees that *none* shall be saved *until* all are saved. The Boddhisattva Paradox is echoed in the western idea of a morally perfect being, the latter defined as so good as to be *incapable* of evil. Since it is logically inconsistent with his nature to *do* evil, he does not *forbear* and indeed he is logically impotent to forbear from evil. As with the mechanical veracity of the lobotomized, the mechanical good-doing of the morally perfect leaves us uncomfortable, since he could not do evil if he wished: good gushes forth irresistibly, but it is a bit like the mechanical purity of the emasculate.

My concern for the moment, however, is less with this than with the confirmation of an intuition that forbearance is in our power just in the case the repertoire of powers we possess includes the power to do. So in general, merely knowing that *m* has not done *a* leaves indeterminate our appraisal of *m* until we have found out whether this is because he forbore, i.e. whether he did *not-a*. I shall leave it open (for the moment) whether forbearancy is the exclusive interpretation to be given to *doing not-a*, or whether it is only one instance of the latter.

The distinction between not doing *a* and doing not-*a* finds an analogue, not surprisingly, in the theory of knowledge, where we mark a difference between *m* not knowing that *s* – which is a case of ignorance – and *m*'s knowing not-*s* – which is after all a bit of knowledge. Doubtless, if *m* knows not-*p*, it follows that *m* does not know *p*, and indeed that he cannot know *p*: for we cannot know what is false, and *p* must be false if not-*p* is true. This sounds faintly like a violation of what would have to be an analogue to our recent argument, the analogue being that *m* could not know not-*p* if he is impotent to know *p*. But he is automatically impotent to know that *p* if he knows that not-*p*: from which it then ought to follow that neither can he know not-*p*. But this is a transparent sophism. If we do not-*a*, we are of course impotent to do *a*, if this impotency is meant only to be taken as a powerlessness to do and not to do *a* at the same time, a scarcely surprising impotency since it is a logical impossibility. Were we to take this sophism seriously, we would be logically impotent to forbear through the fact that we could not simultaneously forbear and not forbear. Tedious as it is, however, the sophism yields a useful benefit. We may say that if forbearing *a* implies that a man *could do a*, we must mean: could *do a instead*. And we must in addition mean that *at the time* he will have been able to do *a*: for if he could not, then neither could he have been said to have forborne. Obviously, he could not both *do a* and do not-*a* simultaneously. But, simultaneously with doing not-*a* he has to have had the *power* to do *a* instead. This will prove an extremely useful concept in the sequel, but as it needs some antecedent refinement, I shall continue at this point to elaborate the epistemological analogue. The question now is whether there is a parallel to our thesis here, that a man can be said to know not-*p* *only* if he could have known *p* instead.

I think there is, with qualifications, such a parallel. A blind man does not know that a given ball is red. But this cannot be because he *knows* that it is not-red. And he cannot know the latter for the same reason he cannot know the former, namely, that he is impotent, or at least *basically* impotent, to know what color anything is or is not. So his impotency guarantees that he knows neither that it is red nor that it is not-red, though as a logician he might know that it is either the one or the other. Our ability to understand that 'p v not-p' is a logical truth does not entail that we have to be able to understand the disjuncts. The blind man here is like all of us in this respect, regarding the future: for there is a sense in which we are blind to the future, and though we may know that there will be a sea-battle tomorrow or there won't be, we can't know that there will be one, and we can't know that there won't. Such was Aristotle's teaching, but there is a difference, I think, which is worth remarking. It is that there is a deficiency in the blind man, which prevents him from knowing the colors of things, whereas it is not *us* to which the incapacity to know the future must be referred, but to the world. So it is not an impotency in the respect that a corresponding power is possible, but an impotency, if one persist in so regarding it, where a corresponding power is not. Nobody can know what is false, but it is not as though this were a logically remediable defect, so that we *might* come to know what is false! And nobody can know what is neither true nor false, which is what Aristotle supposed was the semantical status of singular propositions regarding the future. Were we to regard these semantical factors as entailing impotencies, then we who are not blind would be impotent, that is, incapable of knowing that a ball were blue when we in fact know that it is red. The fact is that we could have known what color it was had it been blue instead of red. So I think we must conclude that *we* are not impotent to know that p when we know that not-p, the fact that p being semantically disqualified for expressing knowledge (i.e. is not *true*) not counting as incompatible with this. We may, I think, conclude as follows. If F is a predicate such that m is not incapable of knowing that a is F on the basis of experience, then neither is m incapable of knowing that a is G, where G is any predicate antonymic with F. So, if he knows that not-p, where p is a sentence employing such a predicate F, and not-p is formed by employing an antonym of F, then m is not impotent to know that p, even though p is false, as of course it must be. So, with this restriction – and an exactly correspondent restriction must be built into the case of action – it may be argued that m knows not-p only if he is not incapable of knowing – is not cognitively impotent to know that *p*. In general, the truth of *p* is a presupposition for *m* knowing that *p*. But not a presupposition of *m* having the *power* to know! And I suppose in analogy we must say that *a* taking place is a presupposition of *m* doing *a*. But not of his having the power, of his not being impotent to do *a*.

Since the difference between not-*x*-ing and *x*-ing-not seems on superficial glance to be exhibited throughout the domain of intensional, or at any rate of quasi-intensional concepts, it is an interesting question whether the connection between power and *x*-not-ing is everywhere preserved. Consider, in this regard, belief. Belief is already anomalous in that it ordinarily will *not* follow from the fact that *m* believes not-*p* that *m* does not believe *p*. For he may very well believe *p*, believing not-*p*, since we are not immune to believing propositions which in fact are contrary or even contradictory (it does not follow that *m* believes a contradiction, viz. 'p-p' from the fact that he has contradictory beliefs). We *ought* not to believe *p* when we believe not-*p*, but as with most oughts, this one is often breached. But the reason we cannot know both *p* and not-*p* has nothing to do with us, but only with the noted presupposition of knowledge which is disqualified as such if the sentence in question is false. In the case of belief, these external restraints are inapplicable, beliefs being neutral semantically, so we may in fact believe, and so have the power to believe *p* when we believe not-*p*. But this is quite consistent with our principle, which requires only that we not be impotent to believe *p* when we believe not-*p*.

I am not certain that there are any belief impotencies as such, except as otherwise noted in Chapter 5. A blind man may believe that the ball is red, since it is not required that we *understand* what we believe, and in the most contested cases we are acknowledged by partisans at best to see through a glass darkly, and not to understand the deep articles of faith. It is not perhaps wrong, only impudent, to define faith as believing a proposition you do not comprehend. Often a man will suppose by faith that he means a belief he cannot help holding, but as we saw above, this is in a way so with all beliefs, and it does not mean that he is impotent to believe what is incompatible with his given belief. More likely, he means that in his case accumulated contrary evidence does not cause him to pass out of his belief-state into another. There is, that is to say, a kind of doxastic numbness on his part. But this does not preclude the possibility that the belief will fade, and not really be replaced with any relevant contrary: a man may grey off into a disinterested kind of agnosticism, as the issues lose their momentousness to him, the latter, a Jamesian criterion, having nothing to do with strength or weakness of evidence. Even so, he does not remain impotent to believe either of the antiposed propositions, choice between which now strikes him as tiresome.

It would be a pleasant and instructive exercise at this point to canvass a variety of intensional concepts, to see if, in fact, the close tie between negativity and power is everywhere borne out. But I think it most profitable to concentrate on one case, the causal case, where in a way we seem to get a counter-instance. We draw an important distinction between *a* not causing *b* and *a* causing not-*b*, which makes all the difference between saying that *a* is causally inoperative regarding *b*, and that *a* is casually operative, e.g. in *preventing b*: the former implies, without further determination, the absence of a causal episode whereas the latter seems unequivocally to imply the presence of one. But it would amount to a dubious claim of universal homeopathy to say that *a* causes not-*b* only if *a* is not impotent to cause *b*! This sounds very like saying that *p* entails not-*q* only providing it is not impotent to entail *q*. But in fact it is logically impossible for *p* both to entail *q* and not-*q* unless *p* itself is inconsistent; and while inconsistencies are less easily generated in the topic of causality, the claim that *a* may indifferently cause *b* and not-*b* is virtually at odds with our conception of causal independence of *b* from *a*. So though some vaguely supportive examples may be drawn from immunology and such homely antidotive measures as taking whiskey to undo the effects of whiskey, the principle seems largely unacceptable.

This, however, is because we are looking in the wrong place for it. Suppose a man dashes water on what he takes to be gunpowder, claiming credit for having prevented an explosion (= having caused a non-explosion), since the water reached it just before the flame. We may refute his claim by showing that what he dashed water on was not an explosive substance, but only something which *looked* like gunpowder. Indeed, he may be credited with having prevented something from exploding only if the thing in question was not impotent to explode. And the principle, indeed, is a general logical feature of the concept of prevention. The gods need take no preventative measures against danger to their lives, because they are immortal. Antidotes are logically irrelevant to non-toxic substances. And so forth. We may say, then, that *a* causes not-*b* only if there is something *x* such that *x* causes *b*. But this makes sense only if we refer the power to be *b* to the very thing that is not-*b*, since, if we have been right, it is only an interesting fact that it is not-*b* if it *could* be *b*. I mean, saying that it is *not* the case that *o* is *b* is by no means the same as saying that *o* is not-*b*. The latter is a negative attribute, whereas the former is just the negation of an attribute. It is not so much a characterization as a non-characterization; and not every negation is a determination. A thing, in brief, which has a negative attribute is one which is not impotent to have the correlative positive attribute under other causal auspices.

We may, I think, use this as at least a sufficient condition for individuating negative events. In other words, not-*b* is an event in *o*'s history only if *b* could be an event in *o*'s history. What happened to me last night is that I did not sleep. There are many other things of which it would be true but uncharacterizing to say that they did not happen to me last night, e.g. I did not pass into Nirvana, I did not give birth to a giraffe, I did not turn into a pillar of pistachio ice-cream, and so – endlessly – on. But these are all things I am incapable of having happen to me, and so their absences are not part of *my* life.

I shall, then, suppose there are negative events, but shall use our general principle that not-*b* is a negative event in a history of *o* only if *o* is not impotent to have *b* as an event in its history. Since there are negative events, there may be causal laws with negative events as their antecedents, e.g. laws of prevention and of prophylaxis. And so we may suppose that when we say that not-*b* happened, we mean something very different from what is involved in saying that *b* did *not* happen. The latter, indeed, is interestingly true of what it is asserted only if not-*b* is what happened. But '*b* did not happen', though entailed by 'not-*b* happened', is not equivalent to it since we may consistently say that *b* did not happen and neither did not-*b*. What is perhaps of almost equal philosophical interest is this: that it is consistent with saying that *a* caused not-*b* to happen, that *b* could have happened instead, and indeed, the latter is *entailed* by the former, since it would be *false* that *a* caused not-*b* if that in whose history not-*b* figures were impotent to have been, under a different causal dispensation, *b* instead; it must, *at the very time* it was not-*b*, have been capable of *b*!

V

Waiving consideration of whether negative events occur *other* than as embedded in actions, we may note the variety of ways in which they may occur in, or as actions.

(i) There is *direct forbearance*, where a man does not-*a* as a basic action, that is, he does not-*a* without first doing something else which causes not-*a* to happen. A simple illustration is given by an act of disobedience, where a man is told to raise his arm and he refuses. It is true that this negative event is nested in a more complicated action here, namely 'disobeying an order'. The presuppositions for success in such an action, or gesture, are saturated with the apparatus of rules and roles, which the agent in question must be supposed as having internalized: he must appreciate the concept of an order, must recognize that *this* is an order, must appreciate the concept of compliance and counter-compliancy and the differential sanctions attaching to these. It is a highly sophisticated action, but in the end, although his not raising his arm is the *means* by which this elaborate mechanism is activated and the disobedience achieved, at the heart of it lies the basic action, the *positive* production on the rebel's part of the negative event. And the same event would have been performed even were the agent *wrong* in believing he was disobeying a rule, e.g. he failed in disobeying because it was not an *order*, or was not meant for *him*: the agent did what he would have done were he to have disobeyed in fact, but the appropriate context was lacking. It is possible for the context to be present, and for him not to raise his arm, and not disobey an order, because it happens that he misread the context, not understanding that it was an order, or meant for him; and though he did not raise his arm, his arm not rising was not something he *did*. Most of the time, when my arm hangs at my side, and I am not raising it, I am not performing any action, and certainly not performing a negative one. Finally, it is not disobedience if I happen to be impotent to raise my arm and am ordered to raise it, although I might not have wanted to raise it if I could, e.g. I would have disobeyed by not raising my arm had this been in my power.

(ii) Let us complicate this case by considering a man with a curious tic, his arm just happening now and again to rise without his raising it. He is ordered to raise his arm, and means to disobey, but just at that moment his arm begins to rise through the mechanism of his wretched tic, and he reaches across and holds his arm down forcibly, *causing it to happen* that his arm does not rise. This is an action, indeed it is disobedience to a command, but it is not direct forbearancy, but a derived negative act. Imagine in general that we are impotent to forbear in certain things, and nevertheless want not to do them. The classical paradigm for this is Ulysses having himself lashed to the mast in order that he should not answer the Sirens' famously irresistible chant. Strictly speaking, of course, he *did* respond, struggling Siren-ward, but so in a way did the man's arm go up in the recent example: what he, as Ulysses, did was *arrest* a motion he *could not abort*. It counts, nevertheless, as a negative event.

(iii) Ulysses' case differs dramatically from that of his men, whose ears were plugged, by his orders as it happened. *Their* not answering the Sirens' chant is a negative event caused by Ulysses, who knew that they would be powerless not to answer it were they to hear it. This is an instance of forestalling, causing something not to happen by the expediency of inducing impotency of response. This is the favored method of those uncertain of their powers of forbearance, and may be called the Early Christian Strategy. Imagine a man haunted by the fear of Sirens, and never certain that one might not sing to him at any moment and from any direction: so he voluntarily induces auditory impotency by making himself deaf. The morality of such radical solutions, here as elsewhere, is moot, as is the individuation and duration of the negative event. Suppose, for example, there are no Sirens: will we want to say that the man who went deaf specifically in order not to answer the Sirens' call actually succeeded in his aim? Or did he fail in that through the ontological failure of Sirens? Suppose Ulysses and his men all plugged their ears when they approached what they believed was the Sirens' rock, and sailed past in self-congratulatory impunity when in fact the belief was false: those were just girls on the rocks, taking the sun. The ship's log for that day might record 'did not answer the Sirens' call' – but is that what really happened? Is that what would appear in the Ideal Chronicle of the History of the World? At best, the latter would take note of their beliefs and precautionary actions, but would be obliged to record the falsity of those beliefs and hence the futility of precaution. The only negative occurrence was the absence of the credited negative occurrence, and the absence of a negative event is obviously not a negative event in its own right. After all, if you cannot disobey an order which has not been issued, you cannot avoid a Siren that is not there. I think that we must in general insist upon these existential presuppositions. A coward who does not flee danger because he fails to perceive that there is danger, cannot be credited with having *done* the not-fleeing. The man who snubs – does not recognize – a man who he thinks is *m* when in fact it is *m'* does not really snub anyone, even if he would also have snubbed *m'* had he known it was him. And a man gets at best credit for creditable intentions who forswears killing a man who unbeknownst to him is already dead. So of the deluded Siren-shunner, we can say that it is not the case that he answered the Sirens' call – which is not the same as saying that he did not answer their call. The denial of the occurrence of a negative event is not the affirmation of the occurrence of another one.

(iv) A man who does not seriously credit that he is impotent to do not-*a* as a direct forbearance, since nobody presumably is potent to do it – like putting out a fire, say, or curing gallstones – may nevertheless do not-*a* when he does that which causes not-*a* to happen. Here his doing not-*a* is a routine non-basic or mediated action, with just the existential presupposition that he does not-*a* only in case, had he *not* done whatever caused not-*a*, *a* would have happened instead. Obviously there are aggravated epistemological problems with this, but I see no shirking them. A man who changed the tire in order that he should not have a blow-out did not cause a blow-out not to happen unless it would have happened had he not changed the tire. Much the same holds with most prophylaxis. But even when a man causes a fire to go out, the assumption is that this is attributed to him only in case the fire would not have gone out *just then* without his having caused it to go out. In general, then, *m* causes not-*a* by doing *b* only if *a* would have happened if *b* had not, everything else remaining constant. This case is at once a stimulant to and a depressant for the counterfactual imagining of untapped history, of roads not followed and options not taken.

(v) A curious case is where it is known that *b* causes *a* and *m* can do *b*. However, he does not do *b*, and so causes *a* not to happen by not causing it to happen. Imagine that it is true that all I have to do is lift my finger and.... But I forbear lifting my finger. So I derivatively forbear.... Obviously, a man may not lift his finger without this being an action, but when it is an action, the non-occurrence of...has to be counted a negative event – even though nothing happens, and the surface of history shows *not a trace* of that negative fact. Things staying the same is a curious negativity, but one we might all rather deeply appreciate if he who could blow it all to ashes by lifting a finger, forbore lifting his finger.

This catalogue of negativities could be extended, but *we* may forbear from doing so. The issues blend quickly with the casuistries of moral assessment and legal responsibilities, and negligences and omissions of various gravities emerge as important blanks in the shape of society, where I am culpable not for doing negative things but for omitting to do positive ones. For our purposes, the case which has chief interest is that of direct forbearancy, where *m* does not-*a* without doing something which causes it to happen: were not-*a* lies within his repertoire of basic powers. In the following discussion, I shall have only this case in mind. And when I speak of someone being impotent to do not-*a*, I similarly shall mean: someone *basically impotent*, not *causally* impotent.

VI

We may enjoy a degree of control over the distinctions which considerations of negativity force upon us, by distinguishing between *descriptive* negativity and *operational* negativity. They differ in just the way in which affirmation of a negative proposition differs from the denial of an affirmative one. Denial, like affirmation, is an operation upon a proposition without penetrating the content or meaning of the proposition operated upon. But *descriptive* negativity is negativity which *is* part of the content or meaning of a proposition, whatever operation may be performed upon the latter. Let us employ the majuscule N for operational, and the miniscule *n* for descriptive negativity, the latter being by way of a prefix. Thus *np* is a negative proposition, and N*np* is the denial of a negative proposition. It is best, however, to enter the proposition in order to appreciate the negative content. Suppose we permit *n* to form negative predicates, e.g. *n*-happy in such propositions as 'Jane is *n*-happy.' The sentence here has a negative truth-condition, in that *n*-happy describes the state Jane is in when she is *n*-happy. This is a far cry from N(Jane is happy), which denies a state to Jane without specifying any state in which she is. Indeed, the latter is an operation on a sentence which has only positive truth-conditions (at least) one of which it asserts not to hold. There is no doubt an inference from 'Jane is *n*-happy' to N(Jane is happy). But it does not run the other way, since the latter is consistent with N(Jane is *n*-happy), since Jane need be neither happy nor *n*-happy, at the moment untouched alike by states of felicity or infelicity, or subject to either but in fact in neither. States, in this sense, or properties in general, resemble semantical values in the sense that it is the very same subject, Jane, which is either happy or *n*-happy or neither, it being Jane which, invariantly, is in the positive or negative or neutral condition. It is doubtless this which leads to the concept of a pure subject, separable from its states and properties, since it remains itself under this sort of quasi-semantical transformation. My purpose here is not to pursue this interesting suggestion, but merely to point out that invariancy of the subject is entailed by our earlier reflection that *m* can be *n*F only on condition that he is not impotent to be F: so neither F nor *n*F can, so to speak, penetrate or form part of the essence of *m*. And this is a far cry from a *pure* subject, since at the very least the subject in question is credited if not identified with a range of powers and capacities. In any case, were *n*F to penetrate the subject, the latter would be a *different* one in the event that it were F, and the principle that the *very thing* which is *n*F is not impotent to be F, would be lost.

I have been arguing for a tight connection between descriptive negativity and potency, so perhaps we might recall that potency and impotency are descriptive concepts in their own right, and are not to be confused with such operational concepts as the modalities of possibility, impossibility, and the like. The relations between the two sets of terms is subtle. Suppose, thus, that *o* is *a*-impotent. This does not entail, though it may be entailed by a modalized sentence to the effect that it is not possible that *o* is *a*-potent. The latter sentence I should interpret to mean that the *sentence* '*o* is *a*-potent' is logically contradictory, which would mean that in some sense '*a*' and '*o*' are inconsistent. We do not ordinarily mean to imply, by '*o* is *a*-impotent', that '*o* is *a*-potent' is logically contradictory; and so the former cannot mean that it is not possible that *o* is *a*-potent, or that it is necessary that *o* not be *a*-potent. I shall suppose that '*o* is *a*-impotent' is consistent with 'It is possible that *o* is *a*-potent' – an innocuous enough concession in view of the fact that it only means we are not dealing with logical or conceptual notions, but mere facts regarding power and its lack. It is an interesting question whether, in parity with a principle we have often invoked, '*o* is *a*-impotent' actually entails that *o* is not impotent to *be* *a*-potent. But seemingly acceptable as that inference is, the issues of iterated potentialities, no less than the connections between powers and modalities, would carry us wide of the path before us. Let us return to elaborate the distinctions we have before us, then, without introducing novel ones.

In the following array of descriptions, which may in proper combinations afford an exact characterization of any state of affairs of interest to us, I shall make these notational assumptions:

(1) I shall regard a as designating a specific event, rather than a *kind* of event, and so with na. If a happens, then na cannot happen as well, so that a entails $N(na)$ and na entails $N(a)$. The descriptions a and na are contraries, however, in that it is possible that neither a nor na occur. That is to say $N(a)$ does not entail na; and $N(na)$ does not entail a. $N(a)$ denies that a occurs, but does not affirm that na occurs. In general $N(a \lor na)$ is a possibly true description, but $(a.na)$ is not a possibly true description.

(2) In the following, m and D will function as before. Now mDa and $mDna$ will describe complex events, and will be contrary descriptions: just as $(a.na)$ is an impossible description, so is $(mDa.mDna)$ – a man cannot both do and forbear a at the same time. On the other hand, he may do neither – which does not mean that *neither* is what he *does*, viz. that he chooses not to choose, since, if he chooses not to do a, he in effect chooses to do na. Rather, it means that he is not always faced with such a choice, or better, that he is not always either doing a or doing na, but rather $N(mDa \lor mDna)$. The latter may be true, for example, when m is asleep and *doing* nothing (= *not* doing *anything*).

(3) I shall introduce the term P as an indicator of potency to do something. P is an incomplete symbol, in that there are no *pure* and unqualified powers, but only powers to do specific things or specific kinds of things. So $mPDa$ will describe the fact that m has the power to do a. I shall regard PDa as a simple, that is, a one-place predicate, so the logical form of mDa and $mPDa$ differ roughly in the way in which a relational sentence differs from a simple predicative one. The miniscule n, since it serves a descriptive role, may work with P as the affirmation of a non-power or impotency, viz. $mnPDa$. The latter does not deny the predicate PDa as being true of the subject – *that* logical task is performed by $N(mPDa)$ – but rather affirms the predicate $nPDa$ of him. It is a negative predication rather than the negation of a predication, and so we may distinguish notationally between denying potencies and affirming impotencies, just in case it should prove philosophically important to do so. We might, however, want to distinguish between the incapacity of a blind man to see from the incapacity of a stone to

see, on the grounds that stones are not impotent to see if they cannot be potent to see either. So denying an impotency is not asserting a potency: indeed, it seems plain, to deny an impotency must entail denying the correspondent potency. Briefly, we might wish, in a development I leave room for but will not pursue, to distinguish between an impotency to be potent from an impotency *tout court*, so that mnPPDa – 'm is impotent to be potent to do a' – actually entails that m is impotent to be impotent to be impotent to do a – mnPnPDa. Iterated impotencies hence do not amount to a potency, even though 'm is impotent to be impotent' can, in ordinary discourse, sustain a reading to the effect that m has a potency he cannot lose, whereas I shall mean that he lacks a potency he cannot achieve. So a straightforward impotency implies at least the potency to be potent – mnPDa implies mPPDa – and there is accordingly always hope for the powerless.

With this, I think, we may turn to our distinctions, all of which, I believe, may be given by means of the following eight descriptions along with their denials.

(1)	mDa	(9)	N(mDa)
(2)	mDna	(10)	N(mDna)
(3)	mPDa	(11)	N(mPDa)
(4)	mPDna	(12)	N(mPDna)
(5)	mnPDa	(13)	N(mnPDa)
(6)	mnPDna	(14)	N(mnPDna)
(7)	mnPnDa	(15)	N(mnPnDa)
(8)	mnPnDna	(16)	N(mnPnDna)

Disregarding the notational curiosities given in (7) and (8) and their negates, which I shall comment on in a moment, let us note a few simple inferences we may generate from an array which it would be amusing but gratuitous to put in some such geometrical configuration as a Square of Opposition.

(i) (1) entails (3) as (2) entails (4). This is licensed by the principle of *ab esse ad posse*. The contrapositive of the latter, *ab non posse ad non esse*, yields inferences from (5) to (9) and (6) to (11). Obviously no licit inference runs from (9) to (5) nor from (11) to (6): (2) and (5), though on different principles, equally entail (9), which cannot distinguish an action from an incapacity without further specification. (9), indeed, is radically underdetermined: from it you cannot tell whether m did nothing, did *na*, did something which was neither *a* nor *na*, sustained impotency, or what.

(ii) (1) entails (10), since (1) and (2) are contraries. Hence (2) entails (9). (9) and (10) are, I think, subcontraries. They can both be true, but cannot both be false.

(iii) I have argued throughout this chapter that (2) entails (3) – or more weakly, that it entails (13). But (13) and (5) are contradictories. From this it follows that (5) and (2) are incompatible. Now (2) entails (9): a man cannot do *a* if he does *na*. (9) *must* be true if (2) is true, but this does not and cannot entail that (5) must be true if (2), because the latter cannot hold. So the logical incapacity of *m* to do *a* when he does *na* in no sense entails that he is impotent to do *a* when he does *na*. Indeed the very opposite is true. Given that one cannot do both *a* and *na*, it follows that one must choose at most one of *a* and *na* at a given time. But (2) describes a *choice* only if (1) could have been a choice instead, which presupposes that (13) is true *at the very time* that (2) is. That is, it was within his power to have done as (1) describes when in fact he does as (2) describes. I underscore in passing that our logical incapacity to satisfy contrary descriptions is not to be counted an impotency, simply because there is no potency, not even in the omnipotent, for doing the impossible.

(iv) (7) and (8) are curiosities, in that they describe incontinences of the sort earlier imputed to the Boddisattva, presumed impotent not to not pass into Nirvana. It seems a reasonable inference that, if *m* is impotent *not* to do *a*, he is impotent to do *na*, so from (7) to (6) is a reasonable inference. And a comparably reasonable inference runs from (8) to (5): if *m* is impotent not to do *na*, he is impotent to do *a*. These inferences nevertheless raise difficulties. For (2) entails (13), which contradicts (5). So (2) entails (16): if a man in fact does *na*, he cannot be impotent not to do *na*. So (8) should entail (10), which at least sounds as though it were contradictory. It certainly sounds odd that a man should at once be impotent not to do *na* and then not be consistently regarded as able to do *na*! So I think we may regard (7) and (8) as impossible cases: if *mDna*, it at least cannot seriously be believed that this is because he is impotent to do otherwise. And so, *pari passu*, when he does *a*.

I shall not seek further inferences here. Nor, which would be more interesting, shall I attempt to generalize the schema, by putting other terms for D – e.g. 'believes' or 'knows' and other still – to determine the extent to which the same pattern of inferences and distinctions may be projected across various domains. Rather, I want in terms of these distinctions to introduce the concept of *full control*.

VII

By *full control* I should like to mean this:

$$[(1) \supset (4)] . [(2) \supset (3)]$$

That is, *m* has control in the full sense providing that, if he does *a* he is able to have done *na*, and if he does *na*, he is able to have done *a*. This formulation, however intuitively it captures the concept I intend, runs athwart some logical difficulties through the fact that it is true when (1) and (2) are false. By itself, this need cause no dismay, for I may be said to have full control, say, with regard to *opening* my eyes or *keeping them shut*, so long as I am able to do both these things, even though I am in fact doing neither, e.g. when my eyes in fact are open, as now, or when I am asleep. The difficulties, rather, are due to well-known features in the concept of material implication, and perhaps these may be avoided by eliminating the conditional antecedents and defining full control by means of (3) and (4) in conjunction. This is the course I shall follow. Among other advantages of following it is that it enables us to give a characterization of *fully lacking control*, which is given by the conjunction of (5) and (6). If *m* fully lacks control, it follows that *a* entails N(*m*D*a*) and *na* entails N(*m*D*na*). Obviously, having full control is consistent with N(*m*D*a*) and with N(*m*D*na*); indeed, having full control is consistent with doing nothing whatever, so that something can at once be omnipotent and *fenéant*.

What is of more immediate conceptual interest, however, is whether there can be *partial* control, of which there would appear in principle to be two varieties, defined thus:

(I) (3).(6)
(II) (4).(5)

It is difficult to see that we can admit case (II). For (2) implies (3), and hence (13), which contradicts (5). So (2) is inconsistent with (II) in the sense that a man cannot both do *na* and have partial control in sense (II), since his doing *na* is inconsistent with one of the conditions for (II) to be satisfied. So at least (2) entails that *m* must have full control.

180

I have hesitated to draw an inference, parallel to the inference from (2) to (3), only running from (1) to (4). Perhaps this is because men often do things they consider themselves as unable not to have done. But we have already shown that it is at least reasonable to infer that the case in which a man is impotent not to do *a* is impossible, so that if he does *a*, he is at least potent to have done *na*. We must after all not confuse weakness of will with absence of power. And I think that when we are convinced in general that a man is impotent to do *na*, then, if *a* happens, it is not the case that *mDa*; he cannot be said to do what he cannot control in the sense of forbearance. It is, I think, unreasonable to demand that a man exercise his powers of forbearancy when his drives are very strong, or when the behavior in question is highly habitual, or heavily reinforced. But none of these entail an impotency to do *na*, only a strong disinclination to exercise the powers that he has. Behavior, indeed, which is defined by case (1) is tropismatic behavior, like the positive heliotropism of the sunflower or the negatively phototropic behavior of the cockroach.

I shall therefore suppose that (1) presupposes and hence entails (4). Since (4) entails (14), which contradicts (6), (1) is inconsistent with partial control as defined by (1).

There is, then, *no* partial control: only full control or its complete absence. So we do nothing, positive or negative, unless we have, at the very time we do it, the power to do the contrary. *It is analytical to the concept of an action that a man acts only if he could have done otherwise.*

From this result it follows that, unless expressions are basic actions, there is no direct forbearance of expression. Still, we may comply with the expectations society has of us by various expedients, crudely typified by stuffing a fist in one's mouth in order not to laugh out loud. Or one may stun the feeling by thinking certain thoughts, and abort that feeling's natural expression: as a woman may induce frigidity by thinking that men are pigs. But the point is less interesting now than the result which it entails. For if it is a conceptual truth that nothing is an action unless he who performs it could at the moment he performed it have forborne instead, we cannot have acted unless we 'could have done otherwise'. But this is a formula which has played a certain role in the contest concerning metaphysical freedom, and we might turn now to that contest, to see if we have gained any advance towards its resolution.

7

FREEDOM

Perhaps the concept of freedom attaches to action in the way in which the concept of truth attaches to belief: pragmatically, rather than logically, in that I believe my beliefs true when I hold them, and my actions free at the moment they are done. Thus *m* believes it up to him whether the world is to be in one state rather than another when he acts, but *not* up to him which state it is in when he holds a belief with regard to that state of the world. This then leaves logical room for false beliefs and unfree actions, though we cannot entertain ourselves as exemplifying this possibility when the beliefs and actions are current and our own.

The parallel is intriguing but treacherous. We have a fairly clear sense of when a belief is false: it is so when *m* believes that *s* and *s* itself is false. But what sense are we to attach to an unfree action? A popular philosophical tradition supposes that 'free' contrasts with and so excludes 'coerced'.[1] But this destroys the parallel, for just to believe that *s* is to believe that *s* is true, though it is doubtful whether just to perform an action is to believe one was not coerced into doing it. We ought to be authoritative as to whether we were coerced or not, and sometimes we know we would not have acted had we not felt coerced. So insofar as the parallel is compelling, the sense of 'free' which is relevant to it is consistent with 'not-free' in the sense in which the latter is weakly synonymous with 'coerced', and so the tradition referred to is irrelevant to our understanding freedom in the former sense. On the other hand, freedom can no more be analytical to the concept of action than truth is analytical to the concept of belief. For something remains a belief when it is discovered to have been false, and so, if the parallel holds, must something remain as having been an action upon discovery that it was not free.

Truth, of course, is conferred upon what is believed in virtue of factors external to the belief itself: that is why, insofar as he believes *s* true, *m* must believe it not up to him that it is so. So perhaps, by a predictable inversion, it is the *lack* of some factor external to the action which makes the action free, or 'up to him' in the agent's view. Then to say it was not free is to say that there was that external factor, believed absent by the agent insofar as he believed himself free to have done it or not. A natural and hardly less traditional candidate for such a factor would be: a cause. Then, in believing that *s* I believe the world such as to make *s* true, and in performing an action I believe the world such as not to have caused me to perform it.

This would be an attractive suggestion, since it implies that a Determinist ought to feel the same sort of tension which the Skeptic sometimes is alleged to feel between his official belief and any other beliefs he may continue to hold. The Determinist would have to hold his actions to be unfree (now 'caused') and at the same time free (now 'uncaused'), the former because of his philosophy and the latter because of the pragmatic connection between the concepts of freedom and of action. And the Skeptic would have to hold his beliefs true through the parallel pragmatic connection, and not true in consequence of *his* philosophy. To be sure, this would be a special sort of Skeptic – one who for whatever reasons believes all beliefs to be not true – but it is striking anyway that there should be a form of Skepticism which enters the theory of knowledge at a point which corresponds to that at which a parallel form of Determinism fits into the theory of action. It would be a pragmatic tension and not, of course, a refutation, but it would be a tormenting one even so, since the Determinist can as little desist from actions as a Skeptic can desist from belief. 'A body-bearing soul', declares the *Bhagavat Gita*, 'cannot abandon actions without remainder.'[2] Neither, one may suppose, may a soul-bearing body then abandon beliefs. But now the parallel begins to cloy. For 'free' and 'unfree' are predicates conferred upon actions by virtue of an external factor of causation, and we would not want to say of just *any* uncaused event that it was free. But we seem to lack something appropriately similar to say about belief and truth.

Except pragmatically, Determinism may be held compatible with the occurrence of actions, since it regards them all as caused, and regards the concept of an unfree act as coherent as we may regard the concept of a false belief. It need not entail some generalized impotency, as it is sometimes felt to do: as when causes are held to necessitate events in such a way as to exclude the possibility of any other event occurring under just those conditions. For then, it may be argued, 'there would be no such thing as an act, nor would anything ever be done'.[3] And this indeed is implied by the result at which we have arrived in connection with forbearancy. If mDb is a basic action, then it must be true that under the identical conditions in which he performed it, m could have forborne instead. Reference to identical conditions is crucial in ascribing the power of forbearance, and hence of action, for should anything in the conditions in question exclude the possibility of forbearing under them, this *ipso facto* excludes the possibility of action as well. Nor is this innocuous. Thus it may be true of a weathervane which points west that it could have pointed east had the winds blown that way instead. But it cannot have been true of that weathervane that all conditions presupposed under which it is a functioning member of its class, that it should have pointed east or any direction other than west when the west wind blew. But just exactly this is required if a man is to be said to have acted. So no form of Determinism which excludes this is compatible with the occurrence of actions, and unless Determinism entails a generalized impotency – and there must be a difference between an incapacity to act, on the one hand, and acting unfreely on the other – the concept of causation invoked by it must be compatible with something different occurring under given conditions than what in fact occurred. We could refute such a Determinism by forbearing from holding up one hand while demonstrating the existence of the External World, in the manner of G. E. Moore,[4] by holding up the other: at once confounding the prophets of universal ignorance and impotence!

If Determinists are committed to claiming that *actions* are caused, they must accept, since this follows from the present concept of an action, that agents always and under identical conditions can behave otherwise than they do behave. Action is not necessitated to the logical exclusion of forbearance. But since the latter seems also to be compatible with an action being caused, it becomes increasingly difficult to appreciate the urgency in insisting that freedom entail the absence of cause. Absence of cause is not entailed by the concept of a basic action, so if freedom conceptually excludes causes, it remains possible that no basic actions are free. This enables us to induce within the soul of the Libertarian a pragmatic tension which is almost parallel to the one just sustained by the Determinist. It becomes a possibility for him that none of his actions are free though he is pragmatically constrained to believe that all of them are. This would be like realizing it to be possible that all of one's beliefs are false while finding it pragmatically impossible to believe this of any of them. Perhaps then freedom does not exclude cause after all? This simultaneously eases the tensions to which Determinist and Libertarian alike are now subject, but at the price of requiring us once more to find out what the concept of freedom means or how it may attach to the concept of action. And it leaves us to wonder in what way there is any longer a contest between Determinism and any theory regarding the freedom of an action. For if the former entails something about actions being caused, and the latter nothing about causation at all, how should the issue be joined? So let us continue provisionally to suppose that those events are free which both are actions and are uncaused.

Suppose there were in fact no free acts under this characterization! Then Libertarianism would be false, unless its advocates were to derive a cold comfort from the possibility that there might sometime be a free action. On the other hand, it would not definitively establish Determinism. That every action were caused would be consistent with the falsity of Libertarianism and Determinism alike. For the latter is an interesting theory only if it is *necessary* that all actions, because necessary that all events, are caused. It is a far cry from the claim that events are necessitated by their causes to the claim that they have causes necessarily. So we can picture a world which leaves both Determinists and their opponents disconsolate, where it is contingent that actions all are caused. Determinism might then be massively confirmed in what it entails – that all actions are caused – but false all the same.

What a shame to leave these ancient antagonists in this unresolved state! All the more so when we think of the hopes with which philosophers began the exploration of the concept of action: that it would unblock one of the great stuck doors to philosophical enlightenment, and enable us to decide whether we were free.

II

It occurs to the Determinist at this point that the quandary just described concerns basic actions taken in the barest sense, where none of the factors of intention or reason apply as they do in non-basic and especially in mediated actions. When viewed as the pivotal components in mediated actions – those actions through which we not only change the world but fit it to our representations – matters stand differently. In such contexts basic actions have causes, and this indeed is entailed by the concept of the mediated action as such. That concept requires that, if mDb is the component basic action in the simplest mediated action mDa, then m intends that a happen and believes that b will bring a about: and he does b – performs the basic action – *because* of his belief and his intention. That there is something *because* of which the basic action occurs is thus analytic to the concept of mediated action. But the 'because' may, the Determinist insists, be appreciated in terms of ordinary causation, elsewhere exemplified by the banal concussion of billiard-ball upon billiard-ball. True, the intention and belief together do not necessitate the component basic action. But his concern is not to insist that causes necessitate their effects, but that it is necessary that events have causes. And here it really is a matter of necessity, of conceptual entailment.

Of course, this does not establish the general case. It will not follow that every event has a cause, only every basic action which is a component in a mediated one.[5] But of what interest to his opponent can it be that there should elsewhere in the universe be uncaused or only contingently caused events, or even uncaused basic actions executed, say, as blank spontaneities? For if we are not 'free' in the presently relevant sense – where our actions have no cause – what use or point can freedom have for us? It brings *us* no metaphysical dignity that elsewhere in the universe uncaused events transpire.

The Libertarian cannot refute this argument by raising an arm. For it will have been done with the intention of refuting the Determinist, and hence be invalidated as an exception. Indeed, no deliberate refutation is possible. On the other hand, and speaking as an outsider to this dispute, one may wonder why the Libertarian should wish to refute such a claim? For what could be a better candidate for the exercise of freedom than acting in such a way as to realize our intentions, to do things because we intend them to have consequences we believe they will, or at least can or might bring about? To be sure, this does not mean that we always do what we *want*. A man may do something because he intends to do it, without it following that he wants to: unless we adjust the meaning of 'want' so as to make it finally mean just what intention means.[6] 'Doing what one wants to do' contrasts with 'acting against one's will', which may pass as near synonym to 'being coerced', and which brings us back to the traditional theory we rejected before as irrelevant. A whole nest of delicious distinctions are available here, of course: where a person is believed by someone to act under threat or coercion when he is being 'made' to do what he wanted to do anyway; or where duty and inclination so coincide that a man who believes in doing things only because he has a duty to do them wonders whether he is complying with or violating his high principles; and so on. These are matters for moral psychology to ponder: intention is neutral as to whether one wants what one intends or not. Still, that an action should be caused by an intention is not a bad explication of what it means for the action to be free. And 'free' would not so much exclude causes as such, but rather causes of a certain kind, namely causes which are not intentions of the agent. This then leaves conceptual room for unfree actions, namely those which are unintentional, or not caused by intentions. Indeed, this may virtually give us the pragmatic connections we began with. To believe one's action is free is to believe one is doing it because one intends to. Just as to believe one's beliefs are true is to believe they are caused by what makes them so.

These adjustments would enable the Libertarian and the Determinists to leave the quagmire together, since they are now more or less identical: Free Will now presupposes and is inconceivable without Determinism, to pre-empt the title of Hobart's famous study, because Freedom and Determinism are one. Or they differ now over areas of the universe which can have no special bearing on the issues over which they believed themselves traditionally divided.

Unfortunately for this admirable and ironic resolution of a clogged and ancient controversy, there is an objection to reckon with, namely that the Determinist, and now the Libertarian, has misread reasons as causes, and been bewitched by the homonymy of 'because' into making grave philosophical errors.[7] Patterns of explanation in which reference is essentially made to reasons differ from and are irreducible to those in which reference is essentially made to causes. By disregarding these differences, and by coarsening the concept of 'cause' as badly as we recently accused someone of doing with 'wants', we have obtained a hollow truce. Reasons *justify*: causes are indifferent to questions of justification. But let us explore the distinction for a moment.

What exactly are the special characteristics of an explanation in which reference is made to reasons is not altogether easy to state, and I shall indicate only in a very casual manner what I believe them to be. To act for a reason is, presumably, to act on the basis of an *argument* which Aristotle's conception of a practical syllogism perhaps crudely illustrates. Let us say that whatever may be the logical form of a practical argument, we may say that a man who acts for reasons does so through having internalized an argument which justifies his action in his mind. It is not necessary to suppose here any fact which may be rebutted by simple introspection, e.g. a man need not have gone through some actual process of antecedent ratiocination; he need not actually have drawn any conclusions or made any inferences. The sort of argument I have in mind may be represented, in the simplest case, as follows. Our man believes that if '*b*' were true, then '*a*' would be true. He intends that '*a*' should be true and because of this he does *b*, which makes '*b*' true. If his belief were correct, '*a*' is true, and he will have achieved a mediated action, having done *a* through doing *b*. *We* explain his doing *b* by ascribing some such argument to him, and it is certainly plain that we do not explain the motion of billiard-balls or the rotation of weathervanes by similarly ascribing arguments to them. Certainly, to act for a reason in some way involves making true something like a minor premiss in something like a practical syllogism in the belief or at least the hope that this will bring that about which will make the conclusion itself true. And how different all this admittedly is, even in this crude approximation to the case, from those episodes in which a basic action is caused by electrostimulation of some center in the brain, where it is absurd to explain the basic action with reference to internalized argument.

It would be fascinating at this point to elaborate on the logic and even the psychology of practical argument, but here our concern is only to ask whether it is after all an exception to or only a species of causal explanation. Philosophers naturally divide on the question, and all I can attempt here is to approach it through the distinctions we have arrived at in this book.

III

If reasons indeed cause actions, they do so through the fact that they are representations of the world, and are effective primarily through their representational properties. A man means for the world to be a certain way through his doing what he believes will make it that way – at least this is so in the simplest mediated actions – and part then of understanding his behavior requires that we come to appreciate the way he represents the world: the more eccentric the representation, the more eccentric, presumably, the action. It perhaps goes against a certain grain to think of *causes* as eccentric in this fashion: or as rational, false, or true: or as good or bad, as these have reference to reasons. But then beliefs, which are *effects*, can also be, since they too are representations, true, false, wayward, or silly. The classical empiricisms were nothing if not theories regarding the causes of the representational properties of our beliefs (or ideas): of how we acquire the idea *of* red or whatever; and even Descartes thought it important to explain, in a precisely causal manner, how certain features of our representations are caused. He thought, for example, that these features of representations must be caused by things which in fact *have* the features in question: the idea of a substance must be caused by a substance, the idea of an accident by an accident, and the like. It was on this principle, however peculiar, that he erected one of his great proofs of God. But the point I am concerned with is only that we have a tradition in which representations are effects, and hence some effects have certain semantical properties: so it is no grave conceptual outrage to think of causes in these terms either. Indeed it is exactly to be expected that reasons, if causes, are such through their representationality. And as we saw already in examining responses and reactions, the laws entailed by supposing that something causes m to react or respond in a certain way, make essential reference to the way in which m represented the event designated the cause, or, more grandiosely, to m's representation of the world. It is this reference in the laws employed in explaining human behavior to the representations of the agent which marks a crucial difference between the Sciences of Man and the Sciences of Nature, as that distinction is drawn within the Continental tradition. That the way in which we represent the world should enter into explanation of our actions, that different persons should act differently under conditions which differ only insofar as their representations differ, is one of the distinctively human things about us. That these representations vary from historical period to historical period and from culture to culture, and even from person to person, is part of what has complicated the discovery of laws of human behavior, and why these laws cannot easily be generalized beyond the era and area in which the cited representations are possible. But none of this yet makes as plain as we require the way in which representations, in the form of intentions and reasons, themselves cause actions, and that is what must mainly interest us.

I must emphasize that if raising an arm is a basic action done for a reason, it is incorrect to describe what happens this way: I raise the arm through having the reason. It is incorrect first of all because this fits instead the model for a mediated action, in which the arm-rise is an effect. But mainly it is wrong because having reasons is not within one's repertoire of possible actions. I cannot intend at will, any more than I can believe at will. This is not because intending and willing are representational, because I have the power to represent at will, even as a basic action. Whenever I wish to, for example, I can picture Paris. This may be an exceedingly inaccurate representation, but so might a child's drawing of a horse be exceedingly inaccurate and still of a horse: indeed, until we have identified what it is of, the issue of inaccuracy cannot begin to be raised: Paris, as such, is neither accurate nor inaccurate. For this reason, I suppose, to imagine *x* is to believe one's representation of *x* to be largely a correct one. This belief may be wrong, and I may discover I have so strange and private a picture of Paris when I confront the real city of Paris that only I could have known, if the representation were communicated, that Paris is what it was of. Perhaps it is only because I first believe certain things about Paris that I imagine Paris as I do; but while this limits the content of the image, imagining itself is a matter of action. After all, those without arms cannot raise their arms at will. *Having* an arm is not in its own right an action, merely a precondition for having the power to perform certain sorts of actions.

There are other cases of representations as actions. We may entertain hypotheses just for the sake of tracing implications: and the latter, inferential activity may be regarded as representational as well. I may genuinely comply with the command to 'consider a rectangle'. My representations may have effects, even physical effects. The picture of Paris may cause a tightness in my throat, my erotic fantasies have their predictable effects. Whatever the connection between an intention and an action, the intention or reason cannot cause the action in the way in which a fantasy causes tumescence. Or perhaps this will be only because the effects remarked upon are not actions, without the causal connection being of a different order. But we will be able better to appreciate the matter after we better understand why intentions are not to be classed as actions in their own right.

It is difficult to see how intending can be an intentional action, namely something which is itself caused by an intention. The difficulty is due to the exceedingly puzzling iteration in the expression 'I intend to intend that *a*', which would presumably describe the cause in question. If it is a correct description of the cause, what room have we for an effect, since it seems plain that I already intend what I intend to intend in the very intending of it? We cannot consistently intend that which we believe is already the case, and in the present strange example the action intended is consummated in the intending of it, and hence has not the separate existence required for an effect. So there can be no such cause. Philosophers have argued on perhaps just this intuition that I cannot predict my intentions, for to say I *will* intend is already to declare the intention in the present, and any further steps taken in order to have the intention, are rendered superfluous.[8] One may then go on to declare the will itself unpredictable and man then free to the degree that Determinism entails predictability. I am not at all certain the Determinism need hold this, nor that one is any the less free if his acts in fact are all predictable, nor even that I cannot predict what my intentions will be. All I am reasonably certain of is that I cannot predict what my intentions will be on the basis of knowing they will be effects of events I intend to bring about: for then I already have the intention and the steps are wasted. Unless they are merely steps taken toward steeling the will: intentions, like beliefs, admitting of varying consistencies, from firm to fluid. I do not, incidentally, think that intending to believe is self-dissolving in quite the way in which intending to intend is, though it seems also to be a conceptual anomaly. If I intend to believe that *s*, I must believe that I do not in fact believe that *s*, which is to say that I do not now believe that *s* in fact is true. I can, to be sure, intend to take steps to find out whether *s* is true, and hence *arrive* at a belief. But it is inconsistent with this program to intend the belief at which I am to arrive. That implies that my mind is already made upon the matter, which renders the program useless – except in the sense of confirming my belief – and is inconsistent with the precondition for intelligible intention, namely, I really do believe that I believe that *s*, which I could not do if I intended to believe it. Such arguments hint at something either very deep or very trivial in the concepts of intention and belief. My own immediate view is that the difficulties arise primarily because, though beliefs and intentions are admittedly states of a person, they never are merely that, but refer us beyond themselves, in the individual's own view, to the world as it is or *as* he means it to be.

It is this, certainly, that rules it out that intentions, again like beliefs, should be *basic* actions in contrast with mediated ones. We had, in our discussions of belief, to suppose it possible in fact that a man should believe *as an action*,⁹ but only incoherent for him to believe that he had done so. This because it cannot be believed by him that it is an accident that he believes, where 'accident' here means only that the fact of his believing has nothing really to do with the belief being a true one. And since he must believe it is true if he really believes it, the doxastic athlete here has the problem of reconciling his knowledge that he believes only because he happened to 'do' the belief, with his knowledge that there is no connection between that which makes the belief a true one and the history of his having come to hold it. *Something* like this works for intention. An intention, after all, refers to an action through which it is to be made true. Frivolously to form an intention is frivolously to be committed through the logic of intention to an action. Intentions, as before, are not mere isolated states of the soul. Why should one really act on the basis of an intention one formed merely for the sake of forming it? This seems discrepant with the concept of commitment. One does not idly choose an intention just as such: one chooses an *action* through an intention.

Writers on the Free Will question have at times supposed that we have freedom only if willing itself is subject to the will: if my will is determined, in what sense can I finally be free? If we understand this to mean that my intentions must themselves be actions, then the matter is settled. But *I* should think the issue is less what the provenance of my intentions is than whether I can execute, or try to execute what intentions I have – much as the question of knowledge is a matter of whether I can determine which of my representations, however they came about, in fact are true as I believe them to be. That beliefs and intentions should be incapable of enactment, should be caused and limited by one's position in the order of reality and history, may *limit* the range of beliefs and intentions. But within these limits, we may have knowledge and may perform actions.

The mark of intending *a* is that *m* try to bring *a* about: that he does something *b* which he believes will, or believes might, or believes could achieve this. One cannot transform this mark into a behavioristic criterion of intending *a*, much less define the latter in terms of the behavioral mark, inasmuch as 'trying to bring *a* about' is a non-basic description of the action, let us suppose it basic, of *m*D*b*. As a non-basic description, it presupposes that *m* intends *a* and hence can hardly explicate or serve as the latter's definition. And given the vagariousness of beliefs, who knows *what* m may intend in doing *b*, or what, in consequence, he is trying. Or finally, whether he is trying anything here at all: for the basic action may be idle or performed with no ulterior intent whatever. Though there is, then, a commitment to do something towards fulfilling it entailed by the concept of having an intention, this is not a commitment which need ever be honored. If a man never tries, one may question the firmness or sincerity of his intention, since the intention itself cannot easily lie side by side with a belief that *a* is impossible of fulfilment or that he is impotent to fulfil it. But opportunities for actualization never may arise, at least as he perceives opportunities. How then, if a man indeed has the intention that *a* come about and has the belief that *b* will bring it about, if he has it in his power and knows he has it in his power to do *b*, has the opportunity and knows he has – how, one may ask, since this is quite consistent with his never doing *b* in the sense of trying *a*, can the former be considered the cause of the latter in case he in fact ever does try *a* by doing *b*? Is not the connection too loose for one to speak of causation here? One *can*, since it is consistent with the concept, have reasons for doing what one never does. But there can hardly be causes without effects. And since something can be a reason without an action follow-ing and cannot be a cause without an action following it, reasons cannot be causes.

This seems to me rather an empty piece of philosophical vaudeville. There should be no more asked of the concept of causation here than we demand of it elsewhere. So let us recall now an especially relevant part of our analysis. If *b* causes *a*, the implicit law does not require that, if *b* instantiates the type β and *a* the type α, that each β-instance be conjoined with an α-instance, but only that every α-instance be conjoined with a β-instance. I would like to read the notion of *con-joinment* here to be replaced with the notion of *following*, and say that the law does not require each β-instance to be 'followed' by an α-instance, but only that each α-instance follow a β-instance. But the notion of 'following' is too readily taken in a temporal sense, and it should be plain that the order of cause-and-effect cannot be explicated in terms of the *temporal* order of the events so described. One could cautiously introduce the temporal feature we obviously feel essential to the concept of causation insofar as we feel that causes cannot temporally succeed their effects, by the following admittedly shallow strategy. We can say the β-instance with which it is conjoined as effect must be simultaneous with or earlier in time than the α-instance, and that there be no episodes in which this is reversed. But without concentrating too heavily upon such complications in the concept of causal structure, it should be immediately plain that the feature just cited is shared by the concept of cause and of reason alike. In a mediated action, the component basic action may always be redescribed as a trying, where *what* is tried is identified through reference to the intention of the agent. The trying may be successful or a failure, depending upon whether *a* happens in consequence of it or not, when *a* is what would fulfil the intention. It will be a success if the structure of the world enables it to be, say if it allows *b* to cause *a*. But it is not this bit of causation which interests us but another, the causation presumed by us to hold between intention and trying. And our claim need not be that whenever there is an intention, then there is a trying; but rather that there is no trying unless there is an intention: and this is a conceptual truth. But no other condition really is required in order that intentions, to be sure against the background of internalized argument, should be causes. Their satisfaction of the status of causes is entailed by the concept of mediated action. If there are mediated actions, there are basic actions, and these are caused by intentions or, speaking more loosely, by reasons.

The basic action embedded in a mediated action is not, of course, the *conclusion* of an argument, it is not *entailed* by the premisses of an argument whose conclusion it may make true. The actual death of Socrates is not, as an event, entailed as an act of logical murder by the premisses of the textbook syllogism whose conclusion, to be sure, it makes true. The connection between premisses and conclusion of a practical (or any) argument are admittedly different from the connections between cause and effect. But it is not clear why reaching, or having reached a conclusion should not cause an action, in just the ordinary sense of causality, even though the admittedly different connection is required in order to relate the premisses to the conclusion which has been reached. And it is, in fact, not even required that the connection between premisses and conclusion in fact hold, or that the argument in question be valid. All that is required is that the man have *believed* it valid for it to serve as an explanation of his action. And *believing*, being a state of a person, can easily be supposed as standing to action as cause stands to effect.

So the Determinist need not be moved by a distinction which leaves his claim regarding the causation of actions quite unaffected. And why should the Libertarian then demur either? For just that quality of dignity which the concept of freedom was supposed to confer upon agents may be instead conferred by the remarkable thought that we are caused to act by our representing the world as in this state or in that. And mediating as we do, between representation and reality, the laws which *we* believe represent reality must ultimately be taken into account by the Determinist who undertakes to explain human action. That *our* representations must be referred to in his representations goes some distance towards clarifying the claim that we stand at once within and without the world.

Those representations which we believe cause us to act, and then through acting to change the world; and those representations we believe caused by the world which then makes them true: these representations together are partial definitions of the world we suppose ourselves to live in. And if we think once more of what in an earlier chapter we spoke of as responses and reactions, where some event stimulated *m* to perform a basic action and was there said to cause that action, we will appreciate that these events were *constituted* as causes by the representations in the light of which the agent responded or reacted.[10] They pick out features of the world as opportunities and as threats, as instruments and as irrelevancies. They impose those existential contours, those shades and lightings, which characterize the world as lived. Without reference to these representations, of the ways in which men read the world and themselves as in the world, we could not explain either their beliefs or their actions. And this would be so even if, as I have argued, the representations are identical with bodily states of men. The way we see the world then gets to be part of the way the world is.

Except as saturated by representations, basic actions would be blind, neutral motions of the body and basic cognitions ephemeral provocations of the senses. But it is through basic cognitions, even so, that such representations of the world as we may arrive at may pretend to the status of knowledge, and through basic actions that such changes as we may induce upon the world become ours. Since all the same components must be reckoned into the analyses of knowledge and of action, it hardly is surprising that parallels between the concepts should exist. Perhaps I have drawn these parallels wrong because I have gotten the structures of the concepts themselves wrong. Still, however different the truth may prove, there will be parallels to draw, and the concept of knowledge will be the mirror-image of the concept of action. To draw the structures in a different way will require, of course, a different way of drawing the world and us. We are the way in which we understand and change the world; we exist in the space between representation and the world.

NOTES

PREFACE

1 James Stubblebine, *Giotto: The Arena Frescoes* (New York; Norton, 1969), pp. 84-5: 'Throughout the Mission cycle a new sense of purpose and drama is built up. One sign of it is the posture of Christ, which is contrived to achieve a certain effect. After the first scene of Christ at the Temple, he is invariably faced toward the right, the direction of narrative development, and his arm is raised in a number of gestures, depending on the sense of the particular episode, and varying in intensity from scene to scene. Thus in the Cana episode, the gesture is so inconspicuous as to suggest that Christ is engaged in a sort of sleight of hand, in the Baptism it signifies acceptance, in the Lazarus scene it is one of command and miracle working, in the Entry it is a blessing and a greeting, and in the Expulsion it is denunciatory.'

CHAPTER I

1 There is a remarkably visionary passage to this effect in Engels, who speaks of the way in which man emerges from bondage to the forces of history when society seizes the means of production and product no longer dominates producer. 'The extraneous objective forces that have hitherto governed history pass under the control of man himself. Only from that time will man himself, more and more consciously, make his own history ... It is the ascent of man from the kingdom of necessity to the kingdom of freedom.' Frederick Engels, *Socialism: Scientific and Utopian*, in Karl Marx and Frederick Engels, *Selected Works in Two Volumes* (London; Lawrence and Wishart, 1950), II, 141.

2 It is standard in the respect at least that most contemporary analyses of the *concept* of knowledge are framed in terms of it. Roderick Chisholm employs 'accepts that' in place of 'believes that' and explicitly identifies *s* with an *hypothesis*, but otherwise his analysis is 'standard'; see his *Perceiving: A Philosophical Study* (Ithaca, New York; Cornell University Press, 1957), p. 16. For further references, see my *Analytical Philosophy of Knowledge* (Cambridge; Cambridge University Press, 1968), p. 73, n. 1.

3 This notation employs 'K' as a relational predicate, and hence may be said to take a stand on a question of logical form. For after all, '*m* knows that *s*' could be parsed differently: 'K*m*' may be taken as an 'epistemic operator', forming sentences out of sentences, as in Jaakko Hintikka, *Knowledge and Belief* (Ithaca, New York; Cornell University Press, 1962); 'K*s*' may be taken as a one-place predicate, as by W. V. O. Quine in his *Word and Object* (New York; John Wiley, 1960), p. 216; '*m*K' – read as 'is known by *m*' – might be taken in similarly Quinian fashion as a one-place predicate

true of the sentence *s*; or the entire sentence, employing '*that*' as a demonstrative might be used as a composite sentence consisting of *s* and '*m* knows that' where a deixis is to be read from the demonstrative '*that*' to the displayed *s*: see Donald Davidson, 'On Saying That', *Synthèse*, xix (1968–9), 130–46. There is no end to philosophical ingenuity in proposing candidates for 'the' logical form, and it is not easily supposed that we are likely to get a decision on logical form until we have a complete analysis: determination of logical form is not the 'first thing' – as Davidson suggests it is – but more or less the last thing to be settled on. For a defense of my own view, see *Analytical Philosophy of Knowledge*, but for criticisms of this, see J. H. Lesher, 'Danto on Knowledge as a Relation', *Analysis*, xxx, 4 (March 1970), 132–4. These issues are clearly not resoluble in a footnote. Meanwhile, I have found the notation itself a perspicuous representation of the structure of knowledge-ascriptions, as will come plain in the sequel.

4 For extended discussion of semantical vehicles in this generalized sense, see *Analytical Philosophy of Knowledge*, ch. 7 *passim*.

5 On representation – and in effect on 'represents-*x*' as a property of *inter alia* pictures, see Nelson Goodman, *Languages of Art* (New York; Bobbs-Merrill, 1969), ch. 1.

6 Goodman is especially stimulating on the distinction I labor toward, between representations as entities with certain properties, and representation as a *relation* between these and their denotata. I differ from Goodman, in the case of pictures, on the dispensability of the concept of *resemblance*. A picture-of-*x* has the positive semantical value appropriate to pictures if it *resembles* what it denotes. Earlier theories overlooked, to be sure, the denotational relation between pictures and the world.

7 I discuss this is detail in *Analytical Philosophy of Knowledge*, ch. 8.

8 Ludwig Wittgenstein, *Tractatus Logico-Philosophicus*, 4.021.: 'Der Satz ist ein Bild der Wirklichkeit.' Wittgenstein speaks accordingly of pictures as true or false, and hence as bearing semantical values, especially at 2.22 and 2.222.

9 Though this hardly is the place to argue such contested matters, my own view is exactly expressed in these words of David Wiggins: 'Nothing that has happened since J. L. Austin's 1950s lectures "Words and Deeds" or their publication seems to me to have undermined the approach or made obsolete the kind of semantical theory typified by Frege or Russell, or, in our own times, Carnap.' 'A Reply to Mr Alston', in D. Steinberg and L. A. Jakobovits, *Semantics* (Cambridge; Cambridge University Press, 1971), p. 48.

10 The least controversial element in the Standard Analysis is that, if *m* knows that *s*, then *s* must be true. Someone with a less correspondentialist conception of truth, e.g. James, Dewey, or Nietzsche, would offer a quite different conception of knowledge. It is only when we take knowledge as an earned representational success that the entailment here goes through *hors de concours*. Pragmatists and Instrumentalists would reject the Standard Analysis totally.

11 *Verbum hoc, quod est 'facere', solet poni pro omni verbo cuiuslibet signicationis, finito vel infinito, etiam pro 'non facere'. Cum enim queritur de aliquo: 'quid facit?': si diligenter consideratur, ponitur ibi 'facere' pro omni verbo, quod responderi potest, et quodcumque verbum respondetur, ponitur pro 'facere'* . . . *Nam cum respondetur: 'legit aut scribit', valet idem ac si dicatur: hoc facit, scilicet legit aut scribit.* This comes from Anselm's *Potestate et Impotenita, Possibilitate et Impossibilitate, Necessitate et Libertate*, the text as established by F. S. Schmitt, 'Ein neues unvollendetes Werk des Hl. Anselm von Canterbury', in *Beiträge zur Geschichte der Philosophie und Theologie des Mittelalters*, 33 (1936), 25. The translation I owe to Ernst Van Haagen. Anselm's brilliant discussion of the concept of action was discovered amongst his papers in Lambeth Palace, and published only in 1936. It is an overpoweringly subtle analysis, as one would expect from the framer of the Ontological Argument, and in view of the impoverished history that the philosophical theory of action has, by contrast with the history of the theory of knowledge, it is difficult not to speculate upon the counterfactual historical development of philosophy had Anselm's analysis entered the discussion and not have been mislaid. I am grateful to my learned colleague, Professor James Walsh, for having drawn my attention to this fragment, and for having gotten Van Haagen to translate it. The entire translation, together with a gloss by Van Haagen, is scheduled for publication in the *American Philosophical Quarterly*.

12 J. L. Austin, 'A Plea for Excuses', in *Philosophical Papers* (Oxford; Clarendon Press, 1961), pp. 126–7.

13 *Ibid.*

14 Edmund Gettier, 'Is Justified True Belief Knowledge?', *Analysis*, XXIII, 6 (June 1963), 121–3.

15 The commentaries on Gettier, and the *riposti* to these, form a long river of sharp argument and subtle distinction. For two recent and exemplary additions to it see Bryan Skyrms, 'The Explication of "X knows that p" ', *Journal of Philosophy*, LXIV, 12 (22 June 1967), 373–89; and Keith Lehrer and Thomas Paxson, Jr, 'Knowledge: Undefeated Justified True Belief', *loc. cit.* LXVI, 8 (24 April 1969), 225–37. In confirmation of the analogies between the concepts of action and knowledge, Lehrer and Paxton distinguish between *basic* and *non-basic* knowledge, employing and acknowledging the distinction I originally introduced between basic and non-basic *actions*.

16 Skyrms defines the class of Gettier-counter-examples thus: (i) X knows that e; (ii) X knows that 'e' is good evidence for 'o'; (iii) X knows that 'o' entails 'p'; (iv) X knows that 'e' is good evidence of 'p' by virtue of (ii) and (iii); (v) X believes that p on the basis of the knowledge referred to in (i) and (iv); (vi) 'p' is true; (vii) 'o' is false. *Loc. cit.* p. 337. I borrow freely from this skeletization.

17 I take this high road in *Analytical Philosophy of Knowledge*, but the criterion is too severe, and in large measure may be imposed only by confusing what belongs to knowledge that *s* and knowledge that one knows that *s*.

18 The introduction into the analysis of empirical knowledge of the concept of explanation may be credited to Gilbert Harman. See especially 'How Belief is Based on Inference', *Journal of Philosophy*, LXI, 12 (11 June 1964), 353–9; 'The Inference to the Best Explanation', *Philosophical Review*, LXXIV, 1 (January 1965), 88–95; and 'Knowledge, Inference, and Explanation', *American Philosophical Quarterly*, 5 (1968), 164–73. The specific introduction of *causal* explanation is suggested by Alvin I. Goldman, 'A Causal Theory of Knowing', *Journal of Philosophy*, LXIV, 12 (22 June 1967), 357–72.

19 Charles Hartshorne and Paul Weiss (eds.), *The Collected Papers of Charles Sanders Peirce* (Cambridge, Massachusetts; Harvard University Press, 1931–5), V, paras. 145–6. These passages are discussed and imaginatively developed in N. R. Hanson, *Patterns of Discovery* (Cambridge; Cambridge University Press, 1958), pp. 85ff.

20 *Logical* omniscience is defended and explored in Hintikka's *Knowledge and Belief*, *passim*.

21 This implies that it is knowledge only if a man has *come to his belief* along a certain route: has *arrived* at belief in the right way. For a fine discussion of this, and an ingenious example of someone who believes the right thing for the wrong reasons, see Gilbert Harman, 'Knowledge, Reasons, and Causes', *Journal of Philosophy*, LXVII, 21 (5 November 1970), 841–55.

22 A diagrammatic representation may serve to make plain the pattern on inversions to those, like myself, given to pictorial *aides-pensée*.

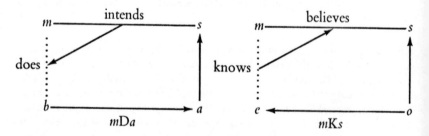

The arrows indicate the direction of explanation, except where they run to *s* from *a* and *o* respectively. There they serve to indicate the truth-making relationship between object and vehicle. The diagrams are otherwise very coarsely grained.

23 The terms 'opacity' and 'transparency' are due to Quine, but I believe they may be misleading, largely in consequence of the suggestion that it is the *same* terms which are transparent in one context and opaque in another, when in fact all that is invariant to the contexts in question is apt to be *shape*. In 'Columbus discovered America', Columbus refers, if anything, to the man Christopher Columbus. In 'Isabella believed that Columbus discovered America', this is not the reference of 'Columbus' any longer. Its reference, rather, is to the subject of the sentence which expresses her belief. And given this divergence in reference, it is false to suppose we have the same term (name) in the two contexts. At best we have a common shape.

24 The example is from William Kneale and Martha Kneale, *The Development of Logic* (Oxford; Clarendon Press, 1962), p. 604.

25 See Wilfred Sellars, 'Belief and the Expression of Belief', in Howard E. Kiefer and Milton K. Munitz (eds.), *Language, Belief, and Metaphysics* (Albany, New York; State University of New York Press, 1970), pp. 146–59. Sellars regards belief here as a settled disposition to think that-*p*.

26 Hence the theory I have advanced in *Analytical Philosophy of Knowledge* that beliefs (and intentions) are 'sentential states' of persons. According to this view, '*m* believes that *s*' is true only if *m* is in a state which the shape *s* replicates, as in a quotation. This would account for the opacities, and it would square well enough with our intuition that what we essentially *are* is a certain representation of the world: a person in a deep sense *is* the way he represents the world.

27 See Bernard Williams, 'Deciding to Believe', in *Language, Belief, and Metaphysics*, p. 96. Strictly speaking, Williams's point is that *saying* 'I believe that *s*' carries an implication that I believe that *s* is true. And the argument is that, as G. E. Moore discovered, it is *somehow* paradoxical to say 'I believe that *s* but *s* is false.' Whether we may infer from this that it is equally paradoxical to *believe* that *s* and to believe that *s* is false is perhaps moot.

28 Since Austin, 'I promise' has been regarded as performative rather than descriptive, and promising consists in such acts as saying 'I promise' rather than in the occurrence of some internal condition which 'I promise' describes. See John Searle, *Speech Acts* (Cambridge; Cambridge University Press, 1969). But neither Searle nor Austin went on from analyzing the *making* to consider the *keeping* of a promise. And from the latter point of view, there is a plausible argument to be made that *something* internal is implied in promising.

29 See my *Analytical Philosophy of History* (Cambridge; Cambridge University Press, 1965), ch. 9.

30 And, as the Stoics and Nietzsche taught, to reconcile ourselves to what we are impotent to alter: to *love* our fate, or at any rate to endure it stoically.

31 Hence two of the routine honorific predicates attributed to God are irreconcilable, namely omnisciency and omnipotency. These may be reconciled by replacing the latter with omnificency, and by supposing *time* in some respect unreal. Everything

that is to be is in effect a *fait accompli* in eternity, outside of time and space. This mean that God does not know the future, of course, but only because futurity, as a tempora concept, marks no distinction in eternity. In the world of time, of course, belief an intention with regard to the same *s* are routinely complementary and exclusive.

CHAPTER 2

1 Adolf Grünbaum, 'Can an Infinitude of Operations be Performed in a Finit Time?', *British Journal for the Philosophy of Science*, xx, 2 (October 1969), 203–12.

2 The distinction between what I term 'mediated' and 'composite' actions is ele gantly made by Myles Brand in 'Danto on Basic Actions', *Noûs*, ii, 2 (May 1968) 187–90. He terms these 'complicated' and 'complex' actions, but the distinctio turns upon whether the components of 'non-simple' actions are causally tied or no See also his comments in his *The Nature of Human Action* (Glenview, Illinois; Scot Forsman, 1970), esp. p. 227. *Gestures* are discussed, though not under that term especially by A. I. Melden in *Free Action* (New York; Humanities Press, 1961), ch. and *passim*.

3 Analytical theories of meaning are typically covert theories of meaningfulness a well, so that if the theory of meaning specifies that the meaning of a term *not in th* base is given through definitions of it by means of terms in the base, this often impli a criterion of meaningfulness according to which a term is meaningful providing is either in the base or definable fully through terms in the base. When the base term are 'observational', the theory of meaningfulness is then empiricistic. The empirici dream, of course, is explicit definition of all non-basic terms through basic terms alon so that the entirety of meaningful discourse is assimilable to the base. This dream h gone shipwreck in recent times, but has not yet gone quite under. Replacement fo mulae other than explicit definition, e.g. reduction schemata, while they appear t allow some margin of extra-basic meaning, are nevertheless so tethered to the bas that this extra-basic margin of meaning can only be explicated via basic terms. Wha ever the case, it is *rules of meaning* which relate composite actions to their basic com ponents. So were the only extra-basic actions composite ones (or gestures), it would b correct to say, via a kind of dictionary (or actionary), that all we ever really *do* basic actions. Mediated actions, involving *causality*, take us outside the sphere meaning.

4 Russell writes: 'We can consider the whole body of empirical knowledge an define "basic propositions" as those of its logically indemonstrable propositions whic are themselves empirical.' *An Inquiry into Meaning and Truth* (London; Allen an Unwin, 1940), p. 139. Since no demonstation of these is possible, it follows that if w know to be true a basic proposition, our so knowing it must be a basic cognition. An in view of Russell's constructionistic program of absorbing the whole of knowledge t basic propositions, the latter are quasi-axiomatic for empirical knowledge. Othe writers, e.g. Schlick and Ayer, held basic propositions (or *Konstatieren*, as Schlic ermed them) to be such that their rules of meaning assure that they are known to be true just when they are understood. For they refer only to immediate experience, and once one understands them, or knows how they are to be used, then one cannot apply the rule of meaning they fall under without their truth or falsity being absolutely determined. See A. J. Ayer, 'Basic Propositions', in Max Black (ed.), *Philosophical Analysis* (Ithaca, New York; Cornell University Press, 1951), p. 72. It follows that no meaningful doubts are available once a basic proposition is understood. They are accordingly 'certain', and held to be such because the conditions under which they are meaningful are those of the basic cognition.

J. L. Austin, *Sense and Sensibilia* (Oxford; Clarendon Press, 1962), p. 116.

Galileo holds that the sole difference between God and us lies in the manner and not the content of knowledge, and not in what we can but only in what we in fact know. We thus can know whatever God knows, and are *practically* omniscient. It is only that all God's cognitions are basic while most of ours are mediated. 'We proceed by argumentation and advance from conclusion to conclusion, while God [apprehends] through a simple, sudden intuition.' *Dialogo sopra i due massimi sistemi del mondo.* I discuss this in *Analytical Philosophy of Knowledge*, p. 65, n. 1. The immediate extension of this to action is plain: we can do whatever God does, albeit not always as a basic action. So we are practically omnipotent. This makes, however, the ways of God inscrutable to man, in large part because we cannot understand how things can be done as basic actions which we can *only* get to happen through causes. On the other hand, to the degree to which we have any basic cognitions and perform any basic actions, we are indeed in the image of God.

George Berkeley, *Three Dialogues between Hylas and Philonous*, II.

'But, besides all that endless variety of ideas or objects of knowledge, there is likewise Something which knows or perceives them; and exercises divers operations, as willing, imagining, remembering, about them. This perceiving, active being is what I call *mind, spirit, soul,* or *myself.* By which words I do not denote any of my ideas, but a thing entirely distinct from them, wherein they exist, or, which is the same thing, whereby they are perceived; for the existence of an idea consists in being perceived.' George Berkeley, *The Principles of Human Knowledge*, pt. I, sect. 2. In sect. 7, Berkeley makes explicit that 'There can be no *idea* formed of a soul or spirit.' He adds, parenthetically; 'It must be owned at the same time that we have some *notion* of soul, spirit, and the operations of the mind . . . inasmuch as we know or understand the meaning of these words.'

'It is intelligible and informative to say that a person's hand moved because he moved it.' D. G. Brown, *Action* (Toronto; University of Toronto Press, 1968), p. 134.

'A thought may have just the same content whether you assent to its truth or not; a proposition may occur in discourse now asserted, now unasserted, and yet be recognizably the same.' Peter Geach, 'Assertion', *Philosophical Review*, LXXIV, 4 (1965), p. 449.

11 Frank Ramsey, 'Facts and Propositions', *Proceedings of the Aristotelian Society*, Sup. vol. VII (1927), 148–87. Of 'It is true (false) that . . .', Ramsay writes: 'They are phrases we sometimes use for emphasis or for stylistic reasons.' Those who follow Ramsey disagree as to the *force* these phrases give without disagreeing that they are not *descriptive* phrases. I have especially P. F. Strawson, A. J. Ayer, and Gertrude Ezorsky in mind.

12 J. L. Austin, 'Other Minds', *Proceedings of the Aristotelian Society*, Sup. vol. XX (1946), 34n.

13 Gottlob Frege, in Peter Geach and Max Black (eds.), *Translations from the Philosophical Writings of Gotlob Frege* (Oxford; Blackwell, 1960), p. 11.

14 G. E. M. Anscombe, in *Intention* (Oxford; Blackwell, 1957), p. 11, proposes only that an action is intentional under one description but not necessarily under all its descriptions. It follows that being intentional is not entailed by the concept of action (though it may be we would not count it an action unless it were intentional under *some* description). Other writers – they are legion – make a stronger claim, namely that an event is an *action* under a description. Hence there are descriptions under which it is not one. It is this stronger thesis I address myself to, a thesis all the more vulnerable because it has no natural basis in the opacities reference to intentions allow.

15 'There are no objects which, by the mere survey, without consulting experience, we can determine to be the causes of any other; and no objects which we can determine in the same manner not to be causes. Anything may produce anything.' David Hume, *A Treatise of Human Nature*, bk. I, pt. III, sect. xv. This is a trivial extension of the fact that we could hardly tell what relations something bore to anything else by examining *it* alone. Cf. 'In reality, there is no part of matter, that does ever, by its sensible qualities, discover any power or energy, or give us ground to imagine, that it could produce anything or be followed by any other object, which we could denominate its effect.' *An Enquiry Concerning Human Understanding*, sect. VII, pt. I.

16 Don F. Gustafson, 'Explanation in Psychology', *Mind*, LXXIII (1964), 280–1.

17 This criticism, directed primarily at Melden (*Free Action*), is made by Donald Davidson in 'Actions, Reasons, and Causes', *Journal of Philosophy*, LX, 23 (November 1963), p. 700.

18 'It is a mistake in principle to attempt to define an action as a bodily happening plus another concurrent event, mental or bodily.' A. I. Melden, *Free Action*, p. 80.

19 C. I. Lewis, *An Analysis of Knowledge and Valuation* (Lasalle, Illinois; Open Court, 1946), p. 183. Lewis's exact words are: 'Subtract, in what we say we see or hear, or otherwise learn from direct experience, all that can conceivably be mistaken: the remainder is the given content of experience inducing this belief.' This neutralization of content and externalization of what makes the difference between 'veridicality' and 'illusoriness' is a standard, fatal, inevitable philosophical move. It is what gives rise to all the major problems of Skepticism. For detailed discussion, see my *Analytical Philosophy of Knowledge*, chs. 8 and 9, and *What Philosophy Is* (New York; Harper and Row, 1968), pt. 3.

20 'Let us not forget this: When "I raise my arm", my arm goes up. And the problem arises: what is left over if I subtract the fact that my arm goes up from the fact that I raise my arm?' Ludwig Wittgenstein, *Philosophical Investigations* (Oxford; Blackwell, 1953), para. 621.

21 I have chiefly in mind G. E. M. Anscombe, Anthony Kenny, and A. I. Melden, whose collective contributions, however profound, are footnotes to paras. 611–60 of *Philosophical Investigations*.

CHAPTER 3

1 The recent turn given to this term of art is due to Roderick Chisholm: 'When one event or state of affairs (or set of events or states of affairs) causes some other event or state of affairs, then we have an instance of *transeunt* causation. And I shall say that when an *agent*, as distinguished from an event, causes an event or state of affairs, then we have an instance of *immanent* causation.' 'Freedom and Action', in Keith Lehrer (ed.), *Freedom and Determinism* (New York; Random House, 1966), p. 17. Chisholm in fact uses immanency to characterize not only basic actions, such as the raising of an arm, but also such occurrences as those in the brain which may *cause* an arm to rise when a man raises his arm. So immanent causation only takes doing (as in basic actions) as an instance. For Chisholm both denies that a man can do something 'to his brain or with his brain' and insists that from this it 'does not follow that the agent is not the immanent cause of some event in his brain'. *Loc. cit.* pp. 19–20. So immanent causation exactly bisects the distinction between basic action and events which are not actions at all. Chisholm finds the distinction in Aristotle, *Physics*, VII, 5, 256a, 6–8.

2 For arguments that this *is* the logical form of causal ascriptions, see Donald Davidson, 'Causal Relations', *Journal of Philosophy*, LXIV, 21 (9 November 1967), 691–703.

3 Richard Taylor, *Action and Purpose* (Englewood Cliffs, New Jersey; Prentice-Hall, 1966), esp. ch. 1. Taylor also makes a distinction between (though he does not use the terms) immanent and transeunt causation. But immanent causation appears to be restricted by him to what agents do as basic actions, in contrast with what *things* 'do'. See ch. 9.

4 Certain metaphysicians ironically excepted, the *rest* of mankind, Hume affirms, are 'Nothing but a bundle or collection of different perceptions, which succeed each other with an inconceivable rapidity and are in a perpetual flux and movement.' *A Treatise of Human Nature*, bk. I, pt. IV, sect. vi.

5 In the tradition, which is somewhat confused, the distinction between immanent and transeunt causation appears largely to do with whether cause and effect are somehow both internal to the subject – in which case we have immanency – or either the cause or the effect is external to the agent – in which case we have transeuncy. See the definition in Blanc, *Dictionnaire de philosophie* (Paris; P. Lethielleux, 1906): 'L'immanence est la proprieté d'une activité ou d'un acte dont le terme est dans le sujet lui-même.' M. Blondel, cited in Lalande's *Vocabulaire technique et critique de la philosophie*, sees immanency as 'l'expression de ce qu'il porte essentiellement en lui', drawing no distinction between things and agents, nor (as with Chisholm) between actions and other events, so long as these are explained with reference to the subject. But C. D. Broad, *Scientific Thought* (London; Routledge and Kegan Paul, 1923), appears to think of immanency as a state of a continuant which happens to resemble very closely another state of it, whereas a *transeunt* causal relation is between events of qualitatively different sorts and belonging to 'a different substance or strand of history' (p. 492). Thus the states of a particle in conformity with the first law of motion are immanent, while accelerations would be transeunt, viz. those due to 'impeding forces'. This is the way, more or less, of the logician Johnson, in his *Logic* (Cambridge; Cambridge University Press, 1924), pt. III. An episode of transeunt causation is where one thing (continuant, in Johnson's terminology) acts on another. In a Leibnizian system, all causation is immanent, but my concern in this note is merely to underscore the extreme chaos of the distinction.

6 Hume, *An Enquiry Concerning Human Understanding*, sect. VII, pt. I: 'An act of volition produces motion in our limbs or raises a new idea in our imagination.' Berkeley holds much the same view: 'I never use an instrument to move my finger, because it is done by a volition.' *Three Dialogues between Hylas and Philonous*, II. Berkeley, incidentally, claims that volitions are *all* we do. Thus, motions are amongst the sensible qualities, and hence cannot be active.'When I stir my finger, it remains passive; but my will, which produced the motion, is active.' This concluded, Hylas is challenged 'whether, motion being allowed to be no action, you can conceive of any action besides volition'. Hylas collapses like a stooge in a platonic dialogue. Thomas Reid, whose *Essay on the Active Powers of the Human Mind* is famously critical of Hume, accepts more or less without demur the concept of volition and draws the distinctions almost exactly as I have ascribed them to Hume: 'The effects of human power are either immediate or they are remote. The immediate effects, I think, are reducible to two heads. We can give certain motions of our own bodies; and we can give certain directions to our own thoughts.' I cite from the edition of his book published at Cambridge, Mass.; M.I.T. Press, 1969, p. 69.

7 Gilbert Ryle, *The Concept of Mind* (Oxford; Blackwell, 1949), pp. 62–9. More or less the same argument is to be found in Reid, *Essay on the Active Powers of the Human Mind*, p. 253, who credits it to Hobbes. If the will is to be itself willed, there is 'an infinite series of wills, which is absurd'. Reid denies that the will in fact is willed.

8 Ryle, *The Concept of Mind*, pp. 64–5. Ryle poses a list of what must be embarrassing questions for volition theorists.

9 It may be argued that we simply have not trained to the sort of dissociative observation required for individuating and identifying volitions. Ryle dismisses this, but even if it can be maintained, it will not help Hume.

10 See Wilfred Sellars, 'Fatalism and Determinism', in Lehrer, *Freedom and Determinism*, pp. 150ff.: 'A volition is an inner episode, a mental act, which is, in the absence of paralysis and granting favorable circumstances, the cause of the corresponding action . . . Volitions are a subclass of *thoughts*.' Lawrence H. Davis, in 'The Individuation of Actions', *Journal of Philosophy*, LXVII, 5 (6 August 1970), speaks of volitions as 'a kind of event which would be first members of sequences or sums of events that are actions' (p. 530). Davis is sympathetic to the idea that a volition is an event in the brain, and that though *we* may describe it with such an expression as 'I willed . . .', another description is in principle available which makes no reference to the agent. He proposes, and I naturally agree, that we may 'explain what an act *is* wholly in terms of bodily and other events which are not themselves acts, or at least not necessarily described as such'. The italicized *is*, I gather, is the 'is' of identity or of material cause, from which it would follow that what an action is *necessarily could not* be described in terms of 'events which are themselves acts'.

11 The point that we do moral philosophy primarily in terms of judges rather than agents, where the question arises more how to evaluate rather than what to do, has been made by Stuart Hampshire in 'Fallacies in Moral Philosophy', *Mind*, LVIII (October 1949) 466–82, and more or less the same posture is endemic to epistomology, viz. that of *testing* whether someone knows something.

12 I discuss erection as a possible action in Chapters 5 and 6. The external resemblances between it and the paradigm of arm-raising were sufficiently and obviously marked for St Augustine to speculate that men might compass voluntary erection in the repertoires of basic competence. See Chapter 5, note 2, below.

13 I have in mind the sort of relation Aristotle hints at in *Nicomachean Ethics*, bk. II, ch. 4, where he speaks of a just or temperate act not being one merely because it satisfies certain criteria, and certainly not because he who performs one follows a certain rule, but rather when it proceeds *from his character*. One may thus learn what justice is by imitating what just men do, but one is not a just man oneself until the action proceeds from one's character. So we judge an action as just finally only in terms of the deep relation to its performance that a man stands in when he does it *as* a just man would do it. This concept has immense implications for linguistic, artistic, as well as moral competence. But I cannot explore these matters here. Father Robert Sokolowski drew my attention to this remarkable passage.

14 I introduce these distinctions in 'Complex Events', *Philosophy and Phenomenological Research*, XXX, 1 (September 1969), 66–77. The formulation there suffers, however, from a bad use–mention confusion.

15 The criterion is due to Donald Davidson: 'Events are identical if and only if they have exactly the same causes and effects.' 'The Individuation of Events', in N. Rescher (ed.), *Essays in Honor of Carl Hempel* (Dordrecht; D. Reidel, 1970), p. 231. Since I claim disjoint classes of causes for the doing of *b* and for *b* itself, I deny that they are the same event, albeit the latter is contained in the former. Hence I dispute Davidson's identification of them elsewhere, viz. 'If a man's arm goes up, the event takes place in the space–time zone occupied by the arm; but if a man raises his arm, doesn't the event fill the zone occupied by the whole man? Yet the events may be identical.' Reply to E. J. Lemmon to his 'The Logical Form or Action Sentences', in N. Rescher (ed.), *The Logic of Decision and Action* (Pittsburgh; University of Pittsburgh Press, 1968), p. 84. Davidson I dare say allows the one zone to be part of the other, but demurs at the suggestion that one *event* might be part of the other.

16 'Actuality is incurably atomic . . . so far as physical relations are concerned, contemporary events happen in *causal* independence of one another.' A. N. Whitehead, *Process and Reality* (London and New York; Macmillan, 1929), p. 95. See also p. 188.

17 Or rather, it is Hume's argument that if *any* cause is contemporary with its effect, *all* are, which means less the destruction of the concept of causation than the 'utter annihilation of time'. *A Treatise of Human Nature*, bk. I, pt. III, sect. ii. 'For if one cause were contemporary with its effect, and this effect with *its* effect, and so on, it is plain there would be no such thing as succession, and all objects must be co-existent.' This is a manifest confusion of causal and temporal succession. There could be succession, albeit the criterion of causal independence now would be that two events were non-contemporary. Richard Taylor points out that if all causes were contemporary with their effects, 'there would be no such thing as a causal chain'. *Action and Purpose*, p. 38. To those who suppose all causes contemporary with their effects, this merely begs the question, I should think. Taylor of course claims that there are causal chains.

18 Douglas Gasking, 'Causality and Recipes', *Mind*, LXIV (1955), 479–87. The asymmetry of cause and effect, which Hume seeks to explicate in terms of temporal asymmetry, Gasking ingeniously suggests is rather due to the asymmetry of means and ends, hence recipes. We call causes what we can manipulate to produce effects. A similar but essentially confused suggestion along these lines is advanced by R. G. Collingwood in *An Essay on Metaphysics* (Oxford; Oxford University Press, 1940), pt. 3–c. A trenchant discussion is found in John Dewey, *Logic: The Theory of Inquiry* (New York; Holt, 1938), pp. 460ff.: 'Propositions that deal explicitly with subject-matters that are connected with one another as means to consequences have a claim to be called causal propositions in a distinctive sense.'

19 Taylor, *Action and Purpose*, allows that some causes may be contemporary with their effects, but that in fact not all are, so that temporal succession is not entailed, nor is non-contemporaneity entailed, by the causal concept. But others have argued that all causes *must* be contemporary with their effects. See Richard Taylor, 'Causation', in Paul Edwards (ed.), *The Encyclopedia of Philosophy* (New York; Macmillan and Free Press, 1967), II, 65. Time cannot, of course, be an irrelevant distinction, since it is generally conceded, whatever may be the reason, that causes cannot temporally *succeed* their effects. See Michael Dummett, 'Bringing about the Past', *Philosophical Review*, LXXIII, 3 (1964), 338–59. It is the basis for an incapacity to reduce the concept of causation to the concept of necessary and sufficient condition, since a sufficient condition may succeed an event, as indeed may a necessary condition.

20 Chisholm employs the expression 'makes happen' in a technical sense, and introduces it in 'Freedom and Action', in Lehrer, *Freedom and Determinism*, p. 31, where he introduces restrictions and suggests as an English paraphrase 'realizes'. ' "Make happen" is to be taken in such a way that we may say, of a man who raises his arm, not only that he makes it happen that his arm goes up, but also that he makes it happen, just before, that certain other physiological events occur inside his body, and that he makes it happen, just subsequently, that air particles move in various ways.' This *sounds* as though 'makes happen' compasses immanent and transeunt causation, basic and mediated action, plus something else, not easily assimilated to these, of the sort we are in search of.

21 There is a familiar argument against identity-claims which Wilfred Sellars endorses as 'going to the heart of the matter' in his frequently cited essay 'The Identity Approach to the Mind–Body Problem', *The Review of Metaphysics*, XVIII (1965), 430–51. He formulates it thus in para. 37: ' "How", it asks, "can a property which is in the logical space of neurophysiological states be identical with a property which is not?" Otherwise put, "How could a predicate defined in terms of neurophysiological primitives have the same use (be synonymous with) a predicate which is not?" To *this* question the inevitable answer is: "It could not." ' I find the argument irrelevant. Indeed, it states exactly what would be the case, and hence ought to be expected, if identity is assumed. Identity would explain non-synonymy.

22 David Hume, *An Enquiry Concerning Human Understanding*, sect. VII, pt. I. I discuss Hume's argument under a different aspect in Chapter 5.

23 Friederich Nietzsche, *Twilight of the Idols*, III, 5. Nietzsche's critique of the concept of the will was astute. For discussion and references, see my *Nietzsche as Philosopher* (New York; Macmillan, 1965), pp. 109–16.

24 Reid, *Essay on the Active Powers of the Human Mind*, combines much the same occasionalism as Hume, with a somewhat more enlightened view of the relationship between action and the physiology of the agent. 'That there is a pre-established harmony between our willing certain motions of our bodies, and the operations of the nerves and muscles which produce these motions, is a fact known by experience. But whether this act of the mind have any physical effect upon the nerves and muscles, or whether it is only an occasion of their being acted upon by some other efficient (*sic*), according to the established laws of nature, is hidden from us.'

CHAPTER 4

1 The distinction between dictionaries and encyclopedias I owe – in a curious way

– to the announced title of a paper which he did not write by Gilbert Harman: 'Dictionaries and Encyclopedias: An Untenable Dualism'. Like the poor librarian of Borges, who wrote the books from the titles on lists sent him by publishers since he could not afford to purchase them, I attempted to work out what Harman could have had in mind, and was disappointed when he told me the paper was never completed. Encyclopedias, I suppose, comprehend the bulk of our causal beliefs, but if a man should reject the entries in the encyclopedia, it is hardly clear that we would speak the same language or have the same conceptual scheme. Thus it is difficult to suppose a man could repudiate every item in the article on apples and still *mean* by 'apple' what we do. So shared meaning supposes shared truths. Hence we necessarily revise meanings when we revise factual beliefs, if we revise them in significant numbers. This, to be sure, is the crux of the view that the distinction between analytic and synthetic propositions is 'an untenable dualism'. The Φ-vocabulary is meant, I suppose, to be neutral with regard to that distinction and that controversy, but I doubt it would itself survive radical transformation either of meaning or of truth.

2 'So far as form is concerned, the issue of non-extensionality does not arise, since the relationship of causality between events can be expressed (no matter how "strong" or "weak" it is) by an ordinary two-place predicate in ordinary extensional first-order language.' Donald Davidson, 'Causal Relations', *Journal of Philosophy*, LXIV, 21 (9 November 1967), p. 702. I will accept this for a moment, but it will be shortly noted that we are in fact dealing with (at least) a three-place predicate relating two events and a law, and that the question of extensionality rises sharply with the third relatum.

3 'It would only be by using "to observe" in a Pickwickian sense that it would be possible to deny that we ever observe one thing breaking, or bending, or killing, or dragging, etc. another thing,' C. J. Ducasse, *Nature, Mind, and Death* (Lasalle, Illinois; Open Court, 1951), p. 120. Hence, in view of the causal implications carried by these terms, it would be only through that 'Pickwickian sense' that *causal relations* are counted non-observable. This is largely correct and irrelevant at once, so far as concerns the analysis of the concept. The Ducassian point is often echoed in philosophical literature, e.g. in A. R. Louch, *Explanation and Human Action* (Berkeley and Los Angeles; University of California Press, 1966), pp. 43, 48: 'It is not necessary to break up this sequence into smaller units in order to be quite sure that the swing of the bat caused the ball to follow its trajectory ... We can see, not merely the discrete and hypothetical elements of visual experience, but objects and relations amongst them as well.' The issue of 'being quite sure' is hardly relevant, nor hardly a motive for 'breaking up' the sequence. The question is *where* in the sequence the *causal* relation is to be located, and to identify it *with* the sequence quite disregards the sort of case I cite.

4 'Le mécanisme de notre connaissance usuelle est de nature cinématographique.' Henri Bergson. *Oeuvres* (Paris; Presses Universitaires, 1959), p. 753.

5 It is this *sort* of point which Descartes is in essence making through the celebrated example of the wax. What makes us say that it is the *same* wax which has *first* one and

then another non-overlapping and contrary set of properties? So change and identity are not elements in our experience of things, but frameworks within which elements are accordingly organized, and hence categorial. Descartes, to be sure, makes the point as a polemical deflection of a criticism which invidiously contrasts the abstract nature of our knowledge of *res cogitans* with the ostensibly concrete nature of our knowledge of physical objects. His purpose is to show the latter to be hardly less abstract. Polemical context notwithstanding, the move in *Meditation* II is in striking anticipation of Kant.

6 This is exemplified in the view that 'causes' is to be treated as a non-truth-functional connective between *propositions* rather than as a relational predicate taking names of events as arguments. See J. L. Mackie, 'Causes and Conditions', *American Philosophical Quarterly*, II (October 1965), 245–64; and Arthur Pap, 'Dispositional Concepts and Extensional Logic', in H. Feigl, M. Scriven, and G. Maxwell (eds.), *Minnesota Studies in the Philosophy of Science*, II (Minneapolis; University of Minnesota Press, 1958), 196–224. Davidson, in 'Causal Relations', advances what he regards as grave difficulties in parsing the logical form of causal sentences thus, but Bernard Berofsky takes a more optimistic view of the Connectivist's options for meeting Davidson's objections. See his *Determinism* (Princeton; Princeton University Press, 1971), pp. 51–3.

7 'The identity and existence of the thing, its being in reality what it appears to be at a certain phase of the perceptual process, depend upon, or, if one prefers, correspond to the perceptual process developing harmoniously, all its phases mutually continuing and confirming one another . . . [Real things] can be posited as existent only with the proviso that later phases of the perceptual process will be in harmony and agreement with one another and with earlier phases.' Aron Gurwitsch, 'The Problem of Existence in Constitutive Phenomenology', *Journal of Philosophy*, LVIII, 21 (12 October 1961), 631. This is exactly a *coherence* theory of existence, and passes over into a verificationist account. Phenomenology is after all radical empiricism, and it is not to be wondered at accordingly that Phenomenologists should attempt to treat existence descriptively, as something *within* experience, even though there is no experience of existence as such.

8 'Truth for us is simply a collective name for verification processes.' William James, 'Pragmatism's Conception of Truth', *Pragmatism* (New York; Longmans Green, 1907), p. 218. 'The concept of truth appears as an idealization of the concept of high degree, and the concept of meaning is the quality of being accessible to the determination of a weight', writes Reichenbach in *Experience and Predication* (Chicago; University of Chicago Press, 1938), pp. 190–1. Pragmatism and Positivism alike undertook a verificationist analysis of truth.

9 'Whenever the repetition of any particular act or operation produces a propensity to renew the same act or operation, without being impelled by any reasoning or process of the understanding, we always say, that this propensity is the effect of *Custom*.' David Hume, *An Enquiry Concerning Human Understanding*, sect. V, pt. I.

10 'It does not follow that we must be able to dredge up a law if we know a singular causal statement to be true; all that follows is that we know there must be a covering law. And very often, I think, our justification for accepting a singular causal statement is that we have reason to believe an appropriate causal law exists, though we do not know what it is.' Davidson, 'Causal Relations', p. 701. In *Foundations of Historical Knowledge* (New York; Harper and Row, 1965), p. 75 and *passim*, Morton White argues the related point that singular causal statements imply the existence of laws, not only even if we do not know what they are but even though we have as yet no clearcut philosophical understanding of the *form* of causal laws as such.

11 William Dray, *Laws and Explanation in History* (Oxford; Oxford University Press, 1957) is able, I think, to question the explanatory character of laws by confusing laws with generalization. 'All *a*'s are *b*'s' goes no distance towards explaining the *b*-hood of the *b*'s unless a causal law is implicit in the generalization. Thus 'All men are mortal' – though true – is unedifying with regard to the mortality of men unless humanity explains, as it does not, mortality.

12 'The very concept of a cause so manifestly contains the concept of a necessity of connection with an effect and of the strict universality of the rule, that the concept would be altogether lost if we attempted to derive it, as Hume has done, from a repeated association of that which happens with that which precedes, and from a custom of connecting representations, a custom originating in this repeated association, and constituting therefore a merely subjective necessity.' Immanuel Kant, *Critique of Pure Reason*, trans. Norman Kemp Smith (London; Macmillan, 1963), p. 44.

13 I borrow the expression, though not altogether the concept he intended by its use, from Nelson Goodman, *Languages of Art*.

14 Karl Popper, *The Logic of Scientific Discovery*, is the *locus classicus* of falsificationism. My own account leaves, as irrelevant, both the inductivist and anti-inductive *psycho-iogical* questions, of which Sir Karl makes so much. In view of the irrelevance of large numbers in my analysis, however, I incline to favor Popper's views in this regard, and his insistence upon the imaginative provenance of causal laws is quite in keeping with my views.

15 One special class of cases under this concept is worked out by Paul Grice in his influential paper, 'Meaning', *Philosophical Review*, LXVI, (3 July 1957), 377–8, in connection especially with what he terms 'non-natural meaning'. In general, to read an event as having been *done* presupposes in these cases that it was intended an audience should read it *as* intended: that recognition of the intention is presupposed in giving a *meaning* to the event. Meaning in this sense is unaffected, I believe, by criticisms of Grice's view which suppose his account relevant to semantical theory.

CHAPTER 5

1 David Hume, *An Enquiry Concerning Human Understanding*, sect. VII, pt. 1. All citations in this chapter are from this source.

2 St Augustine, *The City of God*, xiv, ch. 24. All citations in this chapter are from this source.

3 Something of this order is implicit in the concept of *adequacy*, which Spinoza employs in *Ethics*, iii, defs, i and ii: 'I say that we *act* when anything takes place, either within us or externally to us, whereof we are the adequate cause; that is . . . when through our nature something takes place within us or externally to us, which can through our nature alone be clearly and distinctly understood.' I suspect that Chisholm's concept of 'making happen' (see p. 63 above) is a gloss on this.

4 This is treated exhaustively in the next chapter.

5 'Every great philosophy has so far been . . . the self-confession of its originator, and a kind of unintentional, unaware *mémoires*.' Friedrich Nietzsche, *Beyond Good and Evil*, 6. Cf. 'So I muddied the stream of friendship with the filth of lewdness, and clouded its clear waters with hell's black river of lust.' St Augustine, *Confessions*, iii, 1. Translation by R. S. Pine-Coffin (Harmondsworth; Penguin Books, 1961), p. 55.

6 'I would stand in front of my mirror, concentrating all my powers in a command to my pupils to contract or expand, banishing every other thought from my mind... At first I stood bathed in sweat, my colour coming and going, my pupils would flicker erratically, but later I succeeded in contracting them to the merest points and then expanding them to great, round, mirror-like pools. The joy I felt at this success was almost terrifying and was accompanied by a shudder at the mystery of man.' Thomas Mann, *Confessions of Felix Krull, Confidence Man*, trans. Denver Lindley (New York; Knopf, 1955), pp. 11–12.

7 The history of attempts to condition the pupillary reflex effectively begins with H. Cason, 'The Conditioned Pupillary Reaction', *Journal of Experimental Psychology*, v (1922), 108–46. Cason employed a bell, much as Pavlov had done, but C. V. Hudgins, 'Conditioning and the Voluntary Control of the Pupillary Light Reflex', *Journal of General Psychology*, viii (1933), 3–51, sought to bring the dilation under the *verbal* control of the subject. His results were inconclusive, but the use of shock in conditioning appears definite. A. A. Gerall and P. A. Obrist, 'Classical Conditioning of the Human Pupillary Dilation', *Journal of Comparative Physiological Psychology*', lv (1962), 486–91, explains that the startle reaction to shock, which includes dilation, is prepotent over the pupillary reflex to light. For summary and comment, as well as further references, consult Robert S. Beecroft, *Classical Conditioning* (Goleta, California; Psychonomic Press, 1966), pp. 49–56.

8 Neal Miller, 'Learning of Visceral and Glandular Responses', *Science*, 193 (31 January 1969), 434–45. Miller reports successful conditioning of heart-rate, intestinal reactions, kidney functions, gastric changes, and the like. For a summary of other work, see 'Control by Brain Studied as Way to Curb Body Ills', *New York Times*, 10 January 1971. Miller's paper is especially relevant to us in that he has been very careful to distinguish between what I would call basic, in contrast with mediated control of these responses. 'It is hard to rule out the possibility that, instead of directly learning a visceral response, the subject has learned a skeletal response the performance of which *causes* the visceral change being recorded' (p. 435, my italics). Hence he used curare to paralyze the rats temporarily.

9 Obviously there are more normal senses than five when we reckon in the proprioceptive senses – vestibular and kinaesthic – as well as visceral ones. But the expression 'the five senses' connotes the *normal* equipment, much as 'sixth sense' is explicitly defined as 'a power of perception seemingly independent of the five senses' (*The American Heritage Dictionary of the English Language*). Locke writes: 'I have here followed the common opinion of man's having but five senses, though perhaps there may be justly counted more; but either supposition serves equally to my present purpose.' *An Essay Concerning Human Understanding*, bk. II, ch. II, sect. 3.

10 Leibniz, I believe, expresses what must have been for a long time the canonical view, that 'Axioms and postulates . . . cannot be proved and, indeed, have no need of proof.' *Monadology*, 35.

11 Hence, in the cave episode of the *Republic*, the philosopher who redescends is *obliged* to speak gibberish to those who have never left it. Plato, of course, believed in the theory that we only understand what we are acquainted with. Hence, if we understand general terms there (a) must be general *things* – which yields his most characteristic metaphysical thesis, and (b) we must be acquainted with these – which yields his doctrine that knowledge (of general things) is *recollection*. This almost yields a theory of the immortality of the soul by way of a transcendental argument.

12 'Even as light displays both itself and darkness, so is truth a standard both of itself and of falsity.' Spinoza, *Ethics*, II, xliii, note.

13 David Hume, *A Treatise of Human Nature*, bk. I, pt. I, sect. i, speaks of 'the one contradictory phenomenon' to his general principle that 'all our simple ideas in their first appearance are derived from simple impressions, which are correspondent to them'; and again in *An Enquiry Concerning Human Understanding*, sect. II. The example shows that Hume's principle – which is in effect empiricism as a theory of the acquisition of understanding – is not *necessarily* true. That there is this counter-instance suggests that it in fact is false. For speculations as to why Hume was able to accept with such seeming *sang-froid* a case which ought on sound scientific principles to have thrown his theory out, see Bernard Rollin, 'Hume's Blue Patch and the Mind's Creativity', *Journal of the History of Ideas*, XXXII, 1 (March 1971), 119–28. Hume's case can be generalized if Helmholz is correct in believing that two sensations belong to *distinct* modalities if they have no intermediary. For then each modality is a continuum, although whether this is strictly required by Hume's case is not plain: a series of sensations can be *quantized* although intermediate sensations between two 'just noticeably different' elements would *plainly* not be noticed, and this just *may* entail a continuum. For details of this history of the modality concept, with interesting reference to Hans Henning's work on tastes and smells, see E. G. Boring, *Sensation and Perception in the*

History of Experimental Psychology (New York; Appleton-Century, 1952), pp. 10, 444, 454, and *passim*.

14 Peter Geach, *Mental Acts* (London; Routledge and Kegan Paul), p. 35, n. 1. Geach's remark is embedded in a discussion of *abstractionism*, as he terms it, though I am not certain his being wrong on this point blunts the edges of that polemic.

15 Mrs Stanley is quoted thus in 'Woman Who Tells Colors by Touch Mystifies Psychologist', *New York Times*, 8 January 1964. The psychologist – R. P. Youtz – has a theory of how the discriminations are to be physiologically, i.e. non-mysteriously, accounted for. A portion of the electro-magnetic wave-length spectrum is responded to as light, another portion as heat. Light can penetrate the skin 'to a considerable depth in measurable quantities'. Obviously thresholds vary, and Mrs Stanley has an especially low one. So perhaps the ability is a matter of making fine temperature discrimination, viz. feeling light as heat. R. P. Youtz, *Report to the Psychonomic Society*, 9 October 1964. See also 'Dermo-Optical Perception', in *Science*, 152 (20 May 1966), 1108. Much the same sort of hypothesis may be invoked to account for the 'Mrs G. Phenomenon', in which the subject was converting electric signals into sound signals, and 'hearing' things inaudible to others. See *Newsweek*, 20 January 1964, p. 52. This leaves, of course, the question of the intelligibility of the sensation report unaffected, we still cannot *understand* Mrs Stanley or Mrs G.

16 I discuss 'two-stage predicates' in 'Historical Understanding: The Problem of Other Periods', *Journal of Philosophy* LXIII, 18 (13 October 1966), 566–77; and in *Analytical Philosophy of Knowledge*, p. 46.

17 Descartes, *Meditation* VI; Leibniz, *Nouveaux Essais*, II, ch. xxix, para. 13.

18 Francis Galton, *Inquiries into Human Faculty* (Everyman edition), p. 59; cited by H. H. Price, *Thinking and Experience* (Cambridge, Massachusetts; Harvard University Press, 1953), p. 235.

19 Gilbert Ryle, *The Concept of Mind*, ch. 8.

20 Grey Walter, *The Living Brain* (New York; W. W. Norton, 1953), pp. 214–17. Without this being an *explanation*, of course, it is striking that there should be the strong correlation between persistent alpha rhythms and *no* visualization, on the one hand, and the virtual absence of alpha rhythms with strong visualization.

21 I discuss these questions in 'Concerning Mental Pictures', *Journal of Philosophy*, LV, 1 (2 January 1955), 12–20.

22 The *impotency* of the imagination to produce a simple idea not initially caused by an impression is stressed by Locke in *An Essay Concerning Human Understanding*, bk. II, ch. II, sect. 2, and again in ch. VII, sect. 1: 'This shows man's power and its way of operation to be much-what the same in the material and the intellectual world. For the materials in both being such as he has no power over, either to make or destroy, all that man can do is either to unite them together, or to set by one another, or wholly separate them.' A similar power and impotency are scheduled by Hume, in *A Treatise of Human Nature*, bk. I, pt. I, sect. iii; and in the *Enquiry Concerning Human Understanding*, sect. II: 'All this creative power of the mind amounts to no more than the faculty of compounding, transposing, augmenting, or diminishing the materials afforded us by the senses and experience.'

23 Imagination can in this way be an *action* (whether or not it happens to consist in producing a mental picture): 'Seeing an aspect and imagining are subject to the will. There is such an order as "Imagine *this*", and also "Now see the figure like this"; but not: "Now see this leaf green." ' Ludwig Wittgenstein, *Philosophical Investigations*, II, xi, 213ᵉ.

24 J. L. Austin, 'Ifs and Cans', *Proceedings of the British Academy*, XLII (1956), 109–32.

25 The formulation is Roderick Chisholm's. See his 'J. L. Austin's Philosophical Papers', *Mind*, LXXIII (1964), 20–5.

26 'Having a sense-datum' thus is invariant as between so-called veridical and so-called illusory perception. So one always may retreat to this neutral base, and hence to a (mere) sense-datum claim in the face of perceptual failure. Or one can say: it seemed as though one were sensing. This presumably admits of no further retreat, unless some further neutral element may be a fixed center in the switch from really to only apparently seeming to sense.

27 'I am not lodged in my body merely as a pilot in a ship, but so intimately conjoined, and as it were intermingled with it, that with it I form a unitary whole.' Descartes, *Meditation* VI.

28 'He refused to look at his paralyzed left side. If his paralyzed arm was brought before his eyes, he would declare that it was the hand of another person, "probably from the patient nearby", or would say, "I don't know where it comes from; it is so long and lifeless and as dead as a snake."' Paul Schilder, *The Image and Appearance of the Human Body* (New York; John Wiley, 1964), p. 67. The case, to be sure, is extreme. But it is worth stressing that the patient described here did not take the same attitude towards his good arm. The patient was a left-sided hemiplegic with, incidentally, a complete left-sided hemianaesthesia.

29 In Berkeley, for instance. Berkeley is curiously liable to the criticism of Spinoza, *Ethics*, II, prop. XLIX, *scholim:* 'They look upon ideas . . . as dumb pictures on a tablet.' For a full-scale discussion, see Price, *Thinking and Experience*, ch. 8.

30 It is striking that the Problem of Other Bodies – of accounting for the fact that I cannot move your body as a basic action any more than I can have your sensations – goes largely unnoticed by Maurice Merleau-Ponty in his discussion of the embodied self in *The Phenomenology of Perception* (London; Routledge and Kegan Paul, 1965) especially Part I. Indeed, Merleau, for all his insight into the difference between my relation to my body and my relation to other bodies in the world, works this out in terms of my *representation* of my body, hence exhibiting his characteristic, unacknowledged Cartesian biases.

CHAPTER 6

1 David Hume, *A Treatise of Human Nature*, bk. II, pt. I. To be sure, it seems etymologically implicit in the concept of a *passion* that it *contrast* with an action. 'We can give the general title passions to all those modes of awareness which often arise in us without our soul making them to be what they are, and which in all cases it receives from the things which they represent.' Descartes, *The Passions of the Soul*, art. 17.

2 See the penetrating discussion of believing something (only) because we want to in B. A. O. Williams, 'Deciding to Believe', in H. Kiefer and M. Munitz (eds.), *Language, Belief, and Metaphysics* (Albany; New York State University Press, 1970). I have deeply benefited from discussion of this subject with him. A fine treatment of these and other systematically related matters is in David Wiggins, 'Freedom, Knowledge, Belief, and Causality', in *Knowledge and Necessity*, Royal Institute of Philosophy Lectures, III (London; Macmillan, 1970), pp. 132–54.

3 These examples of illusions are standard in the Indian tradition. They are illusions one *lives through*, and in their own tradition they support certain philosophical claims concerning the world's irreality. To ask *what* the world is, against the claim of its illusoriness, is like asking what became of the snake for which one mistook a piece of rope. Daya Krishna once made the impressive point in conversation with me that one difference between East and West is revealed through the paradigm illusions with which philosophers illustrate their points. A stick which looks bent in water still looks bent when we know that it is not and have mastered Snell's Law in explanation of it. It is purely an intellectual understanding. But we cannot see the rope as a snake when we discover what it is.

4 Ultimately, the brilliant discussion of the logical incapacity to will pain rests upon some version of the private language argument in Brian O'Shaughnessy's marvelous paper, 'The Limits of the Will', *Philosophical Review*, LXV, 4 (October 1956), 443–90: 'So the act of throataching is necessarily private, i.e., it makes no sense to say one witnessed his throataching. Then what would be the process of teaching someone the use of "throatache"? How could we tell that someone could use "throatache", unless he were to tell us, and how could *he* know how to use "throatache" unless we could tell by some other means?' (pp. 451–2).

5 Mental causation is introduced and glossed in G. E. M. Anscombe's *Intention*, sects. 9 and 10. She comments: 'Note that this sort of causality or sense of "causality" is so far from accommodating itself to Hume's explanations that people who believe

that Hume pretty well dealt with the topic of causality would entirely leave it out of their calculations: if their attention were drawn to it they might insist that the word "cause" were inappropriate or was quite equivocal. Or conceivably they might try to give a Humean account of the matter as far as concerned the outside observer's recognition of the cause; but hardly for the patient's.'

6 That sensations are not subject to the will is suggested as a basis for supposing that they are caused by something other than the perceiver, in Descartes, *Meditation* III: 'These ideas are not in any wise dependent on my will, nor therefore on myself.' Descartes dismisses the transcendental argument based upon what he regards as non-controversial, namely that sensations are not dependent on the will. This becomes a commonplace in classical epistemology. 'These simple ideas, when offered to the mind, the understanding can no more refuse to have, nor alter when they are imprinted, nor blot them out and make new ones itself, than a mirror can refuse, alter, or obliterate the images or ideas which the objects set before it do therein produce.' Locke, *An Essay Concerning Human Understanding*, bk. II, ch, ii, sect. 25; and Leibniz, otherwise critical, concurs. It is the incapacity to will sensations which almost certainly requires that they be 'given', which, combined with the theory that all evidence is drawn ultimately from the senses, yields classical empiricism. Plausible attacks on the empiricist notion of evidence, and on the passivity of the mind in cognitive enterprises, while they are just as far as they go, leave unaffected the claim that we cannot sense as a basic action.

7 Sexual impotence, properly so-called, must then be divided into two sorts: (1) a man does not *feel* desire, and so does not *express* desire; and (2) a man feels desire but inhibits the normal expression. Therapy in the latter case consists in removing whatever beliefs, presumably unconscious, are responsible for inhibition, regarded here as unwitting forbearance. But what is to be done for the sexual anaesthetic whom, 'comme le roi d'un pays pluvieux/... rien ne peut l'égayer' (Baudelaire, *Spleen*, iii), 'is logically on a par with the question of what to do to make sighted the blind'. My belief is that it does not fall within the range of competence of psychotherapy, granting always the phenomenon of hysterical blindness in conversion neurosis.

8 Plato, *Republic*, 440. This is a precocious example of *weakness* of will. For a remarkable discussion of Plato's views on this fascinating topic, see J. J. Walsh, *Aristotle's Conception of Moral Weakness* (New York; Columbia University Press, 1963).

9 In the neglected dialogue, the *Lesser Hippias*, Socrates draws a distinction between running slowly voluntarily and running slowly involuntarily. One of whom the former is true *must* be able to run fast: only the good runner can thus lose a race on purpose, so if one cannot win, *losing* is not an action. This rather resembles the point I am making in the text. Socrates sums it up by saying, paradoxically, that only the good man does evil voluntarily, hence 'He who voluntarily does wrong and disgraceful things, if there be such a man, will be the good man' (376).

CHAPTER 7

1 That freedom or liberty contrasts merely with constraint, and hence that it is an empirical matter whether men are in this metaphysically irrelevant sense 'free' or not, is associated typically with Hume. 'By liberty, then, we can only mean *a power of acting or not acting, according to the determinations of the will* . . . Now this hypothetical liberty is universally allowed to belong to everyone who is not a prisoner and in chains.' David Hume, *An Enquiry Concerning Human Understanding*, sect. VIII, pt. I, 10. Cf. *Treatise*, bk. II, pt. III, sects. i and ii. This is of course altogether compatible with Determinism in the causal sense. So much was recognized by Hobbes: 'From the use of the word *Free-Will*, no Liberty can be inferred of the will, desire, or inclination, but the Liberty of the man; which consisteth in this, that he finds no stop, in doing what he has the will, desire, or inclination to do.' *Leviathan*, pt. II, ch. xxi. This brilliant dissolution of the free will controversy has become a commonplace.

2 *Bhagavat Gita*, XVIII, 11; trans. F. Edgerton.

3 Richard Taylor, 'Determinism and the Theory of Agency', in Sidney Hook (ed.), *Determinism and Freedom in the Age of Modern Science* (New York; New York University Press, 1958), p. 216. Cf. 'I can', *Philosophical Review*, LXIX, 1 (January 1960), 78–89.

4 G. E. Moore, 'A Defense of Common Sense', in J. H. Muirhead (ed.), *Contemporary British Philosophy*, second series (London; George Allen and Unwin, 1925).

5 Cf. R. B. Hobart, 'Free-will as Involving Determinism and as Inconceivable Without It', *Mind*, LXIII (1934), 1–27. Cf. Philippa Foot, 'Free Will as Involving Determinism', *Philosophical Review*, LXVI, 4 (October 1957), 439–50.

6 See Alvin I. Goldman, *A Theory of Human Action* (New Jersey; Prentice Hall, 1970), ch. 4.

7 The distinction between reasons and causes is a surface-find, latterly exploited in an effort to overcome the pretended application of the concept of causation to human action. For a review of the relevant literature and the stock arguments, see Keith Donellan, 'Reasons and Causes', in P. Edwards (ed.), *The Encyclopedia of Philosophy*. Donald Davidson's 'Actions, Reasons, and Causes' is the classical effort at rebutting this move, arguing that reasons are a species of cause. The same view is powerfully set forth in the context of a systematic treatment of Determinism in Bernard Berofsky, *Determinism*, pp. 111–13 and ch. 13. The issue is in process of refinement, but has some distance to go before reaching the subtlety of F. H. Bradley's discussion in 'The Cause and the Because', *The Principles of Logic*, second edition (Oxford; Oxford University Press, 1928), II, 535–50.

8 That a man cannot know what his intentions may be until he has in fact formed them is argued in Stuart Hampshire and H. L. A. Hart, 'Decision, Intention, and

Certainty', *Mind*, LXVII (1958), 1–12. Incorporating this into an argument against *anyone* knowing what an intention is going to be, and hence raising a question of whether the will is subject at all to cause, Carl Ginet develops a singular dilemma in 'Can the Will be Caused?', *Philosophical Review* LXXI, 1 (January 1962), 49–55.

9 That believing must be an action is argued in J. R. Lucas, 'Freedom and Prediction', *Proceedings of the Aristotelian Society*, Sup. vol. XLI (1967), pp. 163–72. Cited and criticized by David Wiggins, *Knowledge and Necessity*, p. 135. Lucas argues that we cannot believe our beliefs to have been caused, for that would leave no room for our having held any other. My argument has undercut this, which holds only when we believe that the causes of our belief are independent of what makes the belief a true one. That the will controls belief is, of course, a traditional view. It is advanced forcefully by Descartes in *Meditation* IV, where it is indeed argued that the only thing up to me at all is whether or not to assent to a proposition. The proper exercise of this freedom keeps me from falling into error, which means my mistakes are *my* fault. This is Descartes' quaint extension of the concept of freedom and evil, which we originally owe to St Augustine, to *res cogitans*, for error is the only evil. Lucas's views, meanwhile, I believe must be aimed at those theories which, in discovering that beliefs are caused, supposed them invalidated through this fact. I refer to vulgar marxistic and psychoanalytical theories of belief.

10 This is the concept of freedom which existentialists seem primarily to have in mind. 'There is, then, ultimately nothing that can set limits to freedom, except those limits that freedom itself has set in the form of its various initiatives, so that the subject has simply the external world he gives himself.' Maurice Merleau-Ponty, *The Phenomenology of Perception*, p. 436.

INDEX

Index

Berkeley (*cont.*)
37; on perception, 46, 109; on spirits, ideas, and notions, 36, 203, 216; on volitions and actions, 206
Berofsky, Bernard, 211, 219
bilateral causation, 61–3
blindness, 119, 122, 127, 128, 129, 130, 137, 153, 167
Blondel, Maurice, 206
boddhisatvas, 166, 179
Boddhisatva Paradox, 166–7
bodily movement, and basic actions, 43–50
Boring, E. G., 214
boundaries, of power and knowledge, 118–19
Bradley, F. H., 219
brain-states, 65–72
Brand, Myles, 201
Broad, C. D., 206
Brown, D. G., 203
Buddha, 158

'can', 135–6, 138
Cason, H., 213
causal dependence, 93–4, 96
causal episodes, 56
causal independence, 92–3, 110, 156, 170
causal knowledge and meaning, 79–80
causal matrix, 93
causation, as component in certain actions and cognitions, 12; multiple, 103; and negativity, 120; and reasons for actions, 193–4; theory that there are two species of, 51–63; and simultaneity, 208
causes and objects of feelings, 156
'causes,' logical form of, 81, 90, 156, 210; as of the same type as semantical predicates, 85–7, 90; not a descriptive predicate, 91; as entailing a covering law, 91–6; as semi-transparent, 97–9; as non-basic description, 40, 41
causing someone to do something, 56, non-basic description, 40, 41
104–15
Chisholm, Roderick, 63, 197, 205, 209, 216
Chomsky, Noam, 69
coercion, 182, 187
cognitions, composite, 29; mediated, 28–9, 32, and Ch. 1 *passim*
cognitive impotency, 168
cognizing, instances of, 31

Coherentism, 46–8
Collingwood, R. G., 208
colors, how they feel, 130
comedy, 21
communication, 113, 132
complex events, 56–8, 73–3, 78, 81, 105
compound events, 56, 73, 77, 91, 92, 101
conditional sufficiency, laws of, 96
conditioned reflex, 121, 213
consequences, of actions and cognitions, 14–15
constraint, in the analysis of freedom, 182, 219
control, 116, full and partial, 180–1; over feelings and their expressions, 145–6; and socialization, 161
correspondence, in representationalist theories, 45
Covering Law Models, 100

Davidson, Donald, 43, 198, 204, 205, 208, 209, 211, 212, 219
Davis, Lawrence, 207
depression, 160
Descartes, René, and Problem of External World, 5, 69, 77; on what men are essentially, 1–2, 11, 23, 216; and God, 126, 147; on belief and will, 220; on sensation and will, 159; on causes of our ideas, 189; on categories, 211; and images, 217
descriptions, under which events are covered by laws, 97–8; theory that something is an action only relative to descriptions, 39–44, 204
Determinism, 2, 115, 183–8, 195
Dewey, John, 198, 208
dictionaries, and encyclopedias, 79–81, 209–10
dilation of eyes, whether an action, 120, 213
direct knowledge and action, parallels between theories of, 45–50
Direct Realism, 49–50
'does', descriptive meaning of, 51, 49, 119; said always to be of something, 57, 75
doings, in special sense, 75–9
Donellan, Keith, 219
double negatives, 164–5
Dray, William, 212